We All Want to Change the World

ROCK AND POLITICS FROM ELVIS TO EMINEM

TOM WALDMAN

FOREWORD BY DONOVAN LEITCH

TAYLOR TRADE PUBLISHING

Lanham • New York • Toronto • Oxford

Published by Taylor Trade Publishing
An imprint of The Rowman & Littlefield Publishing Group, Inc.
4501 Forbes Boulevard, Suite 200
Lanham, Maryland 20706

Distributed by the National Book Network

Library of Congress Cataloging-in-Publication Data

Waldman, Tom, 1956–
  We all want to change the world : rock and politics from Elvis to Eminem / Tom Waldman.—1st Taylor Trade Pub. ed.
      p. cm.
Includes bibliographical references (p.) and index.
  ISBN 1-58979-019-7 (hardcover : alk. paper)
  1. Rock music—United States—Social aspects. I. Title.
ML3534 .W27 2003
782.42166'0973—dc21

                                                            2003010314

CONTENTS

FOREWORD

The book you have in your hands will take you on a journey tracing the potent relationship between popular song and politics from the 1950s into the new millennium. From the folksong protest recordings of Pete Seeger and the Weavers, to the overtly sexual and seemingly harmless wails of Elvis Presley, the 1950s' popular song movements entered our daily lives and changed the way the populace would relate to current affairs. Through the new view of televised events, the lyrics and images of singers and songwriters would soon be able to reach right into the living rooms of the Western world.

In tandem with this media awakening, the emerging politicians were slowly realizing their TV skills. Popular songs and politics were now in bed together; one could accurately describe the happening as an "electronic newspaper with sound." I, for one, realized the breakthrough and saw the potential to present the Bohemian Manifesto on the wings of popular song. I was in the forefront of the fusion of folk and pop music in the 1960s and a member of the fraternity that consciously, intentionally introduced ideas of change to the masses through the new openness of the media message. This fusion was the explosive formula that introduced to a sleeping mass the Bohemian Manifesto of change, a program that included free speech, free music, and free thought—all to reach us through the seemingly harmless entertainments of the popular song.

From the 1950s until the present day, the committed singer-songwriter continues a tradition of social commentary that is naturally the work of the poet. Poets are often feared by the establishment, much loved or hated by the populace and sometimes beheaded or interred to shut them up. The popularity of the music star attracts massive audiences, and politicians often wish to bask in such glory—yet star and politician often misunderstand each other's basic drive. The allegiance pledged to a star's music is very different than the allegiance showered upon a political group. It is debatable which effort achieves the evolutionary change in a society's view of reality. Is it the poet who introduces a change of viewpoint and thus a change of life for millions, or is it the political vote?

It is rare when such a star actively promotes a political group. The Socialist movement of the '30s and '40s attracted major writers and performing artists, some of whom began to align with the various political groups who fought for the rights of the working class. Paul Robeson—a hugely popular American singer and film actor who went to the street to show his commitment—is perhaps the best example of such an individual. Robeson's act is all the more amazing in that he was Black and Proud and up against the general trend of the entertainment industry, an institution which at the time downplayed the stature of "colored" female and male artists of the day while encouraging "white" audiences to fantasize on these amazingly influential artists. Here we come up against the question whether Robeson actually aligned with the political "left" or followed his own compassionate drive to use his stardom to some good.

In France in the 1940s, the intellectual literary world naturally aligned with the great Communist movements in Russia and China, the prime manifesto being the overthrow of the establishment and the dawn of a new age for the masses. The dark and satanic forces of Fascism were to be countered by the power of the word, the seduction of song, and the flickering magic of the moving picture.

Jean-Paul Sartre, Pablo Picasso, and many others in the arts thrived in the long-established French tradition of active engagement. These artists presented to their generation the answer to the onslaught of the Greed Barons of Industry, Church, and State. That answer, or so they thought, was the Socialist revolution which would sweep the West, liberating the masses from the yoke of the Tyrant and the Factory Bosses. In this climate of social change it was of course the Socialist political parties that were supported by the artist. The Communist dream would fade as George Orwell's book *Animal Farm* entered the consciousness of the committed artist. From this point on the basic premise of over-throwing one political system for another would be called into question. Freedom was the issue—but freedom from what? The masters of war (as Dylan so wisely put it) were ever-present in the ancient families of wealth, and now modern commerce.

Carl Jung, the pioneer psychologist, was presenting the great affliction of the twentieth century as a mass psychosis that originates in fear and doubt, creating monsters who would become leaders and would play on the masses' insecurity, leading them into war. What political party could then be supported to end such suffering and delusion? Surely this was a spiritual as well as a political question.

After World War II, the 1950s arrived and Europe was rebuilt yet again. Millions upon millions of people were dead or displaced and private money again poured into fallen countries to regenerate the military industrial complex. In this naive decade, the American artists of film were unjustly accused of being Communist in their sympathies, as they lovingly created wonderful movies of the plight of the working man against the greed and oppression of the establishment. The Mc-Carthy hearings are famous enough for me not to elaborate.

The freedom that the American people had fought for in their early days was being forcibly controlled by the new establishment. Popular singers in this decade were not aligning with public political events. Folksingers, however, were—and the maverick artists Pete Seeger and Woody Guthrie were creating a groundswell of influence that would forever alter the future of popular song and political involvement.

One popular actor of the 1950s with an attitude and sensibility consistent with many profiled in this book also appeared. The fiercely rebellious Marlon Brando took the world by storm and his work became the main influence on the singer Elvis Presley. In the 1960s Brando aligned with seemingly non-political groups, the American Blacks and the American Native Tribes. Here was a different act from an artist who wished to use his fame to focus on an issue. Here we would see true selfless support akin to Paul Robeson some decades earlier. And yet one could not pigeonhole Brando with any political party.

It is into the seething cauldron of the 1960s that I arrive and dive in. Fully prepared from the age of sixteen, I headed straight for the Queen of Folk herself, Joan Baez. She introduced me to Bob Dylan and Bob introduced me to the Beatles. Soon I was with Pete Seeger at the Newport Folk Festival, personally invited by Seeger and honored as a new and relevant poetic voice in the fraternity. Now the lyrics of the popular song would be informed with the truth. We had read all the books and studied all the music and we wished to galvanize our generation into awareness. We did not align with any one political party; the political groups of the time were two sides of the same coin, although of course the "left" were on the side of the working class.

Constraints on Western radio, television, and other broadcast media—originally used to control propaganda following World War II—were loosening. Yet our records were still not allowed to be played freely on the airwaves, and many pirate radio stations appeared on ships anchored off the coast of Britain. Even the British Navy was at one point sent to close down the free music being beamed out all over Europe in the early 1960s. But soon commercial interests saw the potential income, and the rest is history.

Twenty years would pass before our generation would grow up and become (incredible as it seemed then) the "older generation." The common experiences that the new politicians shared with the 1960s generation became naturally blended with popular music. John Lennon got it right when he wrote, "We all wanna change the world." Now here was the chance. The president of the United States used to smoke pot.

And now after this short introduction in which I sketched the early beginnings of the unholy alliance between political parties and the radically committed artist, I will leave you in Tom Waldman's most capable hands. *We All Want to Change the World* is thoroughly researched and highlights the ups and downs of the relationship between the political and musical stars of the last fifty years. From Elvis to Eminem, the media has truly proven *itself* to be the message.

As I sign off, the story goes on. This very spring, the Irish singer Bono plans a concert in support of the Iraqi people with none other than world-famous opera maestro Luciano Pavarotti. I ask myself, in this act of support for Iraq, to which political party can Bono and Pavarotti be aligned? None.

It is good that the popular artist aligns with political events, but where is the "left" and where is the "right" when compassion is truly the only way to help our ever-suffering Family of Man?

DONOVAN LEITCH
County Cork, Ireland
April 2003

PROLOGUE: SO HAPPY TOGETHER

I can still remember the first—and last—time that I heard "Dole Man." The television set in the corner was tuned to C-SPAN, which had been providing what seemed to be nonstop reports from the field in the 1996 presidential race. C-SPAN's campaign coverage avoids well-coiffed, highly paid reporters, and instead fills downtime with humorous out-takes, snippets of private conversations picked up by open microphones, and subtle attempts at image making. Minutiae ignored by mainstream media yet indispensable to political junkies. Not even CBS in its glory years was this thorough.

On this particular day, viewers had the privilege of hearing a couple of classic rock and soul hits performed by a perfectly competent band selected as the warm-up act for former Kansas senator Robert Dole, the Republican nominee for president. While you would not mistake the guitar player for the legendary Steve Cropper, the group's brief set included a reasonably faithful version of Sam and Dave's 1967 hit "Soul Man," except that the title was changed to "Dole Man," as in "I'm a Dole Man."

"Dole Man" never cracked the Top 100, and didn't last long on the campaign trail. When "Soul Man" writer Isaac Hayes learned about the play on words, he vehemently objected, presumably for political, musical, legal, and aesthetic reasons. It's bad enough for black musicians when white colleagues rip off their material, but if the offending party is some old Republican presidential candidate's campaign, then that's downright embarrassing. Sam and Dave recorded the song a year before America elected another Republican—Richard Nixon—as president, and the duo would not have imagined that three decades later

"Soul Man" would return in slightly different form to pump up the crowd at GOP rallies. In the late 1960s, Republicans over forty had not even come around to Elvis.

Once Hayes and his lawyers registered their disapproval, the Dole camp dropped "Dole Man," presumably afraid of a lawsuit and of further damaging relations with black voters, although the vast majority of them didn't like the Republicans anyway. No song is so clever that it can withstand negative publicity, at least not in political circles. From that point until the November election, the soul/rock warm-up act changed "Dole Man" back to "Soul Man," when they covered the song at all.

Although Dole filmed commercials for Viagra and Pepsi, does that make him a rock and roll fan? It's not likely. Born in 1926, a World War II veteran, honored member of the Greatest Generation, and a native of Kansas, one might assume Dole leans toward Dixieland and Swing. But running for office in America is not about the "real" you, it's about them—the voters—and what your advisors think the masses want you to be. As presidential politics go, "Dole Man" was a relatively minor attempt at image enhancement, but not irrelevant. The Dole camp had good reason to add rock and roll to their team.

In 1996, Dole was pitted against Bill Clinton, a popular president and a Baby Boomer who had listened to "Soul Man," loved the music of The Beatles, and knew the difference between Sam and Dave and Sam the Sham. Clinton symbolized the coming to power of a generation raised on Elvis, Bob Dylan, and the Rolling Stones, not to mention the Clash, Led Zeppelin, Motown, and funk. What had long been anticipated or feared, depending on one's age and point of view, had now come to pass; ex-hippies, former pot smokers, and forever rock and roll fans were being elected to office and even running big companies. In 1984, President Ronald Reagan could joke about his advanced years, yet Walter Mondale, who hardly represented a passing of the torch, opposed him. But compared with Clinton, Dole was *old*.

Dole predated Little Richard, Chuck Berry, and Buddy Holly, three rock and roll pioneers who might as well have born in the nineteenth century in the minds of most young fans of rap, hip-hop, and the second coming of punk. Dole's era was fading, and quickly. Clinton had a huge advantage in the pop culture category. "Dole Man" was the attempt to level a playing field that in reality could never be balanced.

Thankfully Dole never danced to the music. It was deemed sufficient to have rock music in the vicinity when he appeared around the country. His repackaging as a reasonably hip guy went so far, but no further. You can't fool all the eighteen to forty-year-old voters all the time.

The idea that rock could rejuvenate Republicans is of recent vintage. Richard Nixon didn't attempt it, and neither did Gerald Ford, although the latter did greet George Harrison at the White House in 1974. Reagan embraced Springsteen—particularly the song "Born in the USA"—for a brief period in 1984, until the Boss objected, thereby protecting his reputation as a Man of the People. Bush father and son enlisted a guitar-slinging fellow traveler or two, sandwiched in between "Dole Man."

In a sense, rock and roll has only itself to blame for being co-opted by the other side. If rock and roll had disappeared in the 1950s, as hopeful religious leaders, parents, and music critics predicted, then it would never had the opportunity to sell out to establishment Republicans. There's a price to be paid for success. Rock's amazing staying power, and its massive appeal to generation after generation since the release of "Heartbreak Hotel," virtually guaranteed that it would someday be well received in unlikely places, such as Madison Avenue and political campaigns. In America, nothing is sacred when it comes to marketing and promotion. You would think politically savvy rock fans, so hip to the evils of capitalism, would know this very well. And yet with each new rock-driven TV advertisement they profess to be outraged, clinging to the belief that the Soundtrack of the Revolution must remain pure, and never serve the interests of brands of soft drinks, car manufacturers, or aging Caucasian conservatives. Some children, it seems, never grow up. No one "owns" rock, just as no one owns the movies, television, or Abstract Expressionism. The myth that rock and roll runs counter to good old American values—and is therefore anathema to any politician to the right of center—should have ended when Elvis Presley signed a contract with RCA Records in late 1955.

⌒

You can learn something about American society and culture from 1955 to 1990 by perusing the *Billboard* pop or soul charts from that period, but not enough to be considered an expert, or even well informed. A lot of important issues escaped notice in the Hot 100. For example, few rock, pop, or soul songs directly addressed the Civil Rights Movement, while outside of rap, almost no releases referred to inner-city crime. Both urban and rural poverty got short shrift on vinyl, although attention was paid in the 1980s via the resurgence of benefit concerts. Rock also all but neglected the chief concerns—high taxation and inflation—of what Clinton would later call the forgotten middle class.

It's probably too difficult to write hit songs about these subjects. After all, rock bands have to make a living. Your chances of recording a million-seller are far greater if you stick to sex or love, and leave that other stuff to policy wonks and speechwriters. Ever since Bob Dylan, however, the notion that a rock song could or should say something more than "I want to marry you" or "I want to sleep with you" refuses to die. For one thing, rock critics won't allow it. The older they get, the more they want rock to address serious, adult themes in a serious, adult manner. The rapturous response to Springsteen from many rock and pop culture critics of a certain age is in part an expression of gratitude that he repeatedly tackles political issues, and represents the world beyond videos, drugs, platinum albums, groupies, and fame. Having Bruce around makes it easier for them to go to work in the morning.

Springsteen the composer missed the Vietnam War: his breakthrough album, *Born to Run*, was released a few months after the fall of Saigon on April 30, 1975. The American public, hawks and doves, conservatives and liberals, was sick and tired of hearing about Vietnam at that point. *Born to Run* was a joyous antidote, the famous "future of rock and roll." The LP gave college students in the post-Beatles, post-Vietnam era—the ones who were a little too late for *Sgt. Pepper's* and the March on the Pentagon—their own magic moment. Nine years later, when Bruce recorded "Born in the USA," he focused on the plight of the Vietnam vet. That was his antiwar song.

And yet the war in Vietnam was the single event in the last fifty years that triggered the most rock and r & b songs. The impact of that war on the pop charts is especially apparent by examining hits from the late 1960s and early 1970s. The best of all the antiwar songs, "War" by Edwin Starr, which reached #1 in September 1970, would not have climbed as high in 1977 or 1987, for political rather than musical reasons. The U.S. was not entangled in any military adventures in those years, an historical circumstance that could not have helped the sales of "War," which succeeded partly due to its strong universal message about the futility and brutality of armed conflict. The words were backed up by daily images on the evening news. In peacetime, people don't think so much about the horrors of war.

And by the way, "War" would not have gone over well with the public in the fall of 2001, when the U.S. teamed with the Northern Alliance to rid Afghanistan of the Taliban. Antiwar sentiment captures hearts, minds, and the entertainment dollar when the war in question is perceived as unjust, or a failure.

Political immediacy can be a boon to sales. Record executives may or may not be news junkies, but they won't hesitate to release a song that they think reflects the national mood, especially as expressed by the core audience of 12 to 25-year-olds. In the late 1960s, when more and more Americans turned against the war in Vietnam, the oppositionist viewpoint was reflected in Hollywood, on Broadway, and in the lyrics of selected rock, funk, and soul songs. By contrast, in 1964 and the first half of '65 only a few academics, politicians, and students openly opposed U.S. policy in Southeast Asia.

Though rock wades cautiously into political waters, there are times when it's in sync with the headlines. For example, the emergence of the gay rights movement in the early 1970s coincided with the glitter rock

PROLOGUE: SO HAPPY TOGETHER

scene in Britain and the immense success in Britain and America of David Bowie, then in the midst of his androgynous phase. Would Ziggy Stardust have worked in 1969? I don't think so. The onset of feminism, initially known as Women's Liberation, occurred within the same general period as Helen Reddy's "I Am Woman" (1972) along with a modest increase in the number of all-female bands. Pop songs exploit politics, and politics in turn exploits pop songs. With few appropriate #1 smash hits in the running, "I Am Woman" was designated an anthem of the women's movement, played, sung, or both at pro-choice rallies in the aftermath of the Supreme Court's Roe v. Wade decision (1973).

Other times the connection between popular music and politics is not so obvious, though equally valid. One need not be a Marxist to consider changes in taste and changes in sound within the context of political developments. The reign of disco (1974–1978) neatly coincided with the emergent black middle class and a new sexual assertiveness among urban gay males. Both groups had new places to play, disposable income, and Sister Sledge, Chic, and Donna Summer to get the party started. The first punk era (1977–81) was in part an angry response to the stubborn refusal of the 1960s to make way for something else. And rap is the revenge of the street, the blunt reminder that affirmative action and quotas—which helped to build the black middle class in the 1970s and 1980s—left a lot of people behind.

If politics is used to sell rock or rap, then perhaps it's fair that rock records and rock stars are used to garner votes. That seems obvious today, but it wasn't until the early 1990s that campaigns took the chance. Now you're as likely to hear a classic rock song at a political rally or national convention as you would on the soundtrack of the typical Hollywood big-budget picture. This rule applies to Republican and Democratic campaigns, as well as candidates for city attorney on up. "The soundtrack to modern campaigns is rock and roll," said Nelson Warfield, who served as press secretary in the 1996 Dole campaign.

When compared with focus groups, television spots, or polling, rock comes very cheap; one hundred bucks or so will cover the costs of a stack of anthologies from the 1960s, 1970s, and 1980s. A few of those Time/Warner collections should suffice. And high-priced consultants aren't necessary to the selection process. Anyone in the campaign that knows a bit about rock and roll since the Beatles could peruse Joel Whitburn's pop annuals for the quintessential song or songs. With all the CDs out there, the chances are quite good that the "rock" staff person will find what he or she needs.

And then what? Just like the days of early rock and roll radio, the loyal aide must get the song on the air. But this time payola isn't a prerequisite. The campaign controls the airwaves. The one essential rule is to never send a wrong or even a mixed message. In the post-Gary Hart, post-Clinton era, any song that so much as hints at sex has to be automatically rejected, which would disqualify most of the Rolling Stones' catalogue, not to mention *Led Zeppelin II* and "Afternoon Delight." A campaign also has to be careful with "Revolution" by the Beatles, which has been known to upset righties and lefties, or John Lennon's gentle "Imagine," which seems to endorse the concept of One World Government.

The notion that you can tell a lot about a person by the rock music he or she listens to existed long before modern political campaigns. In the late 1960s, Beatles v. Stones could start as many arguments as Bobby Kennedy v. Gene McCarthy or Mickey Mantle v. Willie Mays. In the mid-1970s, the weird (cool) kids listened to David Bowie, while the reactionaries were partial to Grand Funk Railroad and Lynyrd Skynyrd. In the early 1980s, disco dudes and punk rockers used to get into fights with fists, chains, and occasionally knives in the suburbs of Southern California. The two sides might have agreed on many levels, but that music thing could not be overcome.

Rock songs are employed to define a candidate—check out the number of women running for office that make their way to the podium accompanied by Aretha Franklin's "Respect"—but it wouldn't be politics without a cynical twist. Voters don't know if the candidate actually likes the song that has been chosen for his or her theme. There's no point in asking, because he or she will of course say the song is great, has a fabulous beat, brings back wonderful memories, blah, blah, blah. Even Bob Dole could have been coached to say the right things about "Soul Man."

Can picking the "right" rock song win an election? Of course not. Music plays a much less important role then television in contemporary campaigns, and I'm not convinced that television by itself can make a difference. The economy, foreign policy, law and order, corruption counts as well. Image is important, but not everything. Still, no one born before 1975 can forget when then-candidate Bill Clinton was nominated for president in 1992, and Fleetwood Mac's "Don't Stop" exploded over Madison Square Garden. If Clinton touted his support for welfare reform and business as evidence of a New Democrat, "Don't Stop" said here is a New Candidate, born after World War II and raised on rock. "It was brilliant, it was amazing," said Jean Marie Bunton, one of the younger employees in the Office of Presidential Speechwriting under the first President Bush. "It symbolized his whole message, boiled down to a snappy little song that the whole nation could tap its toes to."

Could picking the "wrong" song cost the candidate an election? Not likely. But who wants to take that chance? The concluding chapters of *We All Want to Change the World: Rock and Politics from Elvis to Eminem*, examine some good and not so good decisions made by staff DJs. The irony is that now that rock is being accorded a modicum of respect by the establishment, it's in a better position to do mischief, if only by accident. Before inserting the CD, a wise campaign will have performed a background check on the song and the performers to guarantee no unpleasant surprises. But as we know, running for office is loaded with unpleasant surprises, despite the presence of experienced strategists hired to make sure such things never happen. As we also know, a mistake, or gaffe, does not go quietly into the night. Just ask Dan Quayle, whose obituary will no doubt include the fact that he once misspelled "potato."

The bulk of this book—the period from Elvis *until* Clinton—considers rock and politics through the impact of historical events, trends, and social or political movements on the music and musicians. The book does not analyze—or even mention—every "political" song, nor does it attempt to match all significant events over the past half-century with their rock and roll counterpart. In some cases, such as the Iranian hostage crisis, few examples exist, while in others, such as the war in Vietnam, there is much to choose from.

Still, one does not have to be a fan of cultural studies to recognize a connection between rock and politics. If handled properly, which means without the excesses of right-wing hysterics on the one hand or burn outs from the 1960s that can't avoid mentioning rock and revolution in the same sentence on the other, politics and history can help chart the progression of rock. Indeed, this method of analysis has been present since the creation. The negative reaction to Elvis in 1956 was directed not only at the singer, but the society that had ostensibly made him possible. He was the evidence that "we" were sick.

We All Want to Change the World holds that the shape, direction, and the history of rock and roll, soul, and rap has been affected by the Vietnam War, women's lib/feminism, gay liberation, black nationalism and self-reliance, the environmental movement, affirmative action, President Reagan, and President Clinton. And we can't forget Baby Boomers, who retain a degree of clout decades after they started buying 45s.

Whether this is a good or a bad thing depends in the end on how you feel about rock and roll. I hope I don't reveal my own bias in the matter by adding that this book is dedicated to those die-hard fans who also vote in every election.

1

R-O-C-K IN THE U.S.A.

Have you noticed the gradual disappearance of "beautiful music," string-laden instrumentals that will be forever associated with elevator rides, supermarket shopping, and the dentist's office? From the 1960s through the 1980s, few Americans could avoid the acute embarrassment of hearing their favorite pop or rock song reinterpreted—to put it charitably—in this inimitable style. These equal opportunity destroyers ruined "Light My Fire," late-period Beatles, and quintessential Stones, along with Motown, funk, and classic R&B. With shocking ease they transformed songs that had outraged elders into light, fluffy productions that could warm the hearts of uptight Middle American parents. Minus Jim Morrison's sensuous vocals and Ray Manzarek's organ riff, "Light My Fire" sounded about as threatening as the theme to the *Beverly Hillbillies*. And don't get me started on the lounge singers that polluted many a mid-priced hotel in the last two decades with their cover versions of rock songs that once blasted from dorm rooms at Berkeley, Michigan, and Harvard.

But rock and roll lovers would have their revenge. As fans of the Beatles grew older, as Stones diehards married and started families, the audience for appalling renditions of rock classics got smaller and smaller. Adults raised on "Satisfaction" do not want to hear a lame cover, even though they ceased having pot parties and one-night stands decades earlier. The sanitized "Satisfaction" was intended for an audience with either no knowledge of the original, or who hated the original and hated the Rolling Stones. "Beautiful music" succeeded—if that's the right word—only with the first few generations of parents whose kids succumbed to the appeal of rock and roll. Born before 1930, these stuffy, intolerant, and envious old folks—as they have been portrayed in film and on record—refused to listen to real rock and roll. Instead, they dug rock and roll Muzak.

Not that it mattered much. Seniors might outnumber young people on election night, but when it comes to pop culture, American youth blow away the competition. In this arena, the voting age is much lower than eighteen. Any kid with a dollar is eligible. And as the years rolled on, the fan base kept expanding. Rock and roll didn't die, and older people bought albums and CDs, long after coming to the sad realization that they were not going to live forever.

Once a Beatles fan, always a Beatles fan; baby boomers in their forties and fifties continue to listen to and find meaning in *Rubber Soul*, *Revolver*, *Sergeant Pepper's Lonely Hearts Club Band*, and the White Album. They also load their car CD players with the Stones, the Who, Jimi Hendrix, and other performers associated with rock's golden period (1964–1970). These rock and roll lifers replace their old albums with new albums, and second vinyl copies with CDs. When they take their kids shopping, the last thing they want their children exposed to is some wimpy "All You Need Is Love" in place of the original 1967 Beatles recording. An easy-listening version of the Stones' 1969 smash "Honky Tonk Women" would have them demanding to see the manager.

It never came to that. "Beautiful music" was destroyed by the very genre it set out to exploit, undermine, and ridicule. In fin de siècle America, rock and roll is everywhere, including your local supermarket and the waiting rooms of dentists and doctors. Not all recordings are permissible; even in the coolest neighborhoods in the city, few markets would sanction playing the Sex Pistols, speed metal, or rap as appropriate background music for shoppers. For the most part, the people that listen to that stuff aren't American society's biggest spenders.

Neil Young, the Beatles, Tom Petty, the Gin Blossoms, and REM will work just fine for the desired demographic.

Like capitalism and democracy, at the beginning of the twenty-first century rock and roll had outlasted its critics and humbled its competitors. Yet many in the old guard asked the question: At what price victory? They had started listening to rock and roll in the 1950s and 1960s, before white-collar employees, Republicans, and anyone else over thirty-five admitted they enjoyed it too. In the opinion of the purists, rock was never supposed to accompany the purchase of tomatoes, or to keep us otherwise occupied while waiting for a root canal. Even worse, by the 1980s and 1990s, original versions of seminal rock songs were being used to sell such lame products as running shoes, wine coolers, and family cars. Those who believed in the artistic integrity of rock and roll, regardless of how many millions and millions of records have been sold over the years, were outraged to hear thirty seconds of "Brown Sugar," "Baba O'Riley," or "Rebel Rebel" borrowed to hustle goods on television. As the critic Jim Miller put it in 1999: "A music that had once provoked the wrath of censors has become the Muzak of the Millennium."[1]

The disgruntled segment of the audience partly holds the performers responsible for selling their songs to corporate America, and thereby selling out rock and roll. Yet most of their ire is directed at the actual advertisers for the unforgivable act of taking the music out of context. It's one thing for record labels to package rock and roll; they own the stuff. Even purists had to understand the commercial motives behind the Monkees or the Partridge Family, although it made them angry and depressed. But how dare big business defile rock's hallowed ground! It was like the desecration of a national monument. The offending companies ought to be fined for vandalism.

The outrage is predictable and naïve, and yet not without some merit. To many adults who attended high school between 1964 and 1975, and to a few who graduated in the 1980s and 1990s, the phrase "rock and roll can free your soul" actually means something. Sociologists and rock critics can argue whether this is a credit to the music, or a sad commentary on the education level and emotional maturity of the American middle class, the group that has shelled out the most money for records and concerts over the years. It's probably a combination of both. Still, rock fans are utterly sincere when they say that their lives would have been much poorer without *Sgt. Pepper's*, "Jumpin' Jack Flash," or the Boss. Rock enlivened dreary landscapes, and made high school bearable, for teenagers from suburban New Jersey to the San Fernando Valley. You don't forget those things as you turn forty or fifty. Middle-aged America feels it owes a huge debt of gratitude to rock and roll. More than a few from that demographic have been quoted as saying something to the effect that "there was nothing before Elvis," or "the Beatles changed my life forever." "Oldies but goodies" is an insulting term for songs from the past that deserve to be called great. "Classic rock" is hardly better.

Most teenagers in the 1950s, 1960s, and 1970s, first heard rock and roll over the radio. Unlike film, theater, concerts, and even television, radio is an essentially private medium. How many people since the 1950s and the rise of TV have invited friends over to listen to the radio? The very idea seems absurd. Listening to the radio is something we do on our own time, and in our own way.

Radio provides its own cherished memories for rock and roll fans. Obscure ballads wafting in and out of an AM station located hundreds of miles away. The super- cool FM DJ who makes a unilateral decision to play twenty Stones' songs in a row simply because the band will be in town tomorrow night. Carrying a heavy, battery-operated machine around throughout the day to hear the Battle of the Bands.

Through radio, listeners established a "personal relationship" with rock and roll, with all the connotations, both religious and American, that that expression implies. Songs such as "On the Radio" by Donna Summer (1980) and "Superstar" by the Carpenters (1971) romanticized the bond between singer and fan, the fantasy of a one-on-one relationship with your idol, who is singing to you alone.

Like followers of opera divas, rock fans could be very paternal towards their favorite performers, treating them as wayward adolescents for the sin of making inferior albums or seemingly bad choices. Rock fans take things personally. When John married Yoko, you would think he had a family of millions, and most of them said, "Why did you do it, man?" Paul got some of the same response when he married Linda. The legions of fans that have visited Graceland since Elvis died in 1977 include middle-aged and senior women who talk about him as if he were their own dearly departed son.

The projecting of one's own dreams, desires, and aspirations on rock music—an unhealthy but very apparent phenomenon—also explains the profound sense of disappointment and shock when songs are used for what the fan considers inappropriate purposes. This is linked to the enduring sense of the 1960s as solely a bastion of liberalism, with the people who share those beliefs supposedly holding the exclusive rights to rock from that, or frankly, any era.

Conservatives have bought into the stereotypical view of the politics of the 1960s, which makes it that much more difficult to offer a counter interpretation. The Republican takeover of Congress in 1994 was fueled in part by anger at the political and cultural legacy of the 1960s, which was still thought to hold sway. And yet the truth is rather different. Republicans in the 1960s *successfully* ran against the 1960s. The conservative backlash that led to the landslide election of Ronald Reagan as president in 1980 actually began with the landslide election of Ronald Reagan as governor of California in 1966. A mere two years later, the American electorate chose Richard Nixon as president, although by a much smaller margin. Here was a guy who in 1962 couldn't get elected governor of California, yet he became president in 1968, the most radical and revolutionary year of the decade. Four years later, the presidential race between Nixon and George McGovern was the most explicit and decisive repudiation of the values of the 1960s, which among other things gave life to the idea that the youth vote would overwhelmingly favor Democratic candidates. And what might that result say about the decade just passed?

But exaggerated claims about rock and roll, radical politics, and people power are as much a part of baby boomer culture as diversity training and casual Fridays. This started way back when. "For the reality of what's happening today in America, we must go to rock'n'roll, to popular music." Ralph J. Gleason, who was too old to be a boomer but spoke for them anyway, wrote those words in an article in *American Scholar* in the fall of 1967. A year after Gleason's confident assertion, America woke up one morning and heard Richard Nixon's victory speech, an event that could not have been predicted by listening to Bob Dylan or the Rolling Stones. Today there are still veterans of the 1960s who argue that rock played a not insignificant part in ending U.S. participation in the war in Vietnam, and for a brief period around the release of *Pepper* in June 1967, in uniting Western civilization. There is nothing more boring then hearing Boomers prattle on about what a grand time they had during the 1960s. It's insufficient to tell even tall tales; their experiences have to be linked to something really, really big, like communalism, world peace, or a new spirituality. Everything they did was infused with meaning. Or that's what they would have us believe today. Suspicion is in order here. I am doubtful that the hundreds of thousands who traveled to Woodstock in August 1969 were in search of much more than, yes, sex, drugs, and good rock and roll—needs that were satisfied in any or all of these categories. Humanity hasn't changed that much.

The irony is that a strong case for rock and roll from the 1960s can be made strictly on its merits, without dragging in all that other stuff. The 1960s are to rock and roll what the Elizabethan period is to English drama. There will never be another Shakespeare, and there will never be another Beatles. A disproportionate share of the best singles and albums in rock history were recorded in the period from 1964 to 1969. This view is not at all meant to minimize the contributions of those performers who exerted a profound influence on Dylan and the Beatles, such as Chuck Berry, Little Richard, Buddy Holly, and, to a lesser extent, Elvis Presley. Nor is it meant to downgrade the importance of those many excellent solo acts and groups that came after the 1960s: Bruce Springsteen, Elvis Costello, the Clash, David Bowie— who got started in 1964—REM, Pearl Jam, Beck, and the like. But no all-decade team can equal the Beatles, the Rolling Stones, Cream, the

Beach Boys, James Brown (1962–1970), the Byrds, the Who, and the stable of Motown acts. A collection of rock CDs with few or no selections from this group of performers has got major problems.

The question of why rock performed so well in the 1960s is one of the wonderful mysteries of post–World War II pop culture. When you add the fact that England, of all nations, led the way, there is the potential here for a five-hour marathon discussion in a pub, coffeehouse, or professor's living room. But to ask the question is to introduce politics—legitimately—into the mix. For example, an explanation that England was experiencing a sense of relief or even liberation at relinquishing its empire might have credence. According to this theory, the Beatles and the Stones represented the first generation that was not expected or required to serve the Mother Country in some capacity—the domestic meaning of Harold Macmillan's "Winds of Change." Or maybe it was a desire to escape the reality of the nation's loss of power and influence following World War II and Suez, when the United States finally and seemingly forever dwarfed England as an economic and military power. As an alternative, youths in Liverpool, London, and Manchester absorbed Chuck Berry and picked up guitars.

Here in America, it could well have been the case that the "revolution" meant more to rock than rock meant to the revolution. Vietnam War protesters didn't need rock to succeed; Robert McNamara, napalm, General Westmoreland, and body counts would do just fine. On the other hand, the *sound* of rock from 1965 to 1970 is a kind of symbol for anti-war protests, ghetto riots, and the various liberation movements of the period. Music and politics grew very loud in the late 1960s. A band like Detroit's MC5, one of the few of that or any time honestly committed to radical politics, played super fast and at excruciating volume, the rock equivalent of "We want the world and we want it now." The MC5 is unthinkable without SDS (Students for a Democratic Society) and cities ablaze in the summertime. The rise of Jimi Hendrix and his aggressive, burning style of playing the guitar occurred at the same time as the escalation of the war in Vietnam and the huge increase in the number of protests and protesters against the war. A coincidence? Perhaps. Still, it's hard to fathom Hendrix or a Hendrix-like figure—in performance and image—coming along in 1977 or 1987. Hendrix was ahead of his time in music, but very much of his time in politics and culture.

It must be the case that the circumstance of America's founding has created a never-ending run on the word "revolution." The best examples of its misuse in recent history are the continuing claims that a revolution took place in the 1960s, and the application of the word to the Republicans gaining control of the House of Representatives in 1994. In both cases, the established order teetered, but didn't fall. Profound changes yes, a revolution, no. But these myths endure, spread by people who need to believe they were part of something monumental, and journalists addicted to political hype.

Since the "revolution" never occurred in the 1960s, rock cannot be the soundtrack to that revolution. That's no blot on rock's reputation; the music itself suffices. Former and current left-wingers will just have to accept the truth. Indeed, the romantic version of the 1960s is in no small way responsible for the disillusion felt when the "dream" turned out to be a lie. Having invented a revolution, they invented a counterrevolution that destroyed what was good. There are some who say that the superb folk singer Phil Ochs took his own life in 1976 because he could not manage the transition to a post–1960s world. The same was said of Abbie Hoffman when he killed himself a decade or so later.

By the same token, rock was never dedicated to the wholesale destruction of middle-class morality, as some right-wing conservatives in religion and politics have claimed since the early days of Elvis. Rock is actually more like Middle America, and Middle America is more like rock, than they are adversaries.

Rock groups don't want to overturn the status quo; they want to maintain the status quo, especially the part that equates success with wealth. They also want to get noticed by girls, which is hardly a novel desire on the part of adolescent and young adult males—not to mention those in their thirties, forties, and fifties, but that's another story. Cast in socioeconomic terms, rock is usually performed by white, male, middle-class bands for an audience of (predominantly) white middle-class teenagers.

⌒⌒

By one measure, anyway, the gap between politics and rock narrowed in the 1980s. During the 1984 election, it was noted that a sizable percentage of Bruce Springsteen fans were also backers of Ronald Reagan, which reportedly bothered the musician but delighted the president. Springsteen had made himself out to be a kind of working-class hero and friend of the common man—the rock star as one of us. Reagan was no working-class hero—although he often tried to sound a populist theme—and to liberals such as Springsteen, was no friend to the common man. But there were a lot of young voters who saw no contradiction between supporting Uncle Ronnie and listening to the Boss. Springsteen made great records, and that's what mattered. Political differences were simply not relevant. And besides, what should young Reaganites listen to? Lee Greenwood?

If nothing else, a preference for Springsteen and for Reagan would seem to offer hope to conservative pundits, who have long argued that only bad comes from exposure to rock and roll. Alas, some will never be convinced. Rock is rock, regardless of whether it's embraced by Reagan-lovers. The more ferocious attacks exceed anything the right ever said about Bill Clinton. Roger Kimball, a reasonably young (b. 1953) author, critic, and essayist, fairly ranted and raved in his book *The Long March: How the Cultural Revolution Changed America* (2000). He states that "the triumph of rock was not only an aesthetic disaster of gigantic proportions: it was also a moral disaster whose effects are nearly impossible to calculate precisely because they are so pervasive."[2]

This was how commentators and religious leaders talked about rock and roll in the mid-to-late 1950s, except back then its "triumph" was by no means assured. Kimball, on the other hand, offers a belated and bitter concession speech. It's rather disingenuous for Kimball to bemoan the changes wrought by rock, since he was born after the era of Benny

Goodman or even Patti Page. Kimball is as much a child of rock and roll as is Bono or Springsteen, yet he writes in the cranky vernacular of an old man. In his criticism, Kimball lets himself off the hook; since the effects of rock "are nearly impossible to calculate" he is excused from providing specific examples. We are expected to take his word for it.

A foolish politician would today describe the whole of rock—as opposed to specific rock groups—in the kind of apocalyptic language employed by Kimball. Only the conservative fringe and fundamentalists—excluding Pat Boone—still believe that rock is responsible for the decline of Western civilization. The mainstream, that place where most voters reside, rejected this theory decades ago, if in fact they ever gave it credence. In 1983, when Secretary of the Interior James Watt condemned the decision to invite the Beach Boys to perform in Washington, D.C., on Independence Day, he was castigated by First Lady Nancy Reagan, who defended the group. Both of them were right: the Beach Boys did take drugs, as Watt asserted, and their music was (from 1962 to 1965 anyway) clean and fun, as Mrs. Reagan noted. To no one's surprise, Mrs. Reagan won the argument, and the Beach Boys went on with the show. More important, this incident reflected the internal tension among conservatives about rock and roll and its place in society. Watt called attention to lifestyle; the First Lady cared only about the music, at least in this case. If a poll was taken, you would assume that most Americans would be on Nancy's side on this one.

Like others of its kind, Kimball's book cites rock, the welfare state, feminism, the Great Society, political correctness, and moral relativism as the reasons American society has been in steady decline since 1965. (For younger conservatives, 1965 is tantamount to 1933—the year FDR was elected president—for an earlier generation of right-wing thinkers and politicians: The beginning of the end.) Kimball postulates a strong connection between rock and politics, a belief he has in common with those among his ideological adversaries who argue that rock played a key role in ending support for the Vietnam War, initiating the sexual revolution, and in general making us better people.

Where, one might ask, is music in this debate? Neither side seems much interested in specific songs or albums, but instead issues grandiose claims about this Thing Called Rock. It's not surprising that conservative writers would take this approach; most are unfamiliar with the music and bent on discrediting it. Citing songs or performers only get in the way. Conservatives are notorious for castigating films they have never seen, and albums they have never heard. In his 1987 best-seller, *The Closing of the American Mind*, the late Allan Bloom included an attack on rock music. Yet his index listed only one reference to the Beatles, and none to Elvis Presley or the Rolling Stones.

You wouldn't expect anything different from Bloom, who took a certain highbrow pleasure in despising rock even as he despaired of its influence over the rest of society. But minimizing the music is an unforgivable sin on the part of rock and roll's supposed friends. The influential *Rolling Stone* school of criticism, which trades on highfalutin' theories and pretentious judgments, drains most of the fun, excitement, and energy out of rock and roll. For several years after its 1967 launch, *Rolling Stone* was a welcome alternative to teen mags and the daily press, neither of which had the slightest notion of how to cover rock after the Beatles invasion in 1964, or Bob Dylan's first pop hit a year later. But eventually the *Rolling Stone* formula grew tired and then embarrassing—while remaining hugely influential. Starting in the late 1960s, major newspapers added pop music critics to their entertainment staffs. As a consequence, rock reviews have in many cases been much more about what the writer thinks than how the music sounds. Songs are parsed as if they were novels. In the case of Springsteen, U2, and others, new releases are scrutinized for their sociological or political content. Songs such as "I'm Just a Singer (In a Rock and Roll Band)" by the Moody Blues (1972), and "It's Only Rock and Roll (But I Like It)" by the Rolling Stones (1974), can be interpreted as attempts to get the new wave of critics to lighten up a little. Not every rock song is recorded with the goal of changing—or destroying—the world.

But it's never "only" rock and roll for writers with an agenda. If rock is purely fun, then how can it also lead to moral decline? By the same token, how can it—or did it—help to end the war in Vietnam? And yet any discussion about rock and politics—or rock alone—is incomplete or simply dishonest in neglecting this component of pure fun. When you're seventeen, few things in life provide as much of a thrill as riding in the car—by yourself or with friends of similar musical tastes—when a great song comes over the radio, be it "Jumpin' Jack Flash," "Born to Run," or "Train in Vain." The reaction is always the same; pump up the volume and sing loud. Front-seat passengers may sit in on air guitar and dashboard drums. A raspy throat is a mere pittance to pay for three minutes of absolute bliss.

The high that comes from listening to great rock and roll has nothing to do with drugs. Deadheads may disagree, but the music suffices. The drugs/rock link should not be assumed in all or even in the majority of cases. Here is where the Left and Right are equally guilty of stereotyping. People on acid were not the only people who dug acid rock. For many listeners, drugs might get in the way of hearing the music, diminishing rather then enhancing the experience.

The forty and fifty-year-olds who still blast the Stones, Led Zeppelin, or the Pretenders from their car stereos have presumably quit dropping acid and smoking pot. Yet they can't quit rock. Perhaps otherwise thin-skinned, they are in this case oblivious to taunts from other baby boomers and some younger critics that they should put away their musical toys and grow up. In a kind of perverse way it bolsters their confidence that the Stones, Paul McCartney, and the Who refuse to retire. If they're still doing it, the aging fans must be telling themselves, then goddamnit so can we. In families across America, fathers and sons—and occasionally mothers and daughters—now argue the relative merits of rock groups from different eras, and each plays his favorite selections to try to win the debate.

A common observation about baby boomers is that they represent the first generation raised on television. They also constitute the first generation raised on rock and roll, and that label is the more appropriate one. After all, Bill Clinton was many times called "the first rock and roll president," but never once called "the first president who grew up in front of the television set," although that's also technically correct. Adults born in the 1940s don't seem all that proud that they were around at the beginning of TV. But mention the debut of Elvis Presley, and they reminisce as if they were the luckiest people in the world to have been alive and aware in 1956.

When is the last time you heard a high school or college student brag because he spent Saturday night watching television? TV is the last resort for people who are either too tired to go out or have no alternative. Cool people attend parties, where rock and roll is played all night long, to paraphrase the lyrics of numerous hit singles from the 1950s. And although baby boomers have an ongoing affection for TV shows from the 1960s, the best rock from that same period is still regarded with awe.

If you have any remaining doubts, compare what boomers—critics and fans—say about *Batman* or *Get Smart* with what they say about *Sgt. Pepper's* or Altamont Speedway. It's the difference between pure nostalgia and intellectual reverence, notwithstanding puffed-up claims for the Beatles album and its impact on the history of Western civilization. For someone who grew up during the 1960s, it might be difficult to recall thirty-five years later what he once saw in *Batman* or *Get Smart*. But he won't have that problem with "Day in the Life" or "Good Vibrations."

Television predated rock and roll as a political campaign propaganda tool by more than two decades. Everybody remembers or has heard of the significance of the Nixon-Kennedy debates in 1960, but how many know the songs used by the campaigns? Kennedy chose Frank Sinatra's recording of "High Hopes," while the Nixon camp picked an original, "N-I-X-O-N: The Man for Us," words and music by Inez Wilson Clark. You can see the sheet music on display at the Richard M. Nixon Museum in Yorba Linda, California.

By contrast, who remembers the commercials used by the Clinton campaign in 1992, or details concerning the candidate's debates against President Bush? Or even if there were debates? But the playing of Fleetwood Mac's "Don't Stop" at the convention—now that they recall.

It's a reasonable assumption that in 1960, more voters watched television then listened to rock and roll, despite Elvis Presley's worldwide fame. Junior high and high school kids purchased rock and roll records in the 1950s; most parents hated the stuff, which didn't exactly upset record labels and DJs. In the early days, buying records mom and dad detested was a relatively safe and easy path to rebellion, as opposed to heavy necking and then some in the back seat of a car, or drinking cheap wine and guzzling sour beer. That's still true today, although the stakes have been raised for sex and illegal substances. Many parents who grew up on Elvis and the Beatles hate rap, which is just fine with their progeny.

I wasn't there, but I would make an educated guess that undergraduates at Columbia, Berkeley, and Michigan didn't have Elvis Presley or Chuck Berry posters in their rooms, and rarely if ever purchased or played their music. We do know that most college students considered rock and roll inferior in every way to folk and jazz. These were the leaders of tomorrow, and they wanted nothing to do with rock and roll. Campaign strategists wanted nothing to do with rock and roll either, both because of its controversial aspects and the fact that you couldn't vote unless you were twenty-one. That law changed with the ratification of the Twenty-sixth Amendment to the Constitution in 1971, which lowered the voting age to eighteen.

In his 1957 book, *America as a Civilization*, the political scientist and pundit Max Lerner described the American election season in words that still hold true a half-century later:

> The history of American political campaigns is studded with outbursts of political passion, rough-and-tumble tactics of political combat, hyperbolic confessions of patriotism, and the assignment of diabolical traits and motives to one's opponents.[3]

Lerner was writing at the height of the Cold War, and yet more than a decade after the fall of the Soviet Union, "hyperbolic confessions of patriotism" and the rest of it are still the norm for American politics. There is no such thing as a post–Cold War campaign, unless one is talking about advances in technology that allow for immediate response to charges and the creation of ever more slick and sophisticated commercials.

Television has dominated political communication from the time of *America as a Civilization*. Rock can never, and will never, be able to compete with TV, which has the advantages of saturation, immediacy, and ability to manipulate the audience. More important, rock is technologically incapable of transmitting negative messages, and every four years we relearn the key role these play in determining the outcome of a presidential race. Rock is used to build up the image of one candidate, not to tear down the image of another—except by implication, as when playing "Don't Stop" reminded voters that President Bush was the old guy in the race. Furthermore, rock on the campaign trail is beholden to television to reach the widest possible audience. I encountered "Dole Man" watching C-SPAN.

Still, campaign staff and candidates are trying hard to capitalize on the exponential growth in the size of rock's audience over the past several decades. This audience certainly cuts across age, gender, racial, and geographical lines as well. Today a familiar rock hit from the 1950s, 1960s, or 1970s can enliven a rally in California, Maine, and Alabama—Democrat or Republican. Occasionally the campaign can hope for more, such as what happened with "Don't Stop" in 1992. The other candidate that year—President George Bush—would have looked foolish if his campaign had picked a rock song for its theme. He was too old and too square. Clinton had the field to himself. It would fall to the next Republican presidential candidate of retirement age, Bob Dole, to try to pull this off.

⌐⌐

Throughout its fifty-year history, rock and roll has either been a political issue itself or addressed political issues. And though it's important not to overstate the case, rock and roll has in some way always been connected to politics. On occasion, the link is easy to establish—the late

1960s, for example—while at other points one must dig deeper—the late 1950s, for example.

We All Want to Change the World provides a look at the sometimes contentious, often opportunistic, and constantly intertwined history of rock and politics from the release of "Rock Around the Clock" in 1954 through the 2000 presidential campaign. Among the questions this book attempts to answer: How has the history of rock tracked American history since the 1950s? Is there any connection between the two? How important is politics to rock and roll, and rock and roll to politics? Why is rock considered a friend of the Left but not the Right? Are rock and mainstream politics in fact closer then either would wish to admit? And finally, how much impact has rock actually had on politics, and politics on rock, through the years?

RUBBER SOULS

Someday a political scientist will study how the media "feeding frenzy" at the turn of the millennium affected the personal lives of young men and women planning to run for office. Did they decline a proffered joint, think twice about premarital, extramarital, or casual sex, or avoid underground clubs because it could ruin their chances later? Seemingly the best advice an aspiring politician could receive today is either to resist temptation, or give in to it under only tightly controlled circumstances. Make sure you know everyone at the orgy, or if you step out of the closet, be certain there are only a few close friends in the room. Political ambition is more effective than a parochial school education in forcing young men and women to adhere to a strict moral code.

It may sound strange given that he was later impeached as president, but Bill Clinton, who at age sixteen shook President Kennedy's hand at the White House, had already figured this out. He did just enough in the 1960s to prove he was there, but not so much that he would be automatically disqualified from running for president some twenty years later. If you're a Democrat, "young and foolish"—the George W. Bush excuse in the 2000 campaign—does not get you off the hook for sexual license and experimenting with drugs. Since Democrats are blamed for the counterculture, they are held accountable for contributing to it as well.

Clinton had known he wanted to be president since high school, and could therefore spin his personal biography from a relatively early age. I'm aware that it's hard to use "Bill Clinton" and "self-control" in the same sentence, but consider that he smoked—but didn't inhale—marijuana, dodged the draft—but wrote a lengthy letter of semi-contrition, and participated in anti-war demonstrations—and never got arrested. (The jury is still out on "smoked but didn't inhale." While none of Clinton's close friends have contradicted his recollection, a lot of former and current pot smokers find it hard to believe).

Clinton did not "Break On Through (to the Other Side)," as the Doors put it in their 1966 hit, and he never made it to "Itchycoo Park," the all-too-beautiful site of the Small Faces' psychedelic single from 1968. Still, he might as well have been a drug-crazed hippie compared to Gray Davis, elected governor of California in 1998, and Davis' Republican opponent that year, Dan Lungren.

As the *Los Angeles Times* described it on September 7, 1998:

> Dan Lungren . . . believes that rock 'n' roll began to die when "a couple of guys from, where were they from, Birmingham?"—well, Liverpool— "thought they could sing as well as Chuck Berry and Jerry Lee Lewis and Elvis Presley." Gray Davis isn't a big Beatles fan either himself, preferring Sinatra and Streisand to rock 'n' roll rebellion. The last time he went to a concert—Linda Ronstadt's—when the singer was dating his boss Jerry Brown a couple decades ago—Davis wore a suit and told the guy in front of him to please pipe down.[1]

Here are two guys who are basically saying you can take the 1960s and throw it all away—sex, drugs, and rock and roll. If Davis and Lungren didn't much like the Beatles, even the group's early, pre-LSD material, imagine their reaction to the Stones, Hendrix, Cream, or the Dead. Even middle-class parents could handle the "I Want to Hold Your Hand"/"She Loves You" Beatles. After *Revolver* came out in 1966, some—mainly people over thirty-five—may well have started to wonder about John, Paul, George, and Ringo. Like Dylan's hapless Mr. Jones, they knew something was going on, but they didn't know what it was. Or maybe they did, and they didn't approve. But Davis and Lungren made no distinctions between pre-and post-*Revolver* Beatles. According to them, none of the songs from 1964 to 1969 are any good. Davis and Lungren either give new meaning to the phrase "overly cautious politicians" or have strange tastes indeed.

Today voters insist upon knowing more about candidates than their positions on the future of Social Security, health insurance, international relations, and tax cuts for the rich. Or maybe the press *believes* voters want to know more, which amounts to the same thing. If sex lives are open for inspection, then why not a candidate's views on films, the theater, rock and roll, and sports? None of these—including sex—is any predictor of success or failure in politics, but that hasn't stopped print and broadcast media from going there again and again.

And when the campaign has ended, in-house media watchers apologize to us on behalf of the profession for "trivializing" the process, a *mea culpa* as unseemly and dishonest as when politicians promise the voters they will always tell the truth. We know, and they know we know, that this kind of reporting will happen again in the next campaign. Their apologies mean nothing.

We have many things to thank for this deplorable trend, ranging from the rise of celebrity-fueled journalism (*People*, *Entertainment Tonight*, and The E! Channel), baby boomer narcissism, lazy editors and reporters, twenty-four-hour cable news channels, boredom (public and press) with the "real" issues, and declining voter participation. Oh, and yes, the 1960s and 1970s, because the popular myth about what went on in those wild times provides a perfect excuse to ask about sex and drugs and rock and roll: the "Are You Now or Have You Ever Been" question of our era.

As men and women who attended high school and college between 1962 and 1975 started to run for office, younger political reporters got very excited. Inspired by Watergate, they had entered journalism to make a difference, only to become frustrated when they realized that making a difference requires hard work. Watergate, from the bugging of Democratic National Committee headquarters to the resignation of President Nixon, took more than two years of digging to fully uncover. And unlike Nixon, most presidents do not have a political death wish, which in Nixon's case included taping damning White House conversations and becoming unhinged at nationally televised press conferences. There was and will always be only one Richard Nixon.

Those lucky guys, Carl Bernstein and Bob Woodward, got the chance to bring down a president. But they didn't stop there; they wrote a best-selling book about the experience, only to see it become a hit movie starring two of the decade's biggest stars, Dustin Hoffman and Robert Redford. The generation of reporters that followed Woodward and Bernstein were like teenagers who had just missed out on the sexual revolution. They arrived at the party a little too late, and it hurt.

It would have made no sense for campaign reporters to ask the three presidents that followed Nixon—Gerald Ford, Jimmy Carter, and Ronald Reagan—about their experiences with drugs and sex, or which song was the greatest ever recorded by the Beatles. If you didn't grow up with rock and roll, then you didn't have a private life worth exploring. That was the rule, written or not. Reagan might have been considered an exception because he spent so many years in Hollywood, a veritable palace of sin where such behavior was as prevalent as haze and swimming pools. Still, no serious reporter would dare ask Reagan about drug use, although at least two of his contemporaries, Robert Mitchum and Cary Grant, had well-publicized experiences with pot and acid, respectively. But Reagan didn't look or act like a man who smoked joints, or took acid hits. As for casual sex, Reagan was spared embarrassing questions due to his age (sixty-nine when he ran against Jimmy Carter in 1980), although some magazine stories had alluded to one-night stands between the end of his marriage to Jane Wyman and his subsequent second marriage to the former Nancy Davis. Yet despite the newly "sexually liberated" society, younger Americans by and large still got queasy thinking about the elderly and sex, even if the people in question were decades younger at the time. Besides, in 1980 Ronald Reagan clearly stood foursquare for moral values, so who cared if he once screwed around and had been divorced?

~~

Senator Gary Hart was a different story. Hart was in his twenties and thirties in the 1960s, and had served as campaign manager for George McGovern in 1972. He wore his hair long at a time when that look suggested loose morals—even criminal behavior—and anti-Americanism to a wide segment of the population. Hart was fair game, even to members of the media who had lived as hippies or wished they had lived as hippies. "Fit for office" became the new criterion for political reporters, on par with abuse of power. The term hid an anti-1960s, anti-liberal bias, which is rather ironic given that the press is often accused of being biased in *favor* of liberals. But in the 1980s and 1990s, it seemed that Democrats were primarily the ones whose past was being scrutinized for evidence of sex, drugs, and rock and roll. Baby boomer Republicans had to answer for avoiding the draft, but they were usually given a pass on hedonistic excess. It's as if the American public— or the American media—could not or would not accept that God-fearing, tax-hating conservatives might have once walked on the wild side in the counterculture.

If reporters didn't have the means or the evidence to pursue illegal wiretaps, breaking and entering, paying hush money, or major violations of campaign finance laws, then cheating on one's wife or smoking pot would have to suffice. The standards of campaign reporting had changed in the 1980s, although no one bothered to tell Gary Hart. All-news channels, reporters hungry for a big score, fame, and book deals, and political consultants quite willing to pass on rumors and hearsay created a scandal-dependent environment. The channels craved high ratings—a reason to keep viewers watching every day—reporters needed their name associated with the uncovering of a major scandal, and consultants had to win in order to get more clients. With these "needs," the unholy trinity of modern American campaigns began

In 1984, there had been talk on the campaign trail about Hart's womanizing, but he fell back in the race before reporters could make much progress on the story. Nobody wants to read about the peccadilloes of a loser. Heading into 1988, however, Hart started as the Democratic Party front-runner. Unlike four years earlier, he did not sneak up on the press, who had all but written him off early in that campaign. This time, reporters were ready and waiting with rumors of Hart's extramarital affairs. It was clear that Hart would have to address the issue at the beginning and with clarity, or it would never disappear. In mid-1987, he made a fatal mistake, daring reporters to follow him to gather evidence of carousing. When he was "busted," not once but twice, he decided reluctantly to withdraw from the race.

It has never been adequately explained why a leader who cheats on his spouse is necessarily unfit to serve. Apparently the view is that if you lie to your wife or husband, you will lie to the voters. The theory is preposterous; Richard Nixon, arguably the most notorious liar in the history of the American presidency, was faithful to his wife, Pat. Still, the media think they are performing a public service by interviewing old girlfriends, trailing new ones, and in general pursuing any lead that will produce conclusive or hazy evidence of sexual improprieties. But the "theory" was a smokescreen anyway; the mainstream media just wanted an excuse to go after a juicy story.

Hart re-entered the 1988 campaign several months after his abrupt departure, although having defined him as a reckless womanizer the media were not about to pay attention to anything of substance that he had to offer to voters. Journalists are more reluctant even then politicians to admit they could have been wrong.

Outside of the Hart situation, sex, drugs, and rock and roll were virtually absent from coverage of the 1988 race. The two nominees that year, Michael Dukakis and George Bush, presented themselves to voters as good fathers and monogamous husbands who live by the credo of all work and very little play. A lengthy national effort to get the press to write about an alleged extramarital affair on the part of Mr. Bush produced only a largely unsubstantiated story in *LA Weekly*, a local alternative publication, but died quickly. Neither of the candidates was any help to practitioners of the new brand of political reporting.

Reporters covering the 1988 contest had to be satisfied with writing about a racist commercial starring a man named Willie Horton. After exhausting that subject, they filed stories on right-wing attacks on liberals (the "L" word) for coddling criminals, sucking up to the ACLU, and allegedly mocking Old Glory; the incredibly inept Democratic campaign; and the apparent lack of smarts of the Republican candidate for vice president. This was fun stuff, to be sure, but nothing scandalous. Maybe the next election would be better.

And it was. In 1988, Arkansas governor Bill Clinton delivered an interminable speech at the Democratic convention, the boring beginning to a depressing campaign. He made it up to political reporters in 1992, providing them with a plethora of goodies during his own run for the presidency. If Michael Dukakis was the Bobby Goldsboro of Democratic presidential candidates, Bill Clinton was Mick Jagger. His "dull" moment behind him, Clinton soon became one of the most exciting—if that's the right word—presidential candidates in recent American history. From denying an affair with Gennifer Flowers to playing the saxophone on *The Arsenio Hall Show*, you never knew what he might do next.

Throughout the 1992 campaign, rumors, whispers, and innuendo followed Clinton's every move, most of them falling in the category that reporters and TV anchors commonly refer to as "sexual improprieties." It was Gary Hart all over again, except for two important differences: Clinton didn't dare reporters to follow him home, and Clinton stayed in the race. He had learned from the Hart debacle. While the governor didn't thrive on the attention to his sex life, he sure as hell wasn't going to quit just because of *that*.

Born in 1946, Clinton had the ambiguous distinction of being the first major baby boomer contender for president. He could presumably speak with authority about Elvis, the Beatles, Motown, and Woodstock. Reporters and voters fifty and under had to be somewhat pleased if not proud that here was a candidate who could recall what he was doing when he first heard "I Want to Hold Your Hand." But the press also had a job to do. And while Clinton was never a practicing hippie or a full-fledged radical, neither did he spend the 1960s as a member of Young Americans for Freedom. He had circulated in the decade, and that was enough for reporters to start asking "probing" questions.

A centrist on most policy issues, Clinton also sought the shelter of the safe middle in recounting his experiences with drugs. But owning up to one's past is not the same thing as touting welfare reform or putting more police on the streets. The political and the personal are not always intertwined. In this case, the politics of having it both ways didn't work out very well. Former and current marijuana users found it hard to believe that Clinton smoked but didn't inhale; the people they knew did both. Why bother with the stuff otherwise? "Everyone who didn't smoke dope during that time was a total creep; why would you elect (someone like that)?" said Jeff Ayeroff, a record executive and co-founder of Rock the Vote. And Reagan Democrats, Republicans, and white southern males didn't care whether Clinton had inhaled or not; to them he would always be a draft-dodger, a pleasure-seeker, and an ultra-liberal. A decade after Clinton gave his explanation—and at the conclusion of a presidency known for many tragicomic events—people of different political viewpoints are still amused and amazed by his apparently ambivalent relationship with marijuana.

But Clinton's "drug problem" was nothing compared to his sexual adventures before and after he became commander-in-chief. The irony is that the president's enemies cited his relentless pursuit of women through the decades as another example of the self-indulgence, immaturity, irresponsibility, and immorality of baby boomers, even though he was hardly the first chief executive to conduct extramarital affairs and trysts. And that includes those from both parties; Warren Harding and Dwight Eisenhower were two twentieth-century *Republican* presidents who reportedly had not been faithful to their wives. But conservatives had developed a thesis, and they were not going to let it go under any circumstances: The culture and politics of the 1960s had shaped and molded Bill and Hillary Clinton, and this meant they were bad people. His sins may have included adultery, one of the oldest "vices" known to humankind, but now it was blamed on the moral relativism and permissiveness of the wicked times in which he grew up.

Clinton's travails clearly influenced how the next two baby boomer presidential nominees dealt with issues of character. It's never hip to be square, but Vice President Al Gore and George W. Bush would take their chances in 2000. Although both the 2000 presidential candidates were close in age to Bill Clinton, they presented themselves to the voters as having rarely strayed from Main Street USA. Gore, the Democrat, was especially eager that voters understand that he didn't live the life of Clinton. At the same time, Gore let it be known that he was a big rock fan, and that his favorite member of the Beatles was John, the subversive one. Could Gore have it both ways?

During the campaign, Gore reminded voters again and again that he had been married for thirty years, had four wonderful children, and would always, yes always, be true to his wife. The long, passionate embraces he and Tipper shared in public literally sealed the deal with a kiss.

It was understandable that Gore would draw an obvious contrast to Clinton once or twice, but did he have to do so twenty-five times? His campaign was one long public service announcement on behalf of monogamy and good parenting. Once or twice, this kind of thing can be effective, but when voters are hearing it for the twenty-fifth time, they usually become suspicious. Yet even Bush, asked during one of the debates to say something good about his opponent, thought about it for a moment and answered, "the man loves his wife." The Gore marriage enjoyed bipartisan support.

The love-my-marriage-love-me message, which both Bush and Gore offered voters, was an obvious contrast to Clinton's having lobbied for support while admitting he had not behaved perfectly in his marriage. Bush and Gore were asking to be judged in part on their private lives, while Clinton asked that we look beyond his.

Gore, who admitted smoking (and even inhaling) pot, was more forthcoming than Bush, who refused to provide much detail at all concerning his extracurricular activities during the 1960s and 1970s. Bush used a

quaint, archaic phrase—"Young and foolish"—to describe how he behaved in his twenties and thirties. But "young and foolish" could mean
anything from stealing candy from a store or pulling the fire alarm at
school to taking drugs, if in fact that's what Bush was trying to hide. He
did acknowledge that he drank too much in his younger days, but he usually made that unflattering admission to demonstrate how his life
changed for the better when he accepted Jesus Christ into his heart. Bush
went so far as to call Jesus Christ his favorite philosopher, a preference
expressed publicly by no other presidential candidate in recent American
history, except perhaps the Reverend Pat Robertson.

Having knocked Clinton around, directly and by extension, the
2000 candidates were nonetheless eager to appropriate some of his
groundbreaking techniques for getting elected. First and most important: use pop culture to communicate with the masses. Clinton was extremely effective at this, although he should have never answered a
question from an MTV viewer on whether he wore "boxers or briefs."
From now to eternity, we can assume any question about a candidate's
underwear is a plant. Outside of that unfortunate exchange, however,
the symbolism of Clinton's appearance on MTV has resonated with
both parties. He went to the kids, instead of the kids coming to him,
and engaged in a discussion that for the most part kept to the high
road. And though every campaign does its best to exert control, this
was not one of those fantasy land scenarios concocted by Republicans
in the late 1960s and 1970s, where the preselected young people had
shiny hair, bright white teeth, smart outfits, and unquenchable faith in
"this great country." The MTV audience, to use one of Clinton's pet
phrases, "looked like America," and was concerned for its future.

In the eight years from the first Clinton campaign to Bush against
Gore, MTV declined from cutting edge and hip to the channel of *Real
World*, *Road Rules*, dancing babes in bikinis, and adolescent sex sitcoms that try to be oh-so-daring showing boys kissing boys. In many
ways, MTV had by the late 1990s become your parents' channel, using
time-honored devices of sex, the battle of the sexes, and stage-managed
controversy to entice viewers. Gore's appearance on MTV made little

news; Bush continued the Republican tradition of telling the producers thanks but no thanks.

But free media is a precious thing, and if appearing on MTV could not create a stir, then perhaps appearing somewhere else could. The fact that these appearances were tightly scripted and closely monitored did not keep viewers away, even those who could otherwise care less about politics. In 2000, Oprah Winfrey, who did not in any way invoke the counterculture, played the role of chief facilitator. No one expected interviews on her program to yield breaking news, but seeing the candidates sit down with such a warm and charming hostess was meant to make them "human," a vital ingredient in winning support from female voters. This was the time you got to imagine having Bush or Gore over for dinner.

Neither of the candidates would ever be considered media stars, but they emerged from their sessions with Oprah Winfrey in good shape, even receiving praise for their performances from cynical media types. True to the tenor of their campaigns, Bush and Gore played it safe, revealing neither too much nor too little about themselves or their plans for the country. In the history of presidential campaigns and television, the 2000 *Oprah* interviews merit a few paragraphs, and nothing more.

If only they could all be like Bill Clinton, the Republicans' nightmare and the media's dream. In 1992, Clinton also appeared on a talk show hosted by an African American, in this case Arsenio Hall. On that night, Clinton didn't just cross the line between politics and pop culture; he obliterated it—mixing rock and roll and television in one never to be forgotten sequence.

Like a master MC, Arsenio gave no indication of what was about to happen. He announced his "next guest," and out came Clinton, although for a few moments even that fact seemed in dispute. The presumptive Democratic nominee emerged from the shadows, wearing dark shades, and strutted down a flight of stairs while performing a saxophone solo of Elvis Presley's "Heartbreak Hotel." How many people across the United States stared at the screen in disbelief? Rock stars are supposed to be outrageous, not politicians, and yet the Clinton team

had concocted a pop culture moment that was as radical—and calculating—as the Sex Pistols saying "fuck" on British television in the
1970s. Next to Clinton's turn on Arsenio, Madonna's overpriced cof-
fee-table book of her own nude photos and controversial homo/
hetero/bisexual videos were about as transgressive as Winnie the Pooh.
She was walking a well-tread path for an entertainer; he had gone
where no man or woman running for president had ever gone before—
and may never again.

The song "Heartbreak Hotel" may have been thirty-six years old by
then, and yet in this context it sounded as fresh as rap or grunge. Clinton had catapulted rock and roll into politics in a way that his Democratic and Republican predecessors could have never imagined. This
was not a photo op or a cautious and passing reference in a longer
speech, but an act of open defiance, in the best tradition of rock and
roll itself. As in those classic movies where teenagers gyrate with
abandon to rhythm and blues while their fearful parents stand to the
side, Clinton was effectively taunting President Bush and his supporters, sending an unmistakable message that they are all too old and too
uptight to try something like this on national television. He was going
over their heads to the masses that had grown up with Elvis, or the
Beatles, or Led Zeppelin, or the Clash, voters from twenty-one to fifty
who took pride in doing or having done crazy things in conjunction
with rock music. Along with promising a tax cut for the middle class
and assorted other political goodies, Clinton was telling the rock and
roll generation to vote for the candidate who was cool like them.

Adapting a sax-and-shades persona was not without risk. Americans
have voiced their desire for candidates and presidents to act "presidential," although it's never been entirely clear how they define that. Proving the negative is easier then defining the positive. When President
Nixon went on national television and proclaimed "I am not a crook,"
he failed the test, as did candidate Bob Dole who, after winning the
GOP New Hampshire primary in 1988, told then-Vice President Bush,
his chief opponent, to "stop lying about my record." Dole's campaign
went into free fall after he made that sour remark. If there's anything the
American public hates more than a sore loser, it's a sore winner.

But Clinton had one important advantage over Nixon and Dole—the freedom to maneuver. As the first serious candidate to emerge from the generation that turned on, tuned in, and dropped out, he capitalized on the sense of low expectations associated with the idea of baby boomers leading the nation. He started his campaign having to overcome the skeptics, not only because of his personal characteristics, although those didn't help, but also because he was twenty-two in 1968. Late in the 1992 campaign, and after he was elected president, Clinton's alleged fealty to the spirit and ideology of the 1960s was used against him over and over. The impeachment hearings of 1998 were in part a referendum on Clinton's lifestyle, notwithstanding the fact that the president helped dig his own grave. But in the early days, Clinton caught his opponents off-guard, and was more willing to play around with his image.

In 1992, far from shaming the baby boomer voting bloc, Clinton emboldened and legitimized them. Attempts by politicians to bond with youth can misfire, such as Richard Nixon's strained visit in the wee hours of the morning to anti-war protests at the Lincoln Memorial in 1970, or Vice President Al Gore's frenetic dance at one of the 1993 inaugural parties. But Clinton was smart, and stayed close to home. Clinton was no King Curtis, but he could hold his own with the cats, and he was not shy to do so before a national audience. Indeed, one might conclude without being too cynical that he learned the instrument just so he would have one more way to woo voters.

The phrase "out of the closet" may mean one thing in West Hollywood, the Castro District, and along Christopher Street, but it meant quite another to Congressman David Hobson, a conservative Republican from Ohio. In 1997, the Capitol Hill newspaper *Roll Call* "outed" Hobson as an unabashed fan of the Rolling Stones. It had been many years since "Satisfaction," but as long as Keith Richards looked like a man who never met a drug he didn't like, the Stones could never be *that* respectable. Veterans of the culture wars with long

memories might well wonder why Congressman Hobson was so enamored of this particular band.

On October 23, 1997, the Rolling Stones performed in concert before a sold-out crowd at Jack Kent Cooke Stadium in Washington,
D.C. As usual when the Stones come to town—any town—VIPs with
an affinity for the band or those just trying to make the scene, place
calls and collect on IOUs in a concerted effort to wrangle choice tickets or maybe, just maybe, a couple of backstage passes. In Los Angeles or New York, actors and other entertainers are certain to be on the
list to meet Mick and Keith, while in Washington, D.C., politicians or
high government officials call in chits.

Prior to the Jack Kent Cooke Stadium performance, *Roll Call* reported
that Congressman Hobson had scored a photo op with the legendary team
of Jagger/Richards. Once upon a time, a snapshot of these three together
would have been political gold in the hands of a Republican primary opponent. Go back, say, to 1972—the year of McGovern v. Nixon—and
imagine that a Hobson-type congressman quietly makes his way backstage at a Stones' concert, only to find some young staffer from the opposing camp, tipped off in advance, armed and ready with camera in
hand. The resulting shot would be plastered on the front of a massive hit
piece in record time. In those days it would have been political suicide for
a conservative Midwest Republican to appear in a photo with any of the
Rolling Stones, not to mention those two. And make no mistake; Republican Hobson is a conservative Republican. The 1998 edition of the *Al-
manac of American Politics* reported that in 1996 Hobson earned an 80
percent approval rating from the Christian Coalition. In the 1995–1996
session of Congress, the congressman voted against the ban on assault
weapons and for a constitutional amendment against burning the American flag. Hobson's votes are typical of the far-right contingent—led by
former congressman Newt Gingrich—who wrested control of the House
of Representatives from the Democrats in 1994.

Indeed, among many reasons offered for the Republicans' historic triumph that year was their success at exploiting lingering resentment of
mainstream voters over the political and cultural legacy of the 1960s.

Much more than the Beatles, who wore fashionable suits and behaved reasonably well at least through the middle of 1966, the Rolling Stones represented everything conservatives hated about that "vile" decade: sex, drugs, long hair, and contempt for authority.

And yet despite the attempts of Republicans and some liberals to act as if the spirit of '67 still hovers ominously over America, the 1960s were a long time ago. The Stones today are freaks, but not for the reason they were at the time of the 1969 release of "Honky Tonk Women." They are freaks now because they are still touring at the age of sixty. Simply by outliving and outlasting the competition, the Stones have earned their right to be crowned as "World's Greatest Rock and Roll Band," though their singles, albums, and concerts from the 1960s and early 1970s certainly justify the title as well. At the beginning of the twenty-first century they continue to perform before sold-out audiences in huge stadium shows, just as they did twenty and thirty years earlier. Mick Jagger, a student at the London School of Economics before going into music, has practiced capitalism with a vengeance. From 1989 to 2002, the Rolling Stones generated $1.5 billion in gross revenues, according to an article in the September 30, 2002, edition of *Fortune Magazine*. Name one conglomerate, movie studio, or country that did as well financially two decades past its prime. The sun never sets on the Rolling Stones.

It can't only be nostalgia that compels rock fans in their forties and fifties, who comprised a big percentage of the Stones' concertgoers during the 1990s, to pay extravagant ticket prices for a two-hour performance. Not that the Stones have ever cared what critics or anyone else on the outside thinks. This is the source of their power, and their peculiar brand of charm. In the 1960s, the Stones flipped off parents, educators, and religious leaders, while in the 1990s, the band did the same to all those who considered it an obscenity that a band of over-fifty-five year olds would play their ancient hits at stadium shows around the country. They simply do what they want to do, which is just what their millions of fans expect from them even today. The rest can go to hell.

Still, Mick Jagger at fifty-seven was no longer polite society's Public Enemy number one, as was the Mick Jagger of twenty-seven. And despite Keith Richards' ghoulish appearance and slurred speech, or Jagger's habit of siring children out of wedlock, the Stones are not regarded anymore as rock's reigning bad boys.

By 1998, Hobson hardly put his political future at great risk by sidling up to the Stones. At best, such a photo might have drawn a collective "so what" from the voters in his district. And maybe the congressman and the band had more in common then they knew. The politics of the Stones—individually and collectively—have never been entirely clear. Through the years, the band has deliberately refrained from saying much about political or social issues. Perhaps they don't wish to offend their fans, perhaps they don't care one way or the other, or perhaps they believe that rock bands should stick to playing rock. Everyone does not share this view; Bruce Springsteen is an obvious example of a rock and roll star who insists on expressing his political opinions, through both his lyrics and on-the-record conversations with journalists. It's hard to conceive of Springsteen writing a song with the title "It's Only Rock and Roll," even if he meant to be ironic. To Springsteen, rock and roll has always been more, so much more, than the sum of its parts.

In the 1970s, the Stones fled their native country for the south of France to escape England's punishing tax system, which might well be the most profound political statement ever made by this band. Shedding the burden of excessive British taxation is one act of rebellion any good Republican could embrace. After all, the two overriding issues that have united Republicans, at least since the 1970s, are mistrust of Big Government and disgust with higher taxes. On others, including abortion, gay rights, education policy, and crime, the GOP evinced wide and politically damaging divisions.

Viewed in this light, the photo could almost have come from the Hobson campaign: "Congressman joins noted anti-tax crusaders backstage before the big show."

⌒

The Stones' original manager, Andrew Loog Oldham, cunningly cast his band as the un-Beatles—surly rather than charming, scraggly rather than well-groomed, sullen rather than engaging. This pose served them well in 1964 and 1965, until acid, Carnaby Street fashions, and unimaginable fame eradicated any meaningful distinction between the world's only two super groups. By the end of 1965 the Stones released *December's Children (And Everybody's)*, an LP whose liner notes included several lines of verse written by Oldham that barely rise to the level of mediocre. The "poem" included references to a number of major political events of the time. By contrast Beatle albums speak only of the Beatles and their music. In the never-ending quest to needle the champs, Oldham was playing the "relevance" card at a time when rock and roll and its audience were entering adulthood. Calculating though they were, Oldham's lines first revealed to me the possibility that rock and politics enjoyed some kind of connection. That was in 1973, many years after the fact.

3

CONNECTION: A PERSONAL STORY

I began to pay attention to rock and roll in the fall of 1966, when *The Monkees* debuted on NBC. I had just turned 10 and was a master of sports trivia, but even if pressed I could not have named five of the top rock groups at that time. I had no help in this regard. My parents didn't listen to rock and roll, I was the oldest child in the family, and the price of records far exceeded my allowance of twenty-five cents per week. I could tell you more about World War II than the British Invasion. The Beatles appearance on *The Ed Sullivan Show* might have changed the world, but it didn't change my home.

A typical weekday in the mid-1960s found me watching television after my homework. I'm tempted to say that I tuned in to *The Monkees* because I thought it was pure slapstick, or a documentary about the United States Congress, but I simply can't remember the reason. It was probably just an accident. You never hear the debut of *The Monkees* cited as a seminal event in the history of rock and roll; it's always Elvis at Sun Studios, the Beatles arriving in New York, Dylan going electric at Newport, or the gathering of the tribes at Woodstock. I know I'm in the minority, but here's at least one vote for that TV show about a struggling rock band with long hair and friendly dispositions. It certainly worked for me.

In more than three decades of steady TV viewing, I can recall only four programs I liked immediately: *Batman*, *Cheers*, *Friends*, and *The Monkees*. Rock and roll is for the young, but not the very young. At the age of eight, *The Monkees* would have done nothing for me, but by the age of ten they had me from the first episode. I knew what I would be doing every Monday night at eight, even during summer reruns. I once had a girlfriend who told me that she would refuse to blink each time she watched the show, for fear she would miss seeing Davy Jones. As a boy, I didn't go that route, but I did buy all the Monkee magazines I could afford. I especially looked forward each week to seeing the band perform its songs on the program. Plot, character, and the steady stream of silly jokes mattered, but not as much as the music. By Christmas 1966, *The Monkees* had overtaken the Los Angeles Rams and become as important in my life as the Dodgers.

I soon realized that my allowance and birthday money could go toward items other than baseball cards, comic books, and candy. Eventually I saved a sufficient amount of cash to actually buy an album by you-know-who. On the afternoon I purchased *More of the Monkees*, the band's second LP, I played it so many times over the next several hours that I couldn't get "Mary Mary," "She," "Sometime in the Morning," and "(I'm Not Your) Stepping Stone" out of my brain. With guitars, drums, and vocals trapped inside, it took me several hours to fall asleep—my first bout with insomnia—and it was entirely the fault of the Monkees.

I spent the following months playing only the Monkees as slavishly as if I had taken a vow of fidelity. None of the other groups caught my ear. But even a starstruck fifth-grader gets restless after awhile. The same twenty or thirty songs repeated for months start to lose their appeal. You forget why you fell in love with them in the first place. The Monkees meant a lot to me, but not that much. I began to stray, first with the Beatles and then moving on to countless others.

It would be many years before I could acknowledge that the Monkees were merely a slick imitation of the Beatles; rightly tagged as the "Pre-Fab Four." By the middle of 1967 even I had to admit that the Beatles were the better group on record. I took a crash course in Beatles 101, listening to everything from "Please Please Me" and "I Want to Hold Your Hand" to "Tomorrow Never Knows." As a ten-year-old I was able to maintain the necessary critical distance. I had no personal stake in having others concede that the Beatles were brilliant. I merely thought they had good songs. And having not followed the Beatles when they were four lovable moptops, I had no appreciation for the impact on their American fans when they grew beards and affected the hip look of London in the mid-1960s. As far as I was concerned, they had been scruffy, trendy, and hip for years. I was also too young to regard *Sgt. Pepper's Lonely Hearts Club Band*, released in the summer of 1967, as a landmark in the history of pop music. To my mind it was simply a neat-looking album—including the helpful step of printing the lyrics on the back cover—with a bunch of cool songs. Nothing more and nothing less.

I could get enough of the Monkees, I could even get enough of the Beatles, but now I couldn't get enough of rock and roll. This meant turning on the radio, where every hour or so one could hear songs by the Turtles, Byrds, Lovin' Spoonful, Donovan, Jefferson Airplane, the Who, and the Rolling Stones. I quickly discovered Top 40 in particular, which at that time was virtually the only outlet for providing hit singles and occasional album cuts to the general public. I developed something of an addiction to the format, locking the dial on the same spot for two or three hours at a stretch. I didn't want to miss any songs. When riding in the car with my parents I would nag them to change their station to my station, a request they granted on occasion, though not without mild protest.

I stuck with Top 40 through 1968, 1969, and 1970, even as FM rock stations began to assert themselves. At the age of thirteen, however, I didn't have the patience to listen to a ten-minute Grateful Dead song, or the latest extended jam by Savoy Brown. (As a matter of fact, that's been true my whole life.) Instead, I bought "ABC" by the Jackson 5 (I was sure the lead singer was a girl), as well as singles by Three Dog Night, Edison Lighthouse, White Plains, the Temptations, Edwin Starr, Mountain, and Eric Burdon and War, to name a few. Sure, the Beatles had broken up in early 1970, but I still thought rock and roll had a bright future.

But in the summer of 1973, when I was sixteen going on seventeen, I stopped listening to rock and roll on the radio, whether Top 40 or FM. It seemed to me then—and it still seems to me now—that in 1973 good or even decent rock was rapidly becoming an endangered species. A few examples suffice. In 1972, the Rolling Stones released *Exile on Main Street*, one of their best albums, and in 1973 they released *Goat's Head Soup*, easily one of their worst. Lightweight pop dominated, a sound that had rarely polluted the airwaves since 1965. I am not sure why this happened, although it's curious that the return of fluff occurred in the same year that America formally ended its military engagement in Vietnam. At the very least, it's an intriguing coincidence that rock lost its edge when the U.S. was no longer directly involved in the war. By the same token, one of rock's all-time greatest years happened to be that same 1965, just as hundreds of thousands of American forces were being sent to fight in Southeast Asia.

The number one pop song of 1973 was "Killing Me Softly with His Song" by Roberta Flack; at number two was "Tie a Yellow Ribbon 'Round the Ole' Oak Tree," recorded by Tony Orlando and Dawn. Fittingly, by 1999, a municipal judge in Fort Lipton, Colorado, was inflicting "Tie a Yellow Ribbon" as "musical torture" for young people who violated that city's noise ordinance. Cruel punishment, possibly, unusual punishment, definitely. To be fair, Tony Orlando and Dawn ranked behind Dean Martin and Wayne Newton, each of whom had two songs on the list compiled by that Colorado judge. But these two had long ago ceased to matter in rock or pop music.

In my life, Tony Orlando and Dawn were the anti-Monkees. Thanks to "Tie a Yellow Ribbon" and other songs of the same ilk, I no longer cared which singles made it to number one for the week, which were picked to do well, and whether the Stones were on the verge of recording a new album. "All the hits all the time" meant nothing to me in an era of the Carpenters, Tony Orlando, and "The Night the Lights Went Out in Georgia." I was finished with rock, pop, soul, and all the rest of it.

But having turned off the radio and closed the lid on my record player, I needed another way to fill up my leisure time. I settled on television, which in those pre-cable days offered limited options. Luckily for me, the Senate Watergate hearings convened in the spring of 1973, and continued through the summer. Television provided gavel-to-gavel coverage, the first time I had ever heard the term. As a fledgling Democrat who would have cast a ballot for George McGovern had I been eligible to vote in 1972, the Watergate hearings were a gift. A mere five months after Richard Nixon had been overwhelmingly granted a second term, his presidency was in serious trouble. If only politics could always be like this!

Even at sixteen, I couldn't bear the thought of four more years of Nixon. But now the spectacle of all these arrogant, clean-cut Nixon staffers being humiliated on national television gave me a great sense of satisfaction. I figured the president would survive this, but at a huge political cost. In any event, no longer would I have to sit there fuming while my few remaining Republican friends trumpeted Nixon's landslide victory in 1972.

But best of all, Watergate was fun. Nobody got killed, and the important details and principal players changed almost on a daily basis. Each new witness provided some memorable quote—often without intending to—that epitomized the Nixon White House. Watergate demanded your full attention, yet unlike the Whitewater scandal involving Bill and Hillary Clinton, which seemed to span the entire 1990s, a reasonably intelligent person could follow the chain of events without too much difficulty.

I was mildly disappointed in August 1973 when the acquisition of a full-time summer job—at my parents' urging—prevented me from watching the hearings live. Whereas Watergate has often been blamed for turning people off of politics, in my case it had the opposite effect. Thanks to Watergate, I craved news about politicians and politics, a habit that continues to this day. That fall I spent a portion of my hard-earned money on subscriptions to *The New Republic, The Nation*, and *The Washington Post*'s Sunday edition, which didn't arrive at my California home until the following Thursday.

The excitement of Watergate furthered my estrangement from rock and roll, which might have pleased Nixon, had he only known. The Beatles and the Stones couldn't compare to the travails of Haldeman, Ehrlichman, Dean, Mitchell, Magruder, and so forth. My thirty to forty albums gathered dust on the shelf throughout the summer. By September, I could barely remember what I had in my collection.

During the early fall of 1973, the Senate Watergate hearings officially concluded, although the star witnesses had long since made their appearances before Sam Ervin, Howard Baker, and their colleagues. This was just as well, because I had returned to high school, a senior in search of a good college to attend the next year. I stopped following politics on a daily basis, paying close attention to only two events that fall: the resignation of Vice President Spiro Agnew, and President Nixon's firing of Special Prosecutor Archibald Cox and Attorney General Elliot Richardson in the so-called Saturday Night Massacre.

On another Saturday night, a month or so after Nixon dismissed Cox and Richardson, I was home alone with nowhere to go and nothing to do, a not uncommon occurrence during my high school days. For reasons that remain obscure, late in the evening I started to casually flip through those thirty to forty albums I had been neglecting for months. Having almost reached the end of the line, I paused before a record that I had just about forgotten called *December's Children (And Everybody's)* by the Rolling Stones. I couldn't remember where I got the album, or even why. Originally released in late 1965, *December's Children* featured a stunning cover shot of the band packed together in what appears to be a narrow passageway, the five of them already showing the effects of life lived much too fast. At that point, the Stones were still in their early twenties, with the exception of the bass player, Bill Wyman, who was on the brink of thirty.

Released six months after "Satisfaction" reached number one in Britain and America—the song that made the Rolling Stones a worthy rival to the Beatles and Bob Dylan—*December's Children* was the last album in which the Stones could play the "us-against-the-world" role favored by renegade rock bands on the rise. In a short time, the Stones would become undeniable rock stars, making tons of money and sampling all kinds of goodies. By late 1966, the Stones projected an image of upper-class hedonism, and by 1968, they were cynical and decadent. Through it all they made a number of exceptional records, and would continue to do so into the late 1970s. If nothing else, during their first twenty years the Stones proved to be masters at keeping up with the times. Mick Jagger's talent for accurately measuring the shifts in audience tastes through the years has been underestimated.

December's Children was perfect for an awkward seventeen-year-old who considered politics more important than sex. Songs such as "Get Off of My Cloud" and "I'm Free" beautifully expressed the anti-parent, anti-teacher, and anti-employer fantasies of teenagers in America, and no doubt Britain as well. These songs carried a political message, although not in the sense of taking the "right" stand on a burning issue, which is how rock would subsequently earn points with liberals, radicals, and ordinary concerned citizens. The Stones were simply suggesting another way of looking at things while framing the world in terms of young v. old, hip v. square, conformity v. independence. I wanted to be on the side of the Stones.

The second selling point of this album was an unexpected treat. Andrew Loog Oldham, the Stones' famous and famously reclusive producer—author of one of the best insider accounts of rock and roll, *Stoned* (published in the U.S. in 2001)—wrote that long and winding poem about the Stones and their times. I read it straight; the genuine musings of a member of the newly minted pop aristocracy in Britain. I later understood that the words were in actuality the product of a PR genius taking the opportunity to introduce his clients to a more mature audience, college students to be precise, while holding on to their base: junior and high school kids.

In his liner notes, Oldham referred to the Watts Riots, which occurred in August 1965, the war in Vietnam, and the assassination of President Kennedy:

> But we have no message to our sea of faces
> Of destruction and riots in downtown LA;
> And war in uptown Vietnam.
> Or who really killed that solider of peace in Dallas a year or so ago

Nearly four decades later, I have yet to locate "uptown Vietnam" on a map.

At seventeen, I was enthralled, even if Oldham's specifics were shaky (was JFK "a soldier of peace?" Mr. Castro, not to mention the families of Patrice Lumumba and Ngo Dinh Diem, might beg to differ) and his style was self-consciously derivative of period hipster lingo. I had just begun reading extensively about the 1960s, a decade that meant little to me while it was in progress, though by 1967 I had begun paying reasonably close attention to major stories. I broke news of Bobby Kennedy's shooting to my parents, watched the Democratic Convention in 1968, and remember where I was when I first heard about the murder of Sharon Tate. But I didn't think of these events as part of the 1960s, a single historical entity.

And yet by 1973, the 1960s were already missed, not least by people who had graduated from college in that decade and were now forced to assume adult responsibilities. The point at which nostalgia for the 1960s ends and regret over the passing of youth begins is not easy to determine. Acid, rock, acid rock, antiwar demonstrations, easily available sex and so on had convinced students and their allies that they had built a new world, in opposition to and without any help from their elders. The thought that it could all disappear on January 1, 1970, was too painful to bear. Force-feeding the 1960s to the rest of us has been an obsession of some baby boomers for over thirty years.

Still, those like me who were born too late to experience firsthand the Watts Riots, escalation of the Vietnam War, advent of LBJ's Great Society, and rise of the Black Power Movement, at times regret that we entered the world in 1956 rather than, say, 1949. Perhaps we were the victims of propaganda, or perhaps we were simply curious. The yearning to be part of the 1960s was not, in my case, starry-eyed. I realize I would have been eligible for the draft, forced to confront hard decisions on "tuning in, turning on, dropping out," and suffered through countless nutty debates about how to raise the consciousness of society.

Reading the liner notes of *December's Children* hurled me back into the middle of the 1960s at precisely the moment I was a ready and willing time-traveler. More important, the album marked the first time that I ever seriously considered the possibility that rock and politics might have some sort of connection. Ironically, Oldham mentioned Watts, Vietnam, and the JFK assassination in order to make the point that the Stones would have nothing to say on these or any other burning issues of the day. They were just a rock and roll band playing rock and roll music—and please don't ask any more questions. The answers to society's ills would have to be found somewhere else, or come from someone else. Politics is not what the Rolling Stones did for a living.

Still, Oldham obviously felt the band must take note of current events, even to shrug them off with the rock and roll equivalent of "no comment." Too much was happening outside the insular world of recording studios, clubs, concert halls, and hotel rooms where he and the Stones had spent so much time from 1963 to 1966.

Oldham's liner notes for *December's Children*, combined with the exceptional material on the album—Jagger/Richards were just coming into their own in 1965 as a quality songwriting team—carried me back to rock and roll for good. No longer would my record collection sit on the shelf gathering dust, and no longer would it stay at thirty to forty albums, but instead grow exponentially over the coming months and years. If the Monkees had been just the right band to introduce an innocent ten-year-old to rock and roll, early Stones was ideal for a seventeen-year-old intrigued with the combination of hard rock, contempt for middle-class mores, and vintage '60s political and social turbulence in one neat package.

~~

I don't know for sure that the liner notes on *December's Children* were the first in rock and roll to make reference to recent events, but the album appeared when the rock business was beginning to acknowledge politics, and in several different ways.

A few months before its release, Barry McGuire had a number one hit with the folk/rock song "Eve of Destruction" (lyrics by P. F. Sloan), which was essentially a recitation of the news mixed with a dash of Cold War paranoia, and backed by acoustic guitar, organ, and drums. The phrase "eve of destruction" is timeless—it would have been appropriate after September 11, 2001—although the lyrics of this song were very specific to 1965:

> Think of all the hate there is in Red China
> Then take a look around at Selma, Alabama
> If the button is pushed, there's no runnin' away
> There will be no one to save with the world in a grave

The sentiments are corny and simplistic, and yet the song is absolutely irresistible, even forty years after its release. The Right hated it, in part because of the comparison of Mao's "Red China" with the racism of Selma, Alabama; an egregious example of moral equivalence. The song was also deeply pessimistic, although McGuire's Dylanesque growl veered dangerously close to self-parody. Several radio stations refused to play "Eve of Destruction," which obviously didn't hinder its commercial success, and might well have helped. "The message in the song that change was needed or the world would continue on its suicidal way toward nuclear war, violence, and hatred, did not sit well with establishment values."[1] "Eve of Destruction" was the perfect crime. The sound was stolen from Dylan and the Byrds, who had united rock and folk earlier in the year, and the words were taken from daily headlines. But at a time when the work of rock's premier lyricists—Dylan, Lennon, and Jagger—had gotten more obscure, the genius of "Eve of Destruction" was that it could be understood by anyone over the age of fourteen. That alone made it a threat to the establishment, which didn't know and frankly didn't care what was on Dylan's mind in "Like a Rolling Stone," which reached number two in September 1965. But they didn't want their kids falling under the spell of "Eve of Destruction."

Nothing like this song had ever ascended the charts before, and few have done so since. Recapping the news is not a preferred method of communication in rock, soul, or rap. Still, "Eve of Destruction" and Oldham's contribution to *December's Children* demonstrated that rock could flirt with politics and not only get away with it, but could actually prosper. Performers, record executives, and audiences paid close attention.

Rock and roll turned ten in 1965. The original stars, Elvis Presley, Chuck Berry, Little Richard, Fats Domino had stopped making hit records. Their place at the top had been usurped by the Beatles, the Rolling Stones, the Byrds, and Bob Dylan, who had just recently made the transformation from acoustic to electric instruments, and folk to rock and roll. The original rock and roll audience, most of them between twelve and seventeen when Elvis took off, were now in their middle to late twenties. Songs about going steady or even young lust could not possibly have had the same impact on these older fans, although in most cases they remained attracted to the sound of rock and roll. Their needs were satisfied by the Stones, the Beatles, the Kinks, the Who, and the other bands that entered the field in 1964–65.

By 1968, even Elvis could no longer ignore the trend toward social criticism and politics in rock and roll that had begun some three years before. That year he recorded his most overtly political single, the Mac Davis-penned "In the Ghetto," which in essence marked his own coming to terms with the 1960s.

It's difficult to pinpoint the beginning of the counterculture, but certainly by late 1965 some of the pieces were starting to fall into place. Kids were listening to lots of rock, protesting against the war in Vietnam, calling for change in college curriculums and internal policies, ingesting massive amounts of drugs, and adapting a New Left agenda (soon to include feminism, environmentalism, and social justice.) A more educated audience demanded a new kind of rock and roll, and whether by luck or design they got their wish in the late 1960s.

By contrast, much rock and roll from the 1950s and early 1960s today sounds simple and quaint, both in musical technique and political content. And yet it represented much more than going steady, drinking coke, and cruising. The politics of early rock and roll was not on par with "Eve of Destruction," but you can find it if you try.

"They certainly helped to change the world," veteran Los Angeles DJ Jim Ladd, one of the pioneers of FM radio, says of the rock and roll stars from the 1950s. "But I don't know that they set out to do that. I think that they found this music and went with it. And it happened that this new music was so magnetic to teenagers, and so offensive to adults, that it really snowballed."

SOMETHING NEW

The first debate I recall over the merits of the 1950s v. 1960s occurred in Sam Shepard's 1972 play, *The Tooth of Crime*, and it featured a strong rock and roll subtext. Hoss, a devotee of Chuck Berry, Robert Mitchum, and cruising, squares off against Crow, who looks like Keith Richards and digs Keith Moon and Ginger Baker. Seemingly every other sentence in the play refers to this or that star, hit song, or legendary venue. The history of rock and roll is to *The Tooth of Crime* what high school is to *Grease*. The battle between Hoss and Crow is fought with words and weapons, until the older one, unable to accept that his time has passed, puts a gun in his mouth, and pulls the trigger. It's Crow's show now, or at least until some late 1970s punk rock cat comes along to challenge *him*. But Shepard didn't write that play.

Apart from the stage, the "decade wars" are not usually waged between people wearing leather jackets, but coats and ties. Rock and roll is a tiny part of the discussion, if it figures at all. The positions are easy to summarize. Either the 1960s ruined the 1950s, or the 1960s saved America from the 1950s. These are the two choices. You can usually tell a person's political leanings by which of the two decades he or she favors. Partisans of the 1950s are typically conservative, while Democrats side with the 1960s. The debate has been perpetuated in books,

articles, and on the campaign trial. Advocates—or defenders—of the
1960s tend to be the same people who disparage the previous decade,
while the pro-1950s lobby harbors a bitterness or even hatred for the
following twenty years, arguing that America regained its sanity only
with the election of Ronald Reagan as president in 1980.

Conservatives revere the 1950s as the last time when the Traditional
Values That Made This Country Great prevailed: respect for authority,
basic decency, innocence (always innocence), sexual modesty, a sense
of shame, and an abiding respect for God, family, community, and the
USA. We were engaged in a great struggle then, actually a series of
great struggles, and the vast majority of Americans knew right from
wrong, according to conservative dogma thirty and forty years after the
fact. In those days there was no "Eve of Destruction," songs aimed at
teenagers didn't dare equate racism with communism, or embrace the
pending revolution. In the 1950s, it was Us against Them, capitalism
v. communism, democracy v. totalitarianism, freedom v. oppression.
Presented with a series of unambiguous choices, the American people
knew which way to turn. Never again would it seem so simple.

In its later incarnation, the 1950s cheering section included some of
the most prominent names in American politics. One of them was Newt
Gingrich, former Georgia congressman, Speaker of the House of Representatives from 1995 to 1998, and architect of the Republican takeover
of the House in 1994, the *first time* that had happened since the mid-
1950s. In his 1995 book, *To Renew America*, hastily cobbled together to
capitalize on the stunning victory of the previous year, Gingrich wrote:

> From the arrival of English-speaking colonists in 1607 until 1965 there
> was one continuous civilization built around a set of commonly ac-
> cepted legal and cultural principles. From the Jamestown colony and
> the Pilgrims, through de Tocqueville's Democracy in America, up to the
> Norman Rockwell paintings of the 1950s, there was a clear sense of
> what it meant to be an American.[1]

In response to this all-inclusive paragraph, it's tempting to offer the
period from 1861 to 1865 as one example of a time when the defini-

tion of what it meant to be an American was in serious dispute, but the rebuttal would have made no difference to Gingrich. "As was widely remarked at the time of Newt Gingrich's 'Republican Revolution' of the mid-1990s, one way of looking at the hardline Republicans—especially from the Religious Right—is to see them as motivated by a classical nationalist desire for a return to a Golden Age, in their case the pre-Vietnam days of the 1950s."[2] Gingrich was adamant in his view that in the span of a few short years liberalism had destroyed the idea of America painstakingly constructed during the previous two hundred. A lot was riding on this thesis, and Gingrich simply couldn't allow contrary evidence to get in the way. He and his conservative cohorts argued that the apparent deterioration of American society began with the Great Society programs of the middle 1960s, otherwise known as the expansion of the welfare state, along with the concomitant rise of the counterculture. "For Gingrich, the Great Society represents the political disasters of affirmative action, feminism, community organizing, environmental activism and the like. But the deeper object of his fear and loathing is the 'counterculture,' which represents something everybody knows about and nobody talks about . . . "[3]

For those of us familiar with Gingrich the adult, railing in the House of Representatives and on Fox News against Democrats, it comes as something of a shock to hear him describe the suburban paradise of his youth. How could such an angry man have emerged from such an idyllic background? Probably the 1960s—and Democrats—are to blame. At one point in his book, Gingrich describes a scene from his childhood that's a cross between a Norman Rockwell painting and one of those family-oriented sitcoms from the 1950s. "I was ten years old and my mother allowed me to go to an afternoon matinee in Harrisburg (Pa). That was a safer era, and with bus money in my pocket, no one worried about my getting home."[4] It wouldn't matter to Gingrich, but I knew ten-year-olds from the 1960s, 1970s, and 1980s who also traveled by bus to their destination and returned safely. These kids came from good homes too, where the parents kept an eye on their children. Must have been a fluke.

With this constant refrain, Republicans have created a political dilemma for themselves—praising society in the 1950s while competing in elections in the 1990s. "Back to the Future" might be a clever movie title, but it is an ineffective and even self-defeating campaign slogan. As Bill Clinton noted on many occasions, the candidate who best embraces the future and effectively promotes himself as an agent of change wins elections—no easy task when you're constantly invoking the past as a political paradise. Besides, there were aspects of the 1950s that sane Republicans would find hard or impossible to defend, such as illegal and unsafe abortions, Jim Crow laws, anti-communist hysteria and a general sense that blacks, women, and gays had it worse. Is this what we would be returning to?

Where conservatives are scared of the 1960s, liberals are absolutely terrified of the 1950s. They draw up a list of sins from the decade that would frighten even those in the sensible middle: McCarthyism, nuclear bomb shelters, the Klan run amok, women held as virtual prisoners in their suburban homes, gays in hiding, schlock on the screen, anti-intellectualism in government. Under this scenario it makes perfect sense that *The Twilight Zone* is a product of the 1950s, because its recurrent themes of alienation and displacement accurately describe the feelings of any enlightened person suddenly transported back to those prehistoric times. Although decades tend not to repeat themselves, the unspoken but unmistakable assumption of the left-wing critique is that we can be thankful that the 1960s rescued us from the 1950s.

Liberals assume that you know the 1960s are cool, and so they expand their efforts toward depicting the 1950s as hostile, naïve, and hopelessly retrograde, about as relevant to contemporary society as the Bull Moose Party and the telegraph. Numerous TV programs—including comedy skits—and films from the 1980s and 1990s took subtle and not-so-subtle shots at the 1950s. It would be naïve to assume that these productions had no political agenda, as entertaining as they might otherwise have been. One need not be a flaming conservative to recognize there are more people on the Left than on the Right in Hollywood. This can be easily confirmed by looking at federal or state campaign disclosure forms.

The 1950s bashers are relentless. They rarely miss an opportunity to charge the decade with a variety of crimes against humanity, including racism, homophobia, sexism, repression, oppression, jingoism, and, last but not least, bad television. Furthermore, note the detractors, this was the last decade in which that "demon"—the dreaded white male— exercised total control over government and business. And don't forget that Eisenhower, Nixon, McCarthy, and J. Edgar Hoover held power for much of the decade.

So much of what we know today comes from television. People who mock the 1950s like to get at the decade through its sitcoms, two in particular. One of these is *Father Knows Best*, and the other is *Ozzie and Harriet*, both of which are ridiculed for perpetrating a hopelessly naïve picture of the inner workings of the Middle American family, even for the "simple times" in which they were popular. David Halberstam has written that 1950s television "reflected a world of warm-hearted, sensitive, tolerant Americans, a world devoid of anger and meanness of spirit and, of course, failure."[5]

We think we know so much more about suburbia now, thanks to director David Lynch, the film *American Beauty*, and similar offerings. The oft-expressed view, which has become a cliché of its own, is that moral corruption and sexual hypocrisy lurks just beneath the surface of the neatly manicured lawns, Friday night high school football games, and potlucks of your typical American suburb. If we didn't know that before, we certainly do now. We seem to have reached the point in American pop culture in which a happy suburban dweller without a shocking past or hidden secrets is depicted in TV and film about as often as a proud member of the Communist Party.

Father Knows Best and *Ozzie and Harriet* were popular in their day, but that doesn't automatically mean that the audience bought into the warm and fuzzy image of the programs. After all, *Will and Grace* attracted strong ratings in the late 1990s and beyond, and yet it would be wrong to assume that all or even most viewers of the show subscribed to its particular take on urban gay life in America. And speaking of gays, they were all but invisible on 1950s television, along with blacks,

Latinos, and women with careers—another unpardonable offense in the view of liberals. Of course, blacks and Latinos in particular were still not satisfied that this problem had been adequately addressed in the 1990s, a charge that Hollywood answered with the claim that "we have a long way to go, but we are doing better."

One does not have to be running for office or affiliated with a political party to join this debate. The two sides don't always play fair. It's not a surprise, but politicians, journalists, academics, and the entertainment industry have on occasion manipulated post–World War II American history to suit their own purposes. Omitting key facts, or distorting others, they offer a questionable interpretation in order to make a larger point about contemporary society and culture. Despite their gaping holes in logic, these universal theories can sound quite seductive, both in book form and on the campaign trail. At least since Vietnam, otherwise known as the "first war the United States ever lost," assigning blame for any number of problems and crises—the Arab oil embargo, declining public schools, teen pregnancy—has been a staple of American politics. Pointing a finger or giving the finger is also conducive to thirty-second sound bites, which is how most American voters now get their news about candidates and issues.

↜

Sam Shepard's Hoss and Crow were on to something that liberals and conservatives—for their own self-serving reasons—prefer to ignore. Despite differences in style, and the transfer of power from America to England, rock and roll represents a link between the 1950s and the 1960s, not a clean break. It was fashionable in the mid and late 1960s to deride Elvis Presley, especially on college campuses, but John Lennon, a hero to that crowd, had said that before Elvis there was nothing. Students in the 1960s liked to think they discovered radical politics, free love, and rock and roll, but they were wrong on all three counts. However, the Beatles, Bob Dylan, the Rolling Stones, and Eric Clapton were actually quite gracious in acknowledging their influ-

ences, be they rock and roll or blues musicians from the 1950s, or folk
and blues artists dating from as far back as the 1930s. They understood
that 1960s rock and roll was merely a link in a long chain.

By now the chain has many links. You could argue that there is a direct connection from Elvis Presley swiveling his hips to Marilyn Manson rubbing his crotch. After all, there is only so much a performer has
in his or her repertoire to turn on the audience, given the limitations of
the human body and restrictive local ordinances. The proverbial enve-
lope can be pushed just so far. But to even imply a cultural bond between Elvis and Marilyn Manson would be a sacrilege to fans of the
King, who probably regard Manson and anyone like him as perverse
and disgusting—precisely the way others described Presley in 1956.
However, once Elvis opened the door anyone could come through.
And that door opened in the 1950s, which brings contemporary society closer to that decade than cultural conservatives would like to admit. Most of them get around this by conveniently leaving the birth of
rock and roll off of their list of things to admire about the 1950s. Instead, we get Gingrich's dreamy recollection of taking a bus trip downtown to see a Saturday afternoon matinee.

It's not like conservatives to keep rock and roll out of politics, especially over the past twenty years. Between the fall of communism
and the War on Terrorism, conservatives took many opportunities to
equate rock with the decline of America. You might recall that before
September 11, 2001, we had April 20, 1999: the killing of eleven students by two of their classmates at Columbine High School. In this
case politicians and commentators couldn't blame Islam, Israel, or
American foreign policy, but conservatives did strongly suggest that
the inspiration for this horrible crime came from the perpetrators having listened to Marilyn Manson and other "shock-rock" performers.
The killers themselves, having conveniently committed suicide, were
unavailable for comment.

As far as we know, there has never been a politician who claimed
that the music of Elvis Presley inspired teenagers to commit murder or
suicide. Elvis was instead accused of influencing white teens to "act"

black—a serious charge in the American South in the 1950s—to con-
template or engage in premarital sex—a serious charge everywhere in
America in the 1950s—and to drink and smoke. Each of these "vices"
threatened the established order as represented by small towns which
were ostensibly free of anxiety, fear, and conflict between parents and
their children. It seems almost unnecessary to point out that this environment, if it existed at all, was stifling for teenagers, which is why
they took to Elvis as if he were some kind of savior. The notion of rock
and roll as necessary for a teenager to feel his life has value and meaning has been a recurrent theme over the past four decades. When
Elvis—and rock and roll—stagnated in the early 1960s, the Beatles
"rescued" the next generation from years of boredom and neglect. The
same happened in 1977, when the Sex Pistols and the Clash stepped in
just as rock was in danger of being ruined forever by Journey, REO
Speedwagon, Styx, and Kansas.

If Presley were a politician, he would have switched parties. The rebellious figure of the 1950s is also the guy who desperately desired—
and received—an audience with President Nixon in 1970. He may
have had these political leanings all along, but nobody would have believed it during the days of "Jailhouse Rock," "Hound Dog," and "I
Got Stung." Throughout his fluctuating career, he was either the good-
looking young man in the black leather jacket or that bloated carica-
ture in the plus-size white jumpsuit. And as befits the change in the
color of his outfits, Elvis's music went from black to white as well,
with many more country or pop ballads featured at the end.

But for all the jokes about his weight, his hairstyle, and his clothes,
fifty years after Elvis made his first series of hit records he still seems
like a contemporary figure in rock and roll, if not pop culture. Even in
rock and roll time, which moves with incredible speed, Elvis is still the
standard by which we measure the impact of rock and roll. The 1976
edition of the *Rolling Stone Illustrated History of Rock and Roll*, published twenty years after the release of "Heartbreak Hotel," put it this
way: "He (Elvis) hit like a Pan American flash, and the reverberations
still linger from the shock of his arrival." That feeling has not dimin-

ished in the early part of the twenty-first century. Among the most anticipated CD releases in the fall of 2002 was a newly remastered collection of Elvis's RCA hits. One gets the feeling that the Elvis industry will flourish for many more decades.

The 1960s veterans can disparage all they want the societal attitudes of the previous decade, but the fact remains that 1950s youth was more than ready for the arrival of Elvis. If not for their enthusiastic acceptance of this new, strange music, rock and roll would have died a quick death. After all, there was nothing inevitable about its success. Presley's producer, Sam Phillips, is quoted in almost every history of rock and roll as saying that he believed that if he could find a white kid who could sing and act like black performers, then he (Phillips) could make a million bucks, but things are never so simple. Yet if we accept the picture conservatives painted of 1950s America, then rock and roll would seem like a bad investment. Elvis was as about as far as one could be from Main Street USA and still be considered a member of the white race. He was born in Mississippi, migrated to Memphis, listened to black radio stations, studied the moves of black performers, and dressed like some kind of crazy fool, mixing outrageous colors. Still, the masses of the under-twenties crowd loved him for it. They were looking for something completely different.

I doubt that Sam Phillips or any other savvy record producer would have said in 1955: "If I could just find me a black, bisexual, flamboyant performer who can sing rock and roll like nobody else, I could make a million dollars." That would have been going too far. Elvis was a risk, so how in the world could the youth of America ever accept Little Richard? It was hard enough for white parents that a black man—any black man—might have designs on their daughters, but a black man fancying their sons would be more than any poor suburban mother's heart could take. Promoting Little Richard would be like coming to bat with the count 0-2. He might even scare the hell out of kids with a strong rebellious streak.

But the new audience was trusting their ears more then their eyes. Sound trumped image back then, unlike the 1970s and later, when they

were of essentially equal importance. And not even Elvis could touch
Little Richard as a straight out rock and roll vocalist. "All I know is
that I heard Little Richard's songs on the radio and it was a motherfucker," said Ray Manzarek, the keyboard player of the Doors, who
was seventeen-years-old in 1956, the year Little Richard came out with
"Long Tall Sally," "Tutti-Frutti," and "Rip It Up." Sure, but Ray Manzarek was not your average American teenager. He had cultivated a
strong interest in jazz, avant-garde theater, and abstract art. He had no
allegiance to middle-class morality, and probably believed that offending society was a noble goal for any performer, especially one who was
targeting the masses. A budding piano player, Manzarek had an ulte-
rior motive as well to listen to both Little Richard and Fats Domino. In
1967, Manzarek, by then keyboard player and one of the principal
composers for the Doors, borrowed a riff out of the Domino collection
for the long middle section of "Light My Fire," the group's huge number one single from that summer.

Of course, Manzarek was not alone in his unbridled enthusiasm for
Little Richard's music. "Tutti-Frutti" was released in February 1956,
three months before "Heartbreak Hotel," and it reached number seventeen on the pop charts. In May of that year, "Long Tall Sally" made
it to number six, the best showing of any single ever recorded by Little Richard. Fans of seemingly all backgrounds flocked to Little
Richard's concerts, and sex orgies with overheated female fans after
the show were not uncommon, according to a member of the band
quoted in *Dancing in the Street: A Rock and Roll History* by Robert
Palmer. The same source said that on occasion Little Richard would
have his boyfriends with him backstage. The scene sounds as wild as
the 1970s, the heyday of rock and roll excess, and yet this took place
during the Eisenhower administration! It makes you wonder what was
really going on in the 1950s.

The number of bisexuals, gay men, or lesbians in the early days of
rock and roll was probably small, but not so the number of African
Americans. Other than Elvis Presley, Buddy Holly, and Jerry Lee
Lewis—each of them from the south—the superstars of that era were

African American: Chuck Berry, Bo Diddley, Fats Domino, and Little Richard. As you go further down the line the ratio increases of black to white musicians. Nearly all of the vocal groups and many of the second-tier hitmakers, including Johnny "Guitar" Watson, Larry Williams, Don and Dewey, and Hank Ballard and the Midnighters were black. In 1958 rock and roll had its first Mexican American star, Ritchie Valens, raised in the northeast corner of LA's San Fernando Valley. Alas, his reign was all too brief. A year later Valens, only seventeen, was killed in the same plane crash that took the lives of Buddy Holly at twenty-two and the DJ turned singer J. P. Richardson, who scored a huge hit with "Chantilly Lace" under the moniker the Big Bopper.

There were black stars in American popular music long before rock and roll. Duke Ellington and Louis Armstrong are two that come to mind immediately. Too much can be made of this. For example, it would be false to suggest that every white kid who bought a record by Ellington, Armstrong, or Chuck Berry was by definition not a racist. A teenager could be a huge Little Richard fan and still fervently believe niggers had to stay in their place. Yet there is no denying that Little Richard attacked the racial, cultural, and sexual barriers in place in the 1950s, whether he was aware of this or not. In so doing, he got the 1960s started early. Sexually explicit songs such as "Long Tall Sally" and "The Girl Can't Help It" anticipated the lyrics of hit singles from the Stones through rap, while the singer's flamboyant persona had many imitators but no equals. Mick Jagger in his camp phase was but a pale imitation of the original. Little Richard did his own thing before anyone thought of inventing the phrase. And even now, almost fifty years later, he seems utterly familiar to us.

Whether rock and roll fans thought of Little Richard as homosexual, or even cared, they bought millions of his records. Contrary to the views of the Right and Left, the modern era did not officially begin in 1965, with the Great Society and the Rolling Stones' recording of "Satisfaction." Elvis, Little Richard, Chuck Berry, and the rest were of their time and ahead of their time in the all-important category of American pop culture.

There was no "We Are the World" in the 1950s, and no Farm-Aid, Live-Aid, or Rock the Vote either. In the 1950s, rock and roll stars didn't tell their fans how to vote or what causes to embrace. They didn't offer opinions on the Issues of the Day, nor were they asked. They had no choice. Rock and roll didn't have much breathing space in the 1950s, not when ministers, parents, and local authorities around the country wanted it banned for life. Few people in power had the inclination or desire to come to its defense. Under the circumstances it would have been commercial suicide for the musicians to express their views on political topics. The establishment already had plenty of evidence against Little Richard and Fats Domino. Why make matters worse by condemning segregation in a newspaper interview?

This doesn't mean that these performers and others from that time were politically ignorant. Their silence should not be misconstrued. Still, it would be hard to argue otherwise to fans born after 1960. Since the 1970s, we have grown accustomed to every other rock group having something to say about the state of the world, whether we care to hear it or not. Half of them seem as comfortable in front of an editorial board as they do inside a recording studio. The seemingly well-informed rock star has been commonplace for the past two decades.

Transport Bono, lead singer of U2, back to the 1950s, and you can imagine him speaking out against segregation, against nuclear proliferation, and in favor of Adlai Stevenson. Ditto for Bruce Springsteen. There were many issues in the 1950s that would have been perfect candidates for the rock and roll treatment: a Ban the Bomb concert, a new pro–Civil Rights song, a benefit for peace. But the high school kids that comprised the vast majority of the audience just wanted to dance, and the performers gave them exactly what they wanted—they left politics to the politicians.

It was adults who dragged rock and roll into politics in the 1950s. They couldn't let it alone. Every op-ed piece that blasted rock and roll for turning America's young people into sex-obsessed robots, every fiery condemnation of "Negro" rhythms, and every music professor who bemoaned a generation that preferred "trash" to Beethoven had the effect of politicizing this music. The motives of the angry opponents were understandable. Rock and roll tore apart the cherished *Father Knows Best* myth about life in the 1950s. Not that Newt Gingrich noticed.

It's ironic that this style of music—loud, angry, celebratory, and arrogant—caught on at a time of relative quiet in American domestic and international politics. But in fact, placid political conditions are ideal for a seismic shift in pop culture. That's when people are looking for thrills.

Although I have vivid memories of turmoil being reported on the evening news, I was actually quite content in the late 1960s. I recall that period with fondness, the golden years of a mostly happy childhood. As a result, my personal recollections would not be the most accurate gauge of the mood of America at the close of a turbulent decade. I didn't feel the country's pain. And so it goes for every period in American history. A person born in 1946 and looking back on his elementary school days would not necessarily be qualified to tell us what the United States was really like during the early 1950s. If this observer was lucky, he or she was blissfully unaware of the Cold War, and instead could lead the simple and carefree life of a typical kid, excited about the future and thinking only of one's self.

Instead we turn to adults from that time, and the history books, to provide a better sense of America from 1950 to 1954. It was not a particularly happy period. "Many contemporary observers described the fifties as the Age of Anxiety. Because of the Cold War, the widespread fear of nuclear annihilation, the Korean War, and finally the War in Vietnam, American society had remained, psychologically at least, in a wartime frame of mind."[6] Ex-hippies wouldn't agree, but you could even make the case that 1950–1954 was every bit as traumatic for the nation as 1964 to 1968.

On June 25, 1950, North Korea invaded South Korea, starting the Korean War. Within two days, the United Nations Security Council called on the members of the UN to "render such assistance to the Republic of Korea as may be necessary to repel the armed attack and to restore international peace and security in the area."[7]

Less than five years after the end of World War II, which resulted in the deaths of 400,000 Americans, the United States had become involved in another land, sea, and air war in Asia.

Imagine for a moment that this had happened in the 1990s, when the U.S. waged war using "smart" bombs and computer-guided missiles, and politicians bragged about accomplishing their objectives without "the loss of a single American life," at least in the case of Kosovo. Even the Persian Gulf War, which many predicted would be a bloodbath on both sides, turned out to be a slaughter—with Iraqi ground forces as the targets. The downing of *one* U.S. aircraft—again, as happened in the Kosovo campaign—was the occasion for hours and hours of "breaking" news on the cable channels, although within a matter of weeks the three crew members were set free.

The rules of engagement introduced by American politicians and military leaders in the 1990s consisted of massive bombing campaigns, a public promise not to send in ground troops, and then waiting to see how much destruction would be required before the other guy surrendered. By contrast, in the fall of 1950, America was not only involved in a brutal conflict with North Korea, but Communist China had entered the war on the other side as well. Regarding casualties, every day of the Korean War was the equivalent of the entire Operation Desert Storm. When the truce was signed in 1953, 33,746 Americans had lost their lives.

But Korea was a mere subset of the larger Cold War, which had become quite terrifying by the middle of the 1950s. In 1952, the United States detonated its first thermonuclear device. "It yielded some 10.4 million tons of TNT, or a force a thousand times greater than the Hiroshima bomb."[8] Not much later the Soviet Union responded by testing a thermonuclear device of its own. The policy of nuclear deterrence brought little comfort to the person on the street. The notion that man could "blow up" the world was now a topic of everyday conversation, rather than merely the ambitious plot of a science-fiction thriller. Later generations found a way to assimilate this terrifying prospect, if for no other primary reason than the need to stay sane. Against this backdrop, escapist fare such as *Father Knows Best* doesn't seem ridiculous, but the understandable equating of fantasy with leading a "normal" life.

On February 9, 1950, several months before the Korean War began, Wisconsin Republican senator Joseph McCarthy leveled one of the most famous charges in American history when speaking to a group of Republican women in Wheeling, West Virginia: "I have here in my hand a list of 205—a list of names that were known to the Secretary of State as being members of the Communist Party and who nevertheless are still working and shaping policy in the State Department."

Depending on your own political point of view, what took place over the next four years was either one of the greatest threats to civil liberties in the history of the Republic, or a much-needed and overdue effort to rid the federal government of communists and the influence of communists. The senator has the distinction of being one of the few American politicians whose name signifies a movement— McCarthyism. The term has certainly had a longer life than Reaganomics or Nixonian, both of which faded away with end of the presidencies of Reagan and Nixon. But McCarthyism is still in wide use on both the Left and the Right, a media-friendly synonym for the politics of demagoguery. Indeed, McCarthyism has proven more resilient then either communism or the Soviet Union, which would have delighted the senator had he lived to see it. In 1998 the attorney and media star Alan Dershowitz published a book at the height of the Clinton/Lewinsky scandal entitled *Sexual McCarthyism*, which purported to show how gossip and innuendo about the private sex lives of public figures was increasingly being used to tarnish or destroy reputations and careers. But sexual McCarthyism hardly compares to the real thing.

In the March–April 1999 edition of *The American Prospect*, Joshua Micah Marshall wrote this about McCarthy and the movement to which he gave his name:

> Centering around the communist victories in China and Eastern Europe in the late 1940s, McCarthy charged that Secretary of State (Dean) Acheson had sold the country out to the communists; that the Truman Administration was riddled with subversion; and that the men who guided the country for the previous twenty years were dupes of the communists, or worse.[9]

Many people believed the senator, and many others knew the truth but kept quiet. For a few years, it almost seemed as if he was in charge of Washington.

You won't find a hint of the anguish of those years in the pop songs that ruled the *Billboard Magazine* charts. The tunes were light, pleasant, and went down easy. They seemed to almost deny America's new status—defender of freedom, the most powerful nation on earth—and instead hark back to simpler times, when the U.S. was a second-rate power without the means or the will to bear any burden. It was as if pop music could not acknowledge the cataclysmic social and political changes in America that had taken place since the end of World War II. The image of the 1950s as blithe, carefree, and innocent is a reflection of the hit songs of the early part of the decade. Ralph Gleason, among others, quoted Plato to the effect that "Forms and rhythms in music are never changed without producing changes in the most important political forms and ways." In the early 1950s, the political forms and ways changed considerably, while pop music lagged behind.

In 1950, the number one hits included "Tennessee Waltz" by Patti Page, "Mona Lisa" by Nat Cole, and "Music! Music! Music!" by Teresa Brewer. Only a director with a sense of irony would have those songs on the soundtrack of a documentary about the Korean War. In 1953, Frank Sinatra—who hated early rock and roll with a passion—began his comeback with "I've Got the World on a String," recorded with his new arranger, Nelson Riddle. The title alone would seem to run counter to the prevailing mood. That same year, "(How Much Is) that Doggie in the Window?" by Patti Page remained at number one on the charts for eight weeks. Of the songs I just mentioned, "Doggie in the Window" is certainly the one most familiar to baby boomers. Even today young parents will sing it in order to calm a restless infant.

Author and music critic Donald Clarke calls the early 1950s "one of the most dismal periods in the history of popular music."[10] Clarke's view of that period is not uncommon, partly because Patti Page and the rest had the bad luck to dominate the charts between two vibrant periods in American pop music, swing and rock and roll. Their product can sound ridiculously lame to kids or adults raised on rock. It's not only a question of rhythm or sound, but also the lack of social or political punch in the pop music of the early 1950s. Several generations of fans have grown accustomed to songs that *say something*. At the same time, sex, the need to have sex, seduction, and desire have for years trumped 1950s-style young love in the lyrics of popular songs. Younger audiences are far more accepting of romantic movies from the 1940s and 1950s then romantic music from the 1940s and 1950s.

Still, if songs from that era enabled the listener to forget the Korean War, the Cold War, and the hydrogen bomb for two or three minutes, then perhaps they served a useful purpose. Of course, it could also be that these songs indirectly served the interests of people in power. Concerned about the anti-communism of the Truman administration? Frightened by Stalin? Worried sick about a friend or a relative at the Battle of Inchon? Listen to a record by Patti Page, Teresa Brewer, or Perry Como. For a little while, anyway, you will feel better.

That's apparently what people wanted, and the music business was all too happy to meet their needs. Two decades later, the record labels would do a flip-flop, giving an expectant audience songs that addressed topical issues, though at times they did so awkwardly.

⌒⌒

Due to the convergence of two seemingly unrelated events, April 1954 must be considered one of the significant months in post–World War II American history. On April 8, Decca released "Rock Around the

Clock," by Bill Haley and His Comets, which is typically regarded as the first rock and roll record. Haley, who grew up in Pennsylvania, had a musical background in country and western and rhythm and blues, which are the two styles that meshed to produce rock and roll of the primarily Caucasian variety. Indeed, that same mix of genres can be heard on the *Sun Sessions*, Elvis Presley's seminal recordings from 1954. Even by contemporary standards, "Rock Around the Clock" is a loud record, particularly the high-tone, fast guitar solo and the smash, bang, boom on the drums at the end. In fact, the song may have been too hot to handle for young audiences in the spring of 1954. It cracked the top twenty-five, a respectable showing, but not so high as to herald the arrival of a musical revolution.

A year later, "Rock Around the Clock" got a second chance, this time by being featured over the opening and closing credits of the film *Blackboard Jungle*, with Glenn Ford and Sidney Poitier. Many times in the history of rock and roll the movies have provided a new opportunity to songs that were minor hits the first time around. In 1987, for example, "Do You Love Me" got a tremendous boost from its key role in the soundtrack of the film *Dirty Dancing*, a box office smash. An early Motown hit (1962) by the Contours, "Do You Love Me" enjoyed a major revival as a result of its inclusion in the film, becoming in short order a "get-down standard" at weddings, parties, and clubs. In addition, the song was added to the regular rotation of oldies radio stations around the country.

Thanks to *Blackboard Jungle*, in July 1955 "Rock Around the Clock" went to number one on the charts, where it remained for eight weeks. Haley's song became the third-highest ranked record of the year, and the only number one from the group that could in any way be considered rock and roll. For a short time, Bill Haley was king; no other performer in the fledgling rock and roll field had recorded a song nearly as popular as "Rock Around the Clock." But ten months later, Elvis Presley, much younger and much sexier than Bill Haley, released "Heartbreak Hotel," followed soon after by "Hound Dog" and "Don't Be Cruel." Haley fell back to the middle of the field, while Elvis, Little Richard, Buddy Holly, Chuck Berry, and Jerry Lee Lewis advanced to the front. Haley's last top ten hit, a forgotten song called "Burn That Candle," peaked in December 1955. In 1964–1965, few if any of the English bands cited Haley as an influence on their careers, and none of them covered "Rock Around the Clock." Today Haley is remembered primarily because he recorded the first monster hit in rock and roll — also featured in the opening of both *American Graffiti* and *Happy Days*—and not for being an innovator in the field, although the sociological impact of "Rock Around the Clock" cannot be underestimated.

In the same month that "Rock Around the Clock" first appeared on the charts—April 1954—the Army-McCarthy hearings opened on national television. For five weeks the senator investigated allegations of communist influence within the United States Army. But he went too far when he double-crossed the army's chief counsel, Joseph Welch. "When McCarthy made an indefensible personal assault on one of Welch's young assistants, public sentiment decisively turned from him."[11]

Welch, with a carefully rehearsed and devastatingly effective rhetorical question, challenged McCarthy—"Have you no decency, sir?" — which remains one of the most quoted moments in the history of congressional hearings, in part because it marked the beginning of the end for the Wisconsin senator and his crusade. In June, the Senate voted overwhelmingly to censure McCarthy, who was becoming an embarrassment and a liability to the institution, if not yet to the political fortunes of his Republican colleagues. After the vote, the press lost interest in the story; McCarthy without McCarthyism wasn't news. McCarthy could handle anything but public indifference or neglect. A heavy drinker for years, he died in 1957.

McCarthy's censure and the fall of McCarthyism occurred a year after the end of the Korean War. The United States had fought the Chinese and the North Koreans to a draw, and seemingly ferreted out most or all the communists in the federal government. And when Senator McCarthy crossed the line, he was deposed as well. There were still all those nuclear bombs out there, but the world would just have to learn to live with them. Maybe deterrence actually could keep the men in the Kremlin and the men in Washington from doing something stupid.

For the time being, anyway, America could relax a little. Here is where the myth of the "Fabulous '50s" truly begins, the seemingly innocent and fun-filled era exemplified by the popular TV program *Happy Days*. As opposed to those potheads and acid freaks in the 1960s, we have been led to believe that high school kids from the 1950s might sneak a few bottles of beer or congregate for midnight drag races now and then, but otherwise behave themselves. On those rare occasions when things really got out of hand, when a dance hall was vandalized or gangs fought with chains and knives, it was all rock and roll's fault. Because by then masses of teenagers were listening to a new kind of music. After 1955, Patti Page would have no more number one records. The same was true for Teresa Brewer and Nat King Cole. If politics had turned complacent—compared with the previous few years—then rock and roll would have to provide thrills for the American public.

⌐⌐

In his book *The Age of Empire: 1875–1914*, the British historian Eric Hobsbawm writes: "August 1914 is one of the most undeniable natural breaks in history. It was felt to be the end of an era at that time, and it is still felt to be so."[12] Bearing in mind that rock and roll is not World War I, and the fate of pop music is in no way analogous to the fate of Western civilization, something similar could be said about May 1956, when "Heartbreak Hotel" reached number one.

Of course, easy-listening pop tunes have continued to show up on the charts from time to time since 1956, some of them even selling millions of copies. But these songs— "Honey" by Bobby Goldsboro (number one in 1968), "The Candy Man" by Sammy Davis, Jr. (number one in 1972), and others—are one-shot oddities that caused no change in the status quo. At worst they are an embarrassment to those who would argue that only cool things happened in the 1960s. For fifty years, the vast majority of teenagers in the United States have listened to rock and roll, soul, funk, or rap—much to the chagrin of parents and music teachers. During this time rock and roll has "died"—and been resurrected—as often as the political career of Richard Nixon. Elvis and his crafty manager, Colonel Tom Parker, were on to something, and that's putting it mildly.

Rock and roll seemed much more in sync with America in the 1950s then did its pop music predecessors. Rock did not speak softly, it carried a big stick. It was loud and aggressive, like the United States. There was nothing innocent about Elvis or Little Richard, and there was nothing innocent about the role the CIA played in the overthrow of the Guatemalan government in 1954. Rock and roll, like military bases, democracy, or support for corrupt dictatorships, soon became a symbol of American power—for good or ill—around the globe. In some communist countries, rock and roll was even considered part of the capitalist plot to take over the world, an irony that was little appreciated by right-wing politicians and Christian fundamentalists over here.

The impact of rock and roll was more apparent on the domestic front. In one of those neat historical coincidences, the significance of which would be easy to overestimate, Elvis emerged at about the same time that Dr. Martin Luther King, Jr. launched the modern civil rights movement. In December 1955, Rosa Parks refused to give up her seat to a white man on a Montgomery, Alabama, bus, as "colored folks" were required to do in that place at that time. King, largely unknown to a national audience, led a one-year boycott that culminated in the end of racial segregation on the Montgomery bus lines.

King and Elvis hailed from the South, mocked by the Northern elite for its crude and regressive ways, and yet within the space of several months in 1954 to 1955 they had set a new direction for American society. As historian Bruce J. Schulman wrote about the attitudes of northerners toward the South in the 1950s and 1960s: "The South barely occasioned a thought in the corridors of power, except to elicit smug head shaking over its economic backwardness, gothic politics, and racial caste system."[13] King had intended to radically change southern politics; Elvis just wanted to make hit records. The two were also implicitly linked by their opponents, the defenders of the traditional Southern way of life, otherwise known as segregation. To be sure, King and his followers were treated far more cruelly than Elvis, who was never violently attacked by the Klan, local thugs, or deputy sheriffs. It's one thing for a white kid from Mississippi to admire and emulate the vocal style and on-stage moves of black performers, but it's something else entirely for a black man to seek equal rights for his own people.

Elvis didn't encroach upon politics, but politics encroached upon Elvis. The desire to quell Elvis and condemn his music had an undeniably political motive. "He [Elvis Presley] brought black music into the white mainstream, scaring the shit out of white Southern politicians at the time," said the Monkees' Peter Tork, who regards the Elvis phenomenon as an attack on the Mississippi/Alabama/Georgia version of apartheid. The racists considered Elvis the beginning, not the end of a process that could only result in tragedy for the white race. If whites like Elvis admired and emulated aspects of black culture, then could a general appreciation for the desires and aspirations of the Negro people be far behind? The Southern establishment couldn't afford for that to happen. Elvis had to be stopped before he took everybody down.

Elvis was hardly the first white American performer who borrowed from black music, but the others were not as popular and not from the South. In the 1930s, for example, Benny Goodman and George Gershwin, the latter as composer of *Porgy and Bess*, exhibited an open admiration and appreciation for African American artistry. But Goodman and Gershwin were based in urban centers in the North and Jewish, which meant they could not be trusted to safeguard the future of white America.

Another southern "turncoat" like Elvis was Carl Perkins, a Tennessee native who wrote and recorded "Blue Suede Shoes" in 1956, one of the most influential and best-known songs from rock and roll's first five years. Perkins was targeted even though he didn't "cover" songs by black artists, but wrote most of his own material. Indeed, "Blue Suede Shoes" sounds much more like classic rockabilly than rhythm and blues or blues. Perkins also carried a guitar on stage, which limited his ability to perform the kinds of outrageous moves that got

Elvis into trouble. But these differences in musical form and onstage persona were lost on the authority figures, who could hardly be regarded as experts in rock and roll. "White boys like Presley and Perkins warranted investigation for singing black and bringing young girls to their knees with suggestive gyrations. In short order rock and roll would takes its place in the (white) citizens councils eyes as a threat even more insidious than school desegregation."[14]

Asa Earl (Ace) Carter, head of the Alabama White Citizens Council at the time of "Heartbreak Hotel" and "Blue Suede Shoes," was described in *Go Cat Go* as a "full-time Commie hunter and rabid anti-Semite." He also took some time to denounce rock and roll. Using language more vivid than any heard before or since on the subject, Carter called rock and roll "sensuous Negro music," that was eroding the "entire moral structure of man, of Christianity, of spirituality in holy marriage . . . of all the white man has built through his devotion to God."[15]

Let's see communism try and top that! Leaving the rhetoric aside, Carter was not entirely out of his mind. Although rock and roll as an entity did not actively promote integration in the 1950s, various concerts did bring black, white, and (frequently) brown people together under one roof to hear black, white, and (sometimes) brown performers. In that sense, avowed segregationists had some reason for concern, although a few hundred teens attending a ninety-minute show hardly constitutes a mass movement. The bigger question centered on what these teens of different races would do once the show ended. Form new friendships? Forge new alliances? Or, God forbid, get involved in a romance? Would kids continue to socialize on the street or in each other's homes? Was rock and roll part of the larger movement to destroy segregation forever? Nobody knew for sure.

With their penchant for conspiracy theories, the Right has, since the 1950s, attacked rock and roll with impunity, because its appeal is often a mystery to adults. In the 1950s, parents couldn't understand what their kids saw in Elvis; while in the 1970s seemingly more enlightened parents couldn't understand what their kids saw in Kiss. Some parents laugh this off as a simple matter of bad taste and figure their children will get over it in due time. But for others, rock has pernicious effects on their offspring, and they seek help in curbing its availability and controlling its influence. And if it's true that people fear what they don't understand, then the political justification for a war against rock—or rap—becomes self-evident. Conservatism thrives on the politics of fear. Yet in this case, fear alone is not enough. After all, rock and roll is not a foreign country, or a massive tax increase, but a form of popular entertainment. You need additional evidence to build a convincing case. Its detractors therefore ascribe to rock and roll the power to redirect human behavior, as if it was on a par with communism, atheism, or to be fair, organized religion. The fact that the Right rarely agrees on the precise nature of rock's political agenda is hardly a deterrent to continue the fight.

The "race-mixing" charge had some validity. For example, the legendary Cleveland disc jockey Alan Freed, widely credited with inventing the term "rock and roll," actually went out of his way to bring black and white kids together. In his book, *The Pied Pipers of Rock and Roll: Radio Deejays of the 50s and 60s*, author Wes Smith describes how Freed virtually willed this to happen:

> In no time, he was packing concert halls with racially swirled crowds. At first he recruited area talent to perform. Later, he made excursions to Harlem and the South, peering into gospel churches and honky-tonk bars, one ear cocked for back-stoop pluckers and street-corner quartets, stars waiting to shine. When he became *the* deejay, of course, all he had to do was start the bus up and the biggest acts in the country would pile on, black and white, drunk, and dangerous.[16]

John A. Jackson, author of the 1991 book *Big Beat Heat: Alan Freed and the Early Years of Rock and Roll*, told *The New York Times*: "Here was this guy bringing blacks and whites together to dance in the 1950s. It was unheard of."

Some observers have claimed that Freed deliberately used live rock and roll shows to further his own goal of bringing the races together, which would have made him a valid threat to segregation and segregationists. Freed's foot soldiers danced rather then marched, but his objectives were the same as those of the Freedom Riders.

Other DJs played to integrated crowds without seeking to advance a political agenda, although racists would not have made a distinction. In Los Angeles, a witty, lanky, and rather gentle record spinner who went by the name of Huggy Boy hosted live broadcasts in the 1950s from a record store called Dolphin's of Hollywood, which was located in an area with a large and growing black population. Like Alan Freed, Huggy Boy seemed quite delighted to attract what would today be called a diverse audience to his shows. (Huggy Boy could still be heard on Southern California radio in 2000 playing classic oldies for a predominantly Latino listening audience, although he was in his early seventies. He has outlasted or outlived nearly all of his original competitors.) In the middle and late 1950s, Anglo kids from the San Fernando Valley and Chicano teenagers from East Los Angeles willingly made the sixty to seventy mile round trip drive to attend these live broadcasts, as well as to purchase obscure rhythm and blues records at Dolphin's. That the store was in the black part of Los Angeles did not deter young white fans in 1957 to 1958. Ten years later, they would be too frightened to make the trip.

This form of "white flight" was not the only factor that segregated popular music audiences in the 1960s. During the decade of the Voting Rights Act, the Civil Rights Act, and the rise of the black middle class, the rock and roll and soul music scenes were far more segregated than in the 1950s. Shows such as the ones hosted by Alan Freed or Huggy Boy virtually disappeared after 1966, as black and white audiences increasingly went their separate ways. For the most part, white kids listened to psychedelia, folk-rock, and acid rock, while black kids opted for James Brown, funk, and urban soul. Whites made up probably 90 to 95 percent of the audience for concerts by the Beatles, the Grateful Dead, Cream, and the Doors, but you would be hard-pressed to find any blonde hair or blue eyes at a performance by James Brown. In the late 1960s it became a kind of pop music truism that blacks and whites had very distinct tastes, and anyone who deviated from the norm ran the risk of being ostracized. I can remember seeing a black kid teased mercilessly by his peers for bringing a copy of the Beatles' album *Revolver* to junior high school around 1968 to 1969. Judging by their reaction, you would have thought the student was a Tommy Roe fan.

The musical tastes of black, whites, and Latinos did find common ground in Motown, which cleverly and accurately billed itself as "The Sound of Young America." Berry Gordy, Motown's founder, launched his label in 1960, when inclusion and not exclusion was the goal. He successfully continued the formula through the next two decades, even hooking white kids with funky records that were clearly influenced by the more "black" musical styles of the era. Gordy's genius was to release single after single that appealed to whites without in any way compromising the artistic integrity of the black performers that recorded them.

The term "race-mixing" seems to belong exclusively to the 1950s. Even people today who don't want the races to mix find some other word or phrase to express their feelings. Perhaps the term was supplanted by "integration," which is still used today. In any event, race mixing disappeared with the increasing polarization of the audiences. The "problem" solved itself, without any assistance from racists. During the 1960s, pop music and progressive politics moved in opposite directions on matters of race. Martin Luther King's dream did not resonate with record labels and radio stations, which in the middle of the decade started marketing their product to audiences divided by color. There were other factors that contributed to this trend; the dominance of rock groups from Britain starting in 1964, the steadily increasing influence of European musical forms on rock and roll, the rise of black nationalism, the politicization of soul music, and the effort of radio to capture niche markets. You didn't hear then, and still would not hear today, "Lucy in the Sky with Diamonds" on stations aimed at black listeners, or James Brown's "Mother Popcorn" on one of those really, really hip FM rock stations.

Rock and roll can always count on sex. In every decade since the 1950s rock and roll or R&B songs have garnered the attention of political, religious, or community leaders on account of sexual content. You can't have rock and roll without it, and you can't have it without rock and roll, according to worried parents, ministers, and politicians from coast to coast in the 1950s and 1960s.

Still, the part that rock and roll played in what is routinely called the sexual revolution is purely a matter of speculation. We know how girls reacted to Elvis, but we don't know if that made them more inclined to settle for second best and have sex with their boyfriends. The same applies to females turned on by Mick Jagger, Jim Morrison, or David Cassidy. It could even be argued that rock and roll stars and rock and roll music served as an orgasmic escape for girls at an awkward time in their personal sexual development. As for the boys, they idolized rock stars because rock stars got all those beautiful women, which was a lot different from what teenage males experienced at Ground Zero of an American high school. The promise of unlimited sex is what has propelled many otherwise undistinguished young men into the rock and roll field in the first place. Some of them get laid on occasion and move on; others have enough talent to actually forge a decent career; and a very lucky few become superstars. In any event, the connection between rock and engaging in sex has been put forward as political propaganda by the Right—but where is the incontrovertible evidence?

Looking back on the 1960s, most commentators would argue that the invention and mass distribution of the birth control pill, which occurred in the early part of that decade, played the single biggest role in bringing about the so-called sexual revolution. Fear of pregnancy was and probably remains a deterrent to heterosexual intercourse between unmarried partners. Nonetheless, it would be absurd for rock and roll performers, producers, and promoters to deny the sexual element in the music, and few if any have ever made the attempt. This is one charge that sticks. While rock musicians are loathe to acknowledge that particular lyrics might refer to or condone drugs, they are not so shy when it comes to dealing with sex, the one subject that is consistent from Little Richard through Prince and beyond. Without the allure of sex and the celebration of lust, a billion-dollar-a-year industry would probably be worth only several hundred million.

Rock and roll is the only one of the popular arts that indulges equally the sexual fantasies of both young men and young women. (By contrast, pornography is obviously a guy thing—although some women are fans as well—while romance novels are not a real popular genre with either macho or sensitive males.) Before the arrival of MTV, the flaunting of sex in rock was primarily a one-way street; the men performed for the girls, a kind of burlesque show in reverse, or even stripped, as in the case of one famous incident involving Jim Morrison in Miami in 1969. The women of rock and roll and soul in the 1950s, 1960s, and 1970s tended to be more beautiful (Marianne Faithfull, Linda Ronstadt) or sexy (Mary Wilson, Tina Turner) than overtly sexual. MTV changed pop from a primarily aural medium to an audio/visual medium, which made possible the fabulous success of Madonna, as well as the girls that came along in the late 1990s: Britney Spears, Christina Aguilera, and Shakira. These young ladies could sing decently, but absent the help of their sex-drenched videos they would never have become such massive stars. At the same time, male rockers in the 1980s and 1990s were spending as much time in the gym as they did in the recording studio, preparing to shed their shirts for some music video. It's no coincidence that rock and roll experienced a musical renaissance in the early twenty-first century as MTV drastically cut back on videos in favor of reality shows, spin-offs of reality shows, spin-offs of the spin-offs, and ludicrous sex sitcoms. Now musicians had to get back to actually playing in order to attract a following.

Even more than a happily married and monogamous young actor, a happily married and monogamous rock star is considered something of an oddball. Thanks to countless TV specials, documentaries, and "tell-it-all" articles, we now know that sexual excess on a scale that puts most other straight men to shame is commonplace in rock and roll, at least since the latc 1960s. If this behavior is not exactly condoned by society, it's not exactly condemned either. Angry feminists on a crusade against rampant male heterosexuality spend most of their time monitoring lyrics, videos, and promotional campaigns for hints of sexism, while ignoring what happens in a dressing room or hotel suite after the show. Horny politicians could only wish they had this kind of freedom to act on their desires.

In the 1950s, most of the sex in rock and roll was implicit rather than explicit. The performers themselves were reasonably careful—probably on the advice of their handlers—not to do anything that might create a sex scandal. It's only many years later that we have learned a bit of what went on behind the scenes—such as the wild times after Little Richard's performances—although in most cases it doesn't compare with the rock scene during the late 1960s, 1970s, and 1980s. Elvis Presley had much more action in the 1960s with his career on the wane then he did in the 1950s, when he was the biggest star in the world. According to Albert Goldman's biography of Elvis, the King and his entourage spent much of the 1960s being "entertained" by beautiful women who were invited to parties at his Hollywood residence.

And yet one sex scandal from the 1950s could shock even today's seemingly unshockable audience, because of attendant issues of class, propriety, and what might be termed family ethics, as opposed to family values. In an era of Howard Stern, *Sex in the City*, and *Queer as Folk*, the famous picture from 1958 of a defiant Jerry Lee Lewis with his arm around his thirteen-year-old bride—who happened also to be his cousin—still wins the prize for audacity. The liberals that support Stern on free speech grounds—*Sex in the City* because it's about time women were shown talking dirty, and *Queer as Folk* because it's about time raw gay sex was depicted on television—would have no political category in which to place Jerry Lee. Nor would they want to create one. A God-fearing Southerner who married his pubescent cousin deserved his fate. He could forget getting any moral or financial support from the ACLU or Hollywood.

In May 1958, on a concert tour of England, the tabloid press found out that Jerry Lee Lewis had secretly married his thirteen-year-old cousin. At the time, Lewis was one of the rising stars of rock and roll, having only a few months earlier released two sensational records, "Whole Lotta Shakin' Goin' On" and "Great Balls of Fire." Both of these songs are better than "Don't Be Cruel," "Jailhouse Rock," or Hound Dog," and they also rank with the best of Little Richard and Fats Domino.

Lewis frankly didn't consider it a big deal that he married his thirteen-year-old cousin, but the British public begged to differ. They were outraged by the relationship between Mr. and Mrs. Lewis and the girl's tender age, even though there was a period in American and presumably British history when older men did marry their teenage cousins without incurring the wrath of the people. But times do change.

In their book, *Anti-Rock: The Opposition to Rock'n'Roll*, authors Linda Martin and Kerry Segrave recount what happened when the news broke:

> Many of the people who had come (to the concerts) were openly hostile. From the audience Lewis was greeted with such shouts as "baby snatcher" and "cradle robber." After a couple such shows Leslie Grade, the agent who had booked the tour, met with officials of the Rank Organization, who owned the theaters in which the concerts were to take place. After that meeting Grade announced the remainder of the tour was canceled, saying, "If he had gone on, it might have done irreparable harm to British show business—and pop music in general."[17]

In no position to argue, Lewis and his entourage took the next available flight out of England. They reckoned that he would get a more sympathetic hearing in the States.

Not a chance. For some time after his return, Lewis was shunned by the entertainment business in America, which feared the consequences of providing work to a young man of such dubious character. The marriage confirmed what conservative parents had always suspected about rock and roll and sex, and led for renewed calls to ban the music entirely.

Lewis never recorded any more hits on the scale of "Whole Lotta Shakin' Goin' On" and "Great Balls of Fire," although those songs are of such exceptional quality that it's hard to say whether the scandal is the reason. In any event, Lewis today is regarded as one of the giants of early rock and roll, due both to his studio recordings and his astonishing live performances. And that thirteen-year-old girl, Myra by name, was many marriages ago.

Today's contrived sex scandals in pop music are more about career advancement then getting uptight Americans to loosen up. Taking off one's clothes or simulating sexual acts is done within a controlled environment, and very much according to a plan worked out by the performer and his or her publicity team. No one is fooled, least of all the media, even if they are happy to play along. The "outraged" religious leaders, who make themselves available to any talk show that will have them, capitalize on the furor as well. The Jerry Lee Lewis affair, however, was not pre-planned. Whether he married for love is unclear, but he certainly didn't do so for the attention. When the secret was leaked, his career suffered. Teenagers and their parents may be more sophisticated today than in 1958 regarding sexual behavior, but I don't think that feeling of openness extends to a rock star marrying his thirteen-year-old cousin. Just suppose that in the 1992 campaign, Bill Clinton had been accused of having once been married to his thirteen-year-old cousin, instead of chronic adultery. Not even James Carville or George Stephanopoulos could have saved him.

In America, where there is no minister of culture, specific efforts to restrict popular entertainment are usually undertaken at the local level. Washington will keep tabs on a particular situation, and if sufficient momentum builds around the country, politicians might decide to make a hard line speech or offer symbolic support. But they are loath to do more. The word you will usually hear coming out of Congress or the White House is "voluntary." Elected officials will demand that the film business or the music industry regulate content on their own, threatening to take some sort of action if the response is inadequate.

Entertainment executives, their lawyers, and industry lobbyists alternate worrying about the "chilling effect" of government regulation of content with promises to be more responsible in the future. But this is just to appease the mob. Their real strategy is to wage a political war of attrition and wait patiently until members of Congress and the media move on to something else, which is inevitable. When the storm passes, studios can return to producing the same stuff that got them into trouble in the first place—as long as it continued to generate healthy profits.

The entertainment industry is secure in the belief that even right-wing politicians are wary of being perceived as favoring censorship, which carries a negative connotation with many people in this country, not all of them highly educated and politically liberal. The mayor of a small town in the Midwest or South, however, would not feel as constrained. He has only to please his loyal constituents, and they may overwhelmingly support attempts to curb rock and roll. If ACLU (American Civil Liberties Union) attorneys want to contest an ordinance, just let them come and try. The 1984 film *Footloose*, about a Midwestern town where dancing is banned, seems quite plausible, but you could never convince an audience that America would outlaw dancing from sea to shining sea.

It didn't take long for local authorities across the United States to look at ways of restricting rock and roll within their jurisdiction. In El Monte, California, a medium-sized suburb twenty miles east of Los Angeles, officials conducted hearings in 1956 on whether to ban dances within city limits. Rock and roll had barely passed its first birthday, and already the ruling class in this particular city had stepped in. Officials responded to the concerns of residents that the dances were attracting a "bad" crowd, which in that section of Southern California could well have been a code word for young toughs, Mexican Americans, or both. The strategy of getting at rock and roll through its fan base has been implemented many times over the past several decades. An impression is created that the problem isn't the music per se, but the questionable types that are drawn to the music. By turning it into an issue of public safety, politicians avoid appearing to be censors, and are theoretically in a better position to fend off any legal challenge. It worked for El Monte: over the objections of the American Civil Liberties Union, the city succeeded in imposing a ban on the dances.

In cities across America, police and politicians in the 1950s sought to either regulate or put an end to live rock and roll shows and dances, and they seized on reports of violence or property destruction as a pretext. In Atlanta for example, "Georgia police banned public dances at the City Auditorium and prohibited youths under the age of eighteen from attending public dances at other locations unless they were accompanied by a parent or guardian, or unless they had written permission from the parent or guardian."[18] This condition reads very much like the "R" rating that the Motion Picture Association of America imposed a decade later, when parents and community leaders grew increasingly worried about the trend toward explicit sex and, to a lesser extent, graphic violence on the screen.

Politicians like what they do, and they generally stay away from controversial issues unless it can further their careers. The tough-talking conservatives that beat up on the entertainment industry do so when they are certain that a huge majority of voters is behind them. The only Good Book that guides their actions is the one that's provided by political consultants. Taking the moral stand means doing what will insure your re-election.

In the first few years of rock and roll's existence, politicians could attack the music knowing that the other side had little or no clout of its own. Indeed, there was no "other side," save the kids that bought the music, and they couldn't vote. The idea of a community leader or elected official "standing up for rock and roll" in 1956 to 1957 was pure fantasy, the stuff of "B" pictures aimed at the youth market. It would be another twenty-five years before First Lady Nancy Reagan defended the Beach Boys against harsh criticism of their lifestyle from her husband's Secretary of the Interior, James Watt. But in the 1950s, politicians could exploit the fear of rock and roll, its potential harmful effects, as well as resentment over the fact that it seemed to empower teenagers. "There is a long history of political figures reacting to rock and roll," said Danny Goldberg, president of Sheridan Square Entertainment and Artemis Records and an avowed civil libertarian. "They don't like it when teenagers essentially say 'fuck you.' It (rock and roll) becomes a useful whipping boy."

In Washington they knew that Khrushchev and Mao were far greater threats to the United States of America then were Elvis and Little Richard. Leading anti-Communists of the late 1950s such as Vice President Richard Nixon and FBI director J. Edgar Hoover had very little to say about rock and roll. They were much too preoccupied with the Soviet Union, Red China, and internal security to care about Negro rhythms and race mixing. In his classic 1964 book *None Dare Call It Treason*, author John Stormer, then chairman of the Missouri Federation of Young Republicans, had nothing whatsoever to say about rock and roll music. When Arizona senator Barry Goldwater ran for president on the Republican ticket in 1964, he criticized Martin Luther King and Social Security but ignored rock and roll. The Right couldn't be bothered with rock and roll in the 1950s and early 1960s, and rarely did its leaders suggest some sort of link between it and communism. Concerted attacks on rock tend to occur when there is nothing else going on. That condition didn't apply as long as the Soviet Union remained strong.

Local politicians looked to Washington to protect their towns from communists, but personally kept a close watch on rock and roll. After all, they had to contend with an immediate problem, the attraction of their sons and daughters—literally and figuratively—to this vulgar, loud, and blatantly sexual form of music. This issue had to be dealt with here and now, before a generation was lost forever. A member of the city council couldn't do much about the Soviet threat, but high school record hops were another story. The people in power fought back with ordinances and bans, which may have achieved the desired short-term results, but also helped to create the rock and roll myth that survives to this day—the poor, picked-on performers being persecuted by close-minded, vindictive, and jealous authority figures.

In many small and mid-sized towns across the country, anti-rock spokespeople received support from an unlikely source—local radio stations. Like the media in general, radio caves at the sign of controversy and public protest, especially when it originates with the forces of "decency." Under pressure from the establishment, some station managers in the middle 1950s made a big deal of either banning rock and roll outright, or firing DJs that dared play a rock and roll record now and then. Ten years later many of these same stations had switched to playing rock and roll twenty-four hours per day.

A cover story in the Arts and Leisure section of the December 31, 2000, edition of *The New York Times* carried the headline "No Last Hurrah Yet for Political Rock."[19] The writer, *Times'* pop music critic Ann Powers, discussed a number of contemporary bands—some of them well-known, some of them not—that were writing songs, exploiting their celebrity status, or doing a combination of both to bring public attention to a variety of vaguely left-wing causes. The article presumed a natural bond between rock and politics, suggesting that a talented band whose members openly advertise their position or positions deserves to be taken more seriously than one whose members choose to keep their political opinions to themselves. The writer seemed almost disappointed in those bands whose politics were difficult to discern. The article also strongly implied that hugging the shore is no longer a viable option for any group that wants the respect of "real" fans and critics—that we are being let down by the bands who care only about sex, money, and noise. In the minds of some rock critics and fans, revolution is still on the agenda.

Like interminable guitar solos and stadium concert tours, the rock star/political commentator did not exist prior to the late 1960s, or at least not in the form that is common today. Elvis didn't perform at rallies, Little Richard didn't sign petitions, and Buddy Holly didn't organize benefit concerts. We will never know how they would have responded if approached to take a stand. There was no New Left in the 1950s, and the old left probably had nothing but contempt for early rock and roll, having been raised around jazz, folk, George Gershwin, and political theater. At the same time, rock and roll performers gave little indication of their own feelings on the big issues of the day. You can search Top 40 charts from 1955 to 1960 and you will not find one rock and roll song that *unequivocally* takes a position on war, peace, poverty, civil rights, or denial of civil liberties. There is nothing about Senator McCarthy, President Eisenhower, integration, Rosa Parks, or the Bomb. The political history of the era is told in books, newspapers, magazines, and newsreel footage, but not in the lyrics of rock and roll records.

The absence of politically influenced records or an evident political awareness among audience and performers is a main reason some fans and critics disparage 1950s rock and roll while also acknowledging its historical significance. They regard rock not as an escape from reality, but as a tool to pound reality into our brains. In this view, we need rock to first tell us the world is shit, and then to inspire us to take action. Rock can succeed where politicians, the media, organized religion, and Hollywood have failed. Lack of commitment is inexcusable to people who are accustomed to the Bob Dylan/Bruce Springsteen School of Songwriting, or the "fuck you" stance of the Sex Pistols and the Clash. Anything less is serving the interests of capitalists and the political establishment. Rock and roll is not fun and games or Coca-Cola and cars, but serious business. If you pick up an electric guitar, you must try to change the world. Can't make that commitment? Then move out of the way for someone who can.

That's easy to say now. But in the 1950s, the rock audience didn't expect or insist upon political statements from performers. Folk/rock, Vietnam, the revolution, "Revolution," ghetto riots, assassinations, Reagan, Thatcher, feminism, the ecology movement, and September

11, 2001, were far off in the future. The sole responsibility of rock and roll in the 1950s was to get teenagers out on the dance floor. The job of doo-wop, the slow ballads, was to accompany make-out sessions in a darkened living room or the back seat of an automobile. Nothing else was expected or required. And by knocking bland pop songs off the top of the charts, the performers had already done plenty for their fans. Life was somehow more interesting after "Maybelline." Rock and roll in the 1950s was fresh and it was exciting. How much more relevant can you get?

That would have been enough. And yet Chuck Berry and Little Richard, the two most influential rock and roll stars of the 1950s, encroached on the political, and sometimes even crossed the line. Now it's true neither of them recorded a song like "Eve of Destruction," the lyrics of which could be easily rearranged to fit the 1950s, or marched on Washington. They also don't fit the mold of the political rock star that emerged around the time of Vietnam. Direct action was not their forte. But in Chuck Berry's lyrics and Little Richard's antics it's possible to construct a broad commentary on rock and roll and American society in the 1950s. They also simultaneously disprove the notion that their songs and the songs of their colleagues have nothing for the cultural and educational elite. At his best, Chuck Berry was a better lyricist than the best of Bob Dylan.

The surest way to convince younger listeners of the greatness of Chuck Berry is to simply note that there would not have been the Beatles or the Rolling Stones without him. That can be said of no other performer from the 1950s, even Elvis. Chuck Berry's influence as a lyricist, guitarist, and vocalist on rock in the 1960s is so pervasive that one is inclined to give him credit even where it may not be due. Did Paul McCartney write the line "Well, she was just seventeen" in "I Saw Her Standing There" because Berry's "Carol" was "too cute to be a minute over seventeen"? We know that Marc Bolan of England's T. Rex lifted the line "Meanwhile, I'm still thinkin'" from Berry's "Little Queenie," more than a decade after the fact. But was the Kinks' Ray Davies similarly inspired to borrow the title of their 1966 hit "Well Respected

Man" from that same descriptive phrase in Chuck Berry's "Sweet Little Rock and Roller"? From a band hip enough to exhume Berry's
"Beautiful Delilah" and "Too Much Monkey Business" for their very
first album in 1964, it is more than likely.

The love/hate relationship between Berry and the Stones is a story
in itself. The Stones recorded so many of the master's songs, including
"Bye Bye Johnny," "Talkin' 'Bout You," and "Around and Around"—
that an entire compilation album was later built exclusively around
their Chuck Berry covers. White critics figured Berry would take delight in being acknowledged by the great Mick Jagger, but he reacted
coolly to these compliments, no doubt wondering why *he* should be
grateful to the Stones. From this and other examples relayed by rock
journalists he was construed to be difficult and remote. Berry may well
have been the only man that Keith Richards ever feared. In their mutual appearances, Richards seemed to be trying hard to not offend Mr.
Berry, who once actually kicked Richards off the stage after the
Stones' guitarist came forward for an impromptu jam. You can't take
the spotlight away from Chuck Berry.

No one in rock over the past fifty years has used the English language like Chuck Berry. He coined phrases that might have sounded
very familiar, until you realized you'd never heard them before. It was
as if he recalled every clever expression he heard and mixed them together to create Berryspeak. There are times he would even reverse the
natural order of things, such as the line in "Brown-Eyed Handsome
Man" where the batter faces a "2-3" count, which as any baseball fan
knows is an impossibility. But changing a 3-2 count to a 2-3 count improves the poetry. (I have tried singing the words the other way; it
doesn't work as well.) In a pop music genre not known for subtlety,
Chuck Berry was subtle, at times gentle—and always witty. When he
wrote about women, for example, it was without the sarcastic bite and
macho dominance typical of the Rolling Stones. In Berry's world, females were usually in control. The narrator chased Maybelline, pined
for Carol, and watched Nadine slip away. Berry could never have been
a successful Hollywood director because the male lead wouldn't end
up with the girl at the end of the picture.

Since the early 1960s, nobody has talked about doing away with rock and roll, only particular groups or songs. But at the beginning, when rock and roll itself seemed to be in danger, lyricists had to be especially careful in the subjects they chose. One false move, as they like to say in the movies, and it would all be over. Love, teenage lust, and automobiles were the most popular subjects for a rock and roll song in the 1950s. These were reasonably safe choices, and traditional, although you couldn't come right out and say you wanted to have sex with someone. Instead, Fats Domino found his thrill on Blueberry Hill, Jerry Lee Lewis was left breathless, and Elvis was all shook up. Chuck Berry covered the same ground, only better. Where his competitors expressed raw emotions, Berry wrote short stories, consisting of a beginning, middle, and an end. It isn't enough that the narrator sees a girl and is attracted to her; we are told what she might be thinking, what he is thinking, and the mental games that go on above and below the surface. A writer so sure of his own talents was eventually going to make the transition to more serious topics. At the beginning, Berry was like the journalist who can't wait to start writing books.

One of the new subjects he took on was rock and roll itself, playing the roles of participant and observer simultaneously. Berry was the first astute rock and roll critic. His songs can still tell you as much as Greil Marcus can about the sociological impact of rock and roll, but Berry happens to be a much better guitar player as well. A decade before the debut of *Rolling Stone* magazine, Berry cleverly dissected the burgeoning rock and roll scene in his songs, offering a wry assessment of a phenomenon that few at the time either recognized or could speak about with authority and intelligence.

Like the proverbial big city newspaper, Berry provided a first draft of history— rock and roll history to be precise. More important, he did so minus the over-the-top verbiage and wildly exaggerated claims about "the music" common in rock journalism—and some rock songs—from the mid-1960s on. Berry clearly recognized the value of rock and roll—he became rich and famous playing the stuff—but he didn't need it in order to make life worth living. In fact, some of his lyrics mock those fans who take it all too seriously. It's a shame Berry didn't write a song about the generation of the 1960s, specifically their belief that rock would lead to world peace, making love in the streets, and the inculcation of a new and better system of values. Rock could have used some internal dissent at that time.

The year teen America discovered rock and roll—1956—Chuck Berry turned thirty. And even though the phrase "Don't trust anyone over thirty" would not be invented for another decade, Berry was several years older than the vast majority of his peers, which could have been a liability to his career. For one thing, he was not a young sex symbol like Little Richard or Elvis. Instead of pelvic thrusts, he performed his famed duck walk across the stage. A bit subtler—there's that word again—then the competition. What he did do was turn maturity into an advantage. Berry staked out his own territory, writing songs that reflected a unique perspective and that left a legacy that has not diminished with time. He saw the future of rock and roll with clarity.

In his 1958 song "Sweet Little Sixteen," Berry tackled a new phenomenon, written about many times since: the rock and roll groupie, who was in most cases innocent compared to her counterparts ten and twenty years later. In the early days, getting close to rock stars didn't necessarily mean sleeping with them. "Sweet Little Sixteen" depicts the lengths to which some young girls will go to build a fantasy life around rock and roll, which includes sexy clothes, hot lipstick, and a single-minded determination to see the show and meet the members of the band afterwards.

If teenagers in the 1950s didn't know about these girls before, they certainly did now. In later versions of the groupie song, the girls are not sixteen, and not as sweet. In the 1970s, the Rolling Stones ("Star Star"), Lynyrd Skynryd ("What's Your Name"), Grand Funk Railroad ("We're an American Band"), and Foreigner ("Hot Blooded") wrote about what happened after young ladies met the guitar player or lead vocalist of their vivid dreams.

Two years before "Sweet Little Sixteen," Chuck Berry gave his rock and roll pep talk and called it "Roll Over Beethoven" (1956). The song has been lauded for arrogance, audacity, and sheer bravado, especially since it was written when rock and roll was in its infancy. What did he know in 1956 that no one else did?

"They (the Beatles) scored a colossal hit with Chuck Berry's 'Roll Over Beethoven'—the title of which is a rejection of Western civilization!"[20] British music critic Wilfred Mellers was writing as a fan of the song, and an even bigger fan of the Beatles. A title that "rejects Western civilization" does not trouble him in the way that it would trouble William Bennett. The exclamation point—unusual punctuation for a serious music critic—suggests joy rather than despair. And Berry is not casting aside Beethoven as a Dead White Male whose time is over. The song is actually a quite funny and obviously absurd attempt to make Beethoven get with the program—rock and roll. Kids are not being urged to drop Beethoven in favor of Chuck Berry. In a perfect world they would listen to both.

Considering its widespread familiarity and historical significance it's surprising that "Roll Over Beethoven" only peaked at number twenty-nine on the *Billboard* charts. There have been other cases since when important records did not make it to number one, or even crack the top ten. Promotion, marketing, and public tastes are not concerned with the judgment of history. Still, I'm sure that a greater number of younger rock fans know about "Roll Over Beethoven"—and can sing a few lines—then almost any other song from the 1950s or early 1960s.

Another theme in the music of Chuck Berry is the classic dichotomy between freedom and responsibility. Unlike his peers, who saw rock and roll solely in terms of liberation, Berry recognized that it provided at most a *temporary* high. After all, the girl in "Sweet Little Sixteen" had to go back to class the morning after she got all dolled up for the dance. Rock and roll doesn't excuse you from doing chores or meeting obligations. It's a break in the action—nothing more. In October 1956, Berry released "Too Much Monkey Business," which recites a litany of dreary tasks and expectations confronting the narrator. He doesn't want to do this and he doesn't want to do that, but in the end what choice does he have? "Too Much Monkey Business" is not a whine, but a witty and perceptive commentary on the conservative nature of American society, as valid today as it was when the song was written. As hippies and radicals would discover, for most of us rebellion is a phase, and not a lifelong commitment. In the early twenty-first century, suburbs across the United States are home to ex-hippies and ex-protesters.

⌐⌐

Either firsthand or through the media, anyone born before 1960 experienced gay liberation, black power, rap music, AIDS activism, and the phenomenon of "coming out." All had in common the aim of first offending the sensibilities of middle-class, white, heterosexual America, and through either guilt or fear, goading that huge segment of the population into giving them what they wanted—money, attention, or both. To the great consternation of American conservatives, the strategy worked. By the late 1990s, society saw the creation of *Will and Grace*, the upper middle-class "family" where the "married couple" is a gay man and a straight woman, saw the first generation of angry rap stars either die or become television and film actors, and even saw homosexual Republican members of Congress publicly reveal their sexuality. But though these changes occasioned lots of self-congratulations on the Left, there was an uneasy sense among some true believers that progress could be bad for business. The political activist class, which includes public relations people, development staff, lawyers, lobbyists, and paid media junkies, does not want to do something else for a living. They are round-the-clock agitators, who make a career out of fighting the oppressors, real or imagined. To stay current they suggest that victory is always in reach, but never achievable. There are always enemies to be fought. At a time of unparalleled success for their natural constituents, gay groups in the late 1990s railed against the Christian Right and offensive rap lyrics, refusing to acknowledge that key social indices showed that history was moving their way. The strong language and predictions of doom that continue to emanate from these groups makes them appear ridiculous to Americans of all kinds, as well as motivated not by a desire for change but pure self-interest. I can recall picking up a niche-market magazine in a Washington, D.C., bookstore a few days after September 11, 2001, and reading an eighteen-point headline about a gay pilot who died on one of the planes. The thought that the editorial staff of this publication was desperate to find the homosexual angle in one of the most important and tragic events in American history had me laughing out loud for the first time since September 10.

One of the effects of this profound shift in attitudes is that Little Richard today seems more, not less, daring then when he burst on the rock and roll scene in the 1950s. At this point in our cultural history, it means next to nothing for a performer to combine effeminacy and aggression with being black. You need more than that to move viewers of MTV, who think they've seen it all. But when Little Richard combined those same ingredients in the 1950s, he was not a cliché. Black and gay was not flavor of the month back then, as James Baldwin knew. Little Richard was out in front of the politics and the pop music of his time. And if in the 1990s he could no longer be considered outrageous, due mainly to the proliferation of Little Richard imitators in music, sports, theater, and film over the past three decades, we still couldn't take our eyes off him. More important, we listened to what he had to say because he dared to be outrageous even in the 1950s, when few entertainers had the courage to take it *that* far.

In recent years, his public appearances have mainly consisted of occasional performances, commercials, and guest spots on late-night television talk shows, where he sits at the piano, plays one or two of his biggest hits, and utters words of wisdom about the necessity of individuals remaining true to themselves. Coming from him the message is convincing, if rather commonplace in an age where every other person seems to be in therapy.

As was true of the comedian Lenny Bruce, whose act in the 1950s included aggressive sexuality, brutally honest social and political commentary, and occasional use of four-letter words, Little Richard seems more suited to a different era. Even if we reject Newt Gingrich's storybook version of the 1950s, it's not easy to account for Little Richard. He wore heavy makeup, exuded a sense of both raw and undefined sexuality, and couldn't stop talking about himself. One almost wonders if he didn't parachute into the decade from some time in the future. And yet he was not relegated to the margins, but became one of the most popular performers of the mid-to-late 1950s. Just because Pat Boone's version of "Tutti Frutti" made it to number twelve in 1956 while Little Richard's original only got to number seventeen is no reason to assume the guy had no following with white kids. We have been brainwashed by Hollywood into thinking that all those boys in crewcuts and girls in long skirts were quasi-racists, sexually naïve, or both. They may have liked Ike, but they loved Little Richard.

Little Richard exemplified the mantra from the 1960s; "Do Your Own Thing," which is why he has been such a big influence on several black celebrities who came later, including James Brown, Muhammad Ali ("I Am the Greatest" is pure Little Richard), and Prince. He played the game as if he had nothing to lose, and when you think about it, he didn't, being black, bisexual, and raised in the segregationist South. What choice did he have but to go into rock and roll? Like the theater and movies, it was a refuge for talented people who didn't fit the social norm.

His career was a political statement. But had Little Richard become a star in the 1980s, left-wing groups peddling political correctness and identity politics would have probably tried to pressure him into becoming a spokesperson for gay rights, affirmative action, or some other life or death cause. He may well have succumbed to these kinds of entreaties, as many other rock stars have over the past three decades. And from this we have learned that spending time on politics can inhibit creativity. But in the 1950s, Little Richard was left alone to concentrate on his music.

Whites and blacks bought millions of Little Richard's recordings; his popularity no doubt causing great pain to parents, religious leaders, and politicians across the country. "Long Tall Sally," "Jenny Jenny," "Keep a Knockin'," and "Good Golly, Miss Molly" were top ten singles from 1956 to 1958, while two from 1956 that made it as high as number seventeen, "Rip It Up" and "Tutti-Frutti," are among the best rock and roll singles in history. Whites still listen to him, but that's not generally true of blacks. The same can be said about the music of Chuck Berry. Since the early 1960s, most fans of Chuck and Little Richard have been white, judging by concert attendance and radio airplay. When the Beatles, the Rolling Stones, and other British groups stated publicly how much these two performers had influenced their own music it aroused the curiosity of a younger generation of Caucasians.

I know a number of listeners who discovered Chuck Berry because of the Rolling Stones, and Little Richard because of the Beatles. Today you will not hear "Sweet Little Sixteen" or "Rip It Up" on oldies stations catering to the black community, which is not the case with oldies stations that are geared toward whites. The stations would say they are simply responding to the tastes of their particular audience. The veteran rhythm and blues performer and scholar Johnny Otis has frequently lamented the fact that younger black listeners as a rule are ignorant about the great soul, rock and roll, and rhythm and blues performers from the 1950s and 1960s.

It's not entirely clear why blacks have shunned Chuck Berry and Little Richard. Perhaps it has to do with the two of them being considered insufficiently assertive—musically and politically—on behalf of The Race. After all, they played rock and roll, and ever since the Beatles came to America rock and roll has been associated with whites. But Chuck Berry and Little Richard were hardly quiescent. More than any of their contemporaries, black or white, they blurred the distinction between rock and roll and politics. Bill Clinton has often been referred to as "The first rock and roll president"; Chuck Berry and Little Richard were the first rock and roll stars whose music and image crossed into the realm of politics.

A world-series winner that loses four of its best players in the off-season will probably not return as champions. Something of this kind happened to rock and roll in 1958 to 1959, and the music suffered as a result. The first to leave was Elvis Presley, drafted into the U.S. Army in the fall of

1958. He spent the next eighteen months in Germany and out of the lime-light. That same year Little Richard denounced rock and roll and em-braced Jesus, demonstrating that for all the mascara, hedonism, and brag-gadocio, he was still a child of the South. In May 1958, the news broke about Jerry Lee and Mrs. Lewis, severely damaging his career. And fi-nally, on February 2, 1959, Buddy Holly, the Big Bopper, and Ritchie Valens were killed in an Iowa plane crash. The UPI story filed the next day said the seventeen-year-old Valens had been hailed as "the next Elvis Presley."

Only Chuck Berry remained standing, and he did his part, releasing some of his best recordings in 1958 and 1959, including "Almost Grown," "Back in the USA," and his signature song, "Johnny B. Goode." But in late 1959, Berry was accused by federal authorities of transporting an underage girl across state lines, in violation of the Mann Act. He was subsequently convicted and sent to jail for two years. Berry's conviction, along with the Jerry Lee Lewis scandal and the reasons behind Little Richard's "conversion," provided plenty of ammunition for the persistent lobby that proclaimed rock and roll en-couraged degenerate and immoral behavior. Still, these objections could be overcome. More worrying to fans was the fact that with the best, most innovative performers in retirement, semi-retirement, or prison, where would the next great records come from?

Dick Clark saw the talent drain as a business opportunity. In the summer of 1957 *American Bandstand* made its debut on ABC. *Bandstand* was based in Philadelphia, which was not known as a hotbed of rock and roll. But Clark had other ideas. He would give the teen pub-lic something different from those wild and crazy southerners, and even parents would be happy with these new singers. Comfort would trump outrage. The reviewers could call it rock and roll, they could call it pop, or they could call it junk. The only thing that mattered was that it sold. And it did—quite well. In the Dick Clark era, 1959 to 1963, rock and roll had its first counterrevolution.

"Rock and roll existed from 1955 to 1956 until maybe 1959," said Ray Manzarek. "And then there was that backlash that came from Dick Clark and Philadelphia."

5

COME SOFTLY TO ME

To most middle-aged men, the nickname "World's Oldest Living Teenager" should be considered an insult and a sign of disrespect. But not so Dick Clark, who didn't seem bothered in the least having to carry around that nickname during much of his career. For decades Clark's face remained almost inhumanly free of wrinkles. When Clark was in his fifties he still looked younger then many of the musicians who performed on his show. While Clark would never be confused for the teens that danced on *Bandstand*, he could pass as their self-assured older brother, at least until the arrival of a facial line or two in the mid-1970s. Clark sent a message that listening to rock and roll, or even just being around rock and roll, might be the secret to eternal youth.

Like Chuck Berry, Dick Clark (b. 1929) was long past his teenage years when rock and roll began. But unlike Berry, the wry lyricist, Clark moved in the direction of his audience. He treated them with respect, deference even, and eagerly sought their opinion in the famous rating of records ("It's got a good beat and you can dance to it"). In the 1950s and 1960s, Clark created a persona of the slightly older man, established in his career, who took seriously the hopes, dreams, desires, and most importantly the tastes of adolescents. The average viewer couldn't imagine Clark raising his voice or cutting a deal. He was the male equivalent of America's sweetheart, and he seemed to have an infinite store of patience. For sheer audacity, his performance rivaled anything in rock and roll, including Little Richard's makeup and Elvis Presley's pelvic thrusts. Watching Dick Clark was like reading the *National Enquirer*; you knew it was all b.s., but you had to take a look anyway—the performance was that good. Indeed, Clark has always had a kind of perverse appeal for viewers that otherwise despise everything he represents. He was too slick, too smooth, and too ingratiating to be ignored.

To Clark's credit, if that is the right word, he didn't abandon his look or nice-guy demeanor in the late 1960s, although by then the typical rock star's accoutrements were long hair, attitude, and hard drugs. He put many of the top bands of the 1960s on his show—although not the Beatles or the Stones—and he bantered with them as he did with teen idols in the late 1950s. Still, no one asked Clark to emcee at the 1967 Monterey Pop Festival, or Woodstock two years later. If nothing else, wearing a suit disqualified him immediately. Even before the election of Ronald Reagan as governor of California in 1966 and Richard Nixon as president of the United States in 1968, Clark stood for solid conservative values in the face of the hippie onslaught. Other than booking the Doors on his show, he appeared to make no concessions to the counterculture, and he remained true to his clean-cut self.

Of course, by the late 1960s, everyone knew what to expect from Clark and *American Bandstand*, neither of which was taken very seriously anymore. In the era of Jimi Hendrix, *Sgt. Pepper's*, and the Grateful Dead, it was hard to get worked up about a program that featured hit singles, dancing, and nice young men and women rating records. Clark had become a kind of harmless anachronism.

In the 1950s, however, depending on your point of view he was either the savior of America's youth or the worst thing that ever happened to rock and roll. He embarked on a mission to clean up rock and roll from the inside, making it more palatable to parents, and to kids who didn't want to upset their parents. It's important to remember that this was a business decision; Clark was neither a fiery evangelist nor a grandstanding politician. Yet he was in a better position then either to exert an impact on the actual product.

"But it was network television, specifically the teenage dance show *American Bandstand* that, by beaming bowdlerized rock and roll into America's living room, ultimately legitimized—some would say destroyed—what was viewed by most adults as vulgar, low-class music."[1]

American Bandstand debuted from Philadelphia in August 1957, and for long-time rock fans this remains one of the low moments in rock and roll history, comparable to Pat Boone covering "Tutti Frutti" in March of the previous year, or the success of the Osmonds in the early 1970s. *Bandstand* destroyed—or should have destroyed—any illusion among true believers that rock and roll was different, and that it could both remain pure and withstand the corrupting influences of the entertainment business. Ray Manzarek, for one, checked out when *Bandstand* became popular; he didn't return to rock and roll until he heard the Beatles and the Rolling Stones in 1964.

There were two primary ways in which *Bandstand* altered the landscape of rock and roll. The first was an obvious attempt to make the music and the attendant scene more palatable to white kids and especially to their parents. Clark didn't openly advertise the fact that he and the show's sponsors wanted a predominantly white studio audience, but viewers who tuned in during the late 1950s saw exactly that. At a time when ministers and politicians in the South were expressing their fears that rock and roll invited race mixing, *Bandstand* practiced its own brand of self-selection on the basis of race. None dare called it segregation, but the practical effect was the same. As John Jackson wrote:

"By the time *American Bandstand* appeared in August 1957, featuring the largely black-derived idiom of rock and roll, the show's studio audience remained segregated to the extent that viewers around the country did not have an inkling that Philadelphia contained one of the largest black populations in America."[2] *Bandstand* forced the issue because of rock and roll's move to television. After all, neither government nor the powers at the top of the entertainment industry in the 1950s could have prevented white kids from buying records made by blacks, or stopped small and mid-sized record labels from recording black rock and roll performers. It would have been impractical, not to mention bad for business. Good money was being made off of Chuck Berry, Little Richard, Larry Williams, and Fats Domino. But television was easier to control. In September 1956—a year before *Bandstand* came on the air—Ed Sullivan negotiated a deal with Elvis Presley's manager, Colonel Tom Parker, which stated that Elvis could only be photographed from the waist up during his performance on Sullivan's highly-rated show. If there was a price to be paid as rock and roll went national, the Presley camp was willing to pay it. Colonel Parker wanted Elvis to be a star, and Elvis wanted to be a star, so Ed Sullivan got his way.

While Sullivan attempted to take the sex out of rock and roll, at least for one night, *Bandstand* focused on race, inventing a counter history in which black kids didn't listen to rock and roll or rhythm and blues. Presumably the sight of black and white couples close to each other on the dance floor would have shocked and disgusted viewers across the nation.

Having "lightened" the audience, Clark next turned his attention to the performers, acting as a sort of equal-opportunity employer for white prospects— affirmative action in reverse. Starting in 1958 to 1959, he and his program launched and sustained the careers of Frankie Avalon, Fabian, and Bobby Rydell, who thanks to *Bandstand* will be forever linked. This trio represented the first teen idols in rock and roll, and as such should be considered the forerunners of Bobby Sherman, Donny Osmond, Leif Garrett, and the like. (It's a cruel category because some teen idols have no talent, while others are skilled at playing an instrument or singing. But if you get the girls to scream and are hated by the critics, you're a teen idol, like it or not.) Whenever rock and roll enters a fallow period, teen idols move in and stake their claim to the charts, sneaking in a number one hit or two and several TV appearances before normalcy returns.

Such was the case in 1958, with the end of the first golden era. The teen idols offered rock and roll stripped of sexual suggestiveness and "Negro" influences, which in truth is no rock and roll at all. But why quibble over definitions? Like a savvy political consultant, Clark knew exactly who and what he wanted to sell to the public, which in this case meant wholesome teenagers—mainly females—and their parents. Indeed, rock and roll, much like politics, operates according to cycles. A period of great creativity and forward movement is often followed by a conservative backlash. The transition from Little Richard to Dick Clark was the first example of this; there have been, and will continue to be, others.

Who today can name three singles by Frankie Avalon, or two each by Fabian and Bobby Rydell? In the land of *Bandstand*, the communicator was always more important than the thing being communicated. Still, the record labels had to put out something. Once again, it was all done according to a formula.

"The songs were aimed primarily at teenage girls, the ones in the suburbs who wanted big fluffy candy-colored images of male niceness on which to focus their pubescent dreams. Charming, wholesome dreamboats, the singers were safe and well-mannered, perhaps with a teasing tendency toward wildness."[3]

In hindsight, it's clear that *Bandstand* and its ilk represented an unfortunate but perhaps necessary transition period between Elvis and the Beatles. It was too much to ask of the first generation of stars that they continue to make great records for another five or ten years, but there was also little or no confidence that happy days would ever come again.

Still, those at the time who prophesized the death of rock and roll—more out of sorrow than glee—had the stronger argument. Not only were the teen idols on top of pop in 1958 to 1960, they were also having an obvious impact on one of the good guys—Elvis Presley.

When he came out of the army in 1960, Elvis cut most of his ties to genuine rock and roll. Compared to his new stuff, even his relatively tame RCA singles from the 1950s sounded tough and gritty. Elvis had three number one singles in 1960: "Are You Lonesome Tonight?" "It's Now or Never," and "Stuck on You." The first two were lush, melodramatic pop ballads, with a fair share of hokum mixed in, and the third was a bouncy little number that would not have seemed out of place on Broadway. This new Elvis remade himself by following the trend toward a more conservative, and classically pop sound. Of course, Elvis was a much greater singer than Frankie Avalon, Bobby Rydell, and Fabian, and a superstar to boot, but he and his management were not too proud to get with the program.

Presley's fans didn't seem to mind, or maybe he acquired new ones. According to *Joel Whitburn's Pop Annual 1955–1977*, Elvis was the number three artist of the year in 1960, the number two artist in 1961, and the number one artist in 1962. In 1963, he dropped out of the top ten entirely, which was just as well, because the Beatles were about to come to America and render Elvis obsolete anyway.

But only for awhile. Like Richard Nixon, another public figure who had supposedly passed his prime, Elvis made an extraordinary comeback in 1968. Again like Nixon, the high point was reached at the end of 1972. Beginning with his legendary television special from Las Vegas in 1968, and culminating with the release of an unexpectedly superb single, "Burning Love" (number two in October 1972), Elvis made a triumphant return to rock and roll. Some of the singles he released during this time, "Suspicious Minds" (1969), "Kentucky Rain" (1970), and "Burning Love" are as good or better than most of his hits from the 1950s and early 1960s. And although he was a product of the 1950s, musically and politically, Elvis obviously benefited from the fertile environment of late 1960s rock and roll. The record-buying public liked what it heard: Elvis was the number six *Billboard* artist of the year in 1969 and number two in 1970, the year the Beatles broke up.

What is rock and roll? The people who wear black leather jackets, leave their sunglasses on indoors, or pierce their tongues are certain that it's not *American Bandstand*. And yet Dick Clark has for years hosted a nationally-syndicated radio program called "Rock, Roll, and Remember," has the rights to one of the world's greatest collections of video footage of performances from the 1950s, 1960s, and 1970s, and rates a chapter in many definitive histories of rock and roll. He also guided the career of Chubby Checker, whose recording of "The Twist" is one of the few things laypeople recall about that fallow period between the decline of Elvis and rise of the Beatles. To be sure, rock and roll books are usually not kind to Clark, referring to him sarcastically as "Mr. Clean," among other things. Like Yoko Ono at the time of the breakup of the Beatles, he is seen as having wrecked something beautiful. Clark injected the heterodox notion that rock and roll could be softened, whitened, and scrubbed and still called rock and roll. It is this uncomfortable truth that rock critics through the ages have refused to accept. In 1974, Jon Landau famously wrote "I saw the rock and roll future and its name is Bruce Springsteen." It's OK to say this about Springsteen because, after all, he is the epitome of rock and roll. He wears a black leather jacket, sings songs about cars and girls, and rocks around the clock. But what if someone had written the same thing about Dick Clark in 1959? Would it be less true because *American Bandstand* was for squares?

Rock and roll might free your soul—except when it comes to the actual songs. The intellectual rock fan or rock critic who feels the spirit of his or her beloved music is being tampered with can become uptight, mean, and hysterical, as the Rolling Stones or the Who learn whenever they embark on yet another "final" tour. Classical music and jazz purists have nothing on their rock counterparts. Indeed, the rock scolds are even worse, criticizing not only musical choices but business and political decisions as well. They are deeply wounded when their heroes don't measure up to their standards, whatever those may be. It's as if these people need rock to affirm for them that there is still some good left in the world. The myth of rock and roll as a bastion of truth in a society built on lies has enjoyed a remarkably long life given these cynical times. The enduring strength of the myth is a tribute to the cultural and political power of baby boomers, who are its fervent champions.

American Bandstand is the first and the best-known counterexample to the notion that only cool people—by their own definition—are in command of rock and roll. When left-wing writers refer to the

"Other," they usually mean blacks, gays, women, and Native Americans: groups that were once marginalized or ignored by society at large. In rock and roll terms, however, the "Other" consists of conservatives, born-again Christians, and descendents of the *American Bandstand* formula. These are the participants the rock elite would like to forget. The case of Christian rock is especially revealing, because it makes traditional rock fans uncomfortable on spiritual and political grounds. "(Christian Rock) is based on faith, worship and Christian family values," according to the March 19-25, 2001, edition of *The Los Angeles Business Journal*.[4] Well, we know those values are not compatible with rock family values, and yet the Christian bands have long hair and feature screaming guitar solos, a crashing beat, and narcissistic lead vocalists. Who is to say this isn't rock and roll? Take away the Bible, and these bands could fit into the Sunset Boulevard scene circa 1989.

The most popular Christian rock band ever, Stryper, released "To Hell with the Devil" in the late 1980s, which went platinum. (Not to be confused with "Runnin' with the Devil," a song released in 1978 by Van Halen, whose members only looked like the guys in Stryper.) Videos from the album were featured on MTV and VH-1. "Christian music festivals feature scores of performers of Christian pop music," according to a story in the July 27, 2002, *Los Angeles Times*.[5] "Rock 'n' soul has even made its way into mainline Protestant churches looking for new ways to bring young people into their declining folds." If rock can be used to sell computers, cars, and candidates, then why not Christianity?

But Christian rock bands are not only out to spread the Word. As in the case of the Christian Coalition, they have political points they would like to get across to the rest of us as well. There are Christian rock videos as blatantly political in their way as anything you might see or hear from Rage Against the Machine or Bruce Springsteen. It's just that these videos are shown on Christian television stations only, where secular humanist viewers rarely venture. These videos are literally a case of preaching to the converted, but at least the creators don't have to worry about being the target of politically correct censors, as would be the case if they tried to get their stuff shown on MTV.

For example, I watched one video involving well-groomed and determined kids who want to form a prayer group at a public high
school being prevented from doing so by a villainous administrator.
Not to be denied, the students gather around some common landmark
on the campus, bibles in hand, and begin the day's lesson, while a
band that rocks as hard as Mötley Crüe is heard on the soundtrack.
Within seconds an authority figure appears to disperse the group,
warning the members not to try it again. But faith is strong, and the
students move their prayer group to various parts of the campus, only
to be dispersed every time. They will not be defeated by some administrator, no matter if he represents the power of the evil government. By the end of the video, the administrator knows he's whipped,
but he has also learned something much more important. Armed with
this new wisdom, he walks over to the praying students, takes the
hands of two of them, and joins the circle—the happy conclusion to
a Christian rock video.

The message is in support of prayer in the public schools, one of the
more contentious issues in domestic American politics over the past
two decades. I haven't seen any polls, but I would doubt that most rock
performers are similarly inclined, if for no other reason then it violates
the separation of church and state. Even many Republicans oppose
prayer in schools. But what's memorable about the video is the stri-
dency of its politics, which are the right-wing equivalent of "Anarchy
in the UK." Don't be fooled just because the Christian rockers don't
spit or scream obscenities.

Even the Mr. Cleans of the world must sometimes answer to Congress.
Still, given his crucial role in "civilizing" rock and roll, it's ironic that
Dick Clark was called to Washington to testify in the infamous payola
scandal of 1960, the first time that people who made their living from
rock and roll were hauled before the federal government. Clark testified
in front of the House of Representatives' Legislative Oversight Committee, which was looking into payola, the practice of accepting cash or

gifts in return for radio airplay. Several well-known disc jockeys spoke at the hearings, but Clark was the big catch. He appeared in April.

During the past fifty years, nationally televised congressional hearings have proved a mixed blessing for politicians. They receive the necessary exposure, so crucial to launching or maintaining a successful career in politics, but a skilled witness can also make them look inept or out of touch. This is what occurred when Lt. Col. Oliver North testified regarding the Iran-Contra affair in 1987, and when both Anita Hill and Clarence Thomas testified during his Supreme Court nomination hearings in 1991. Indeed, there is a wide swath of the American public that enjoy these hearings not for the information they yield, but because politicians can sometimes get put in their place. When North lectured his questioners about the extraordinary steps that are necessary to defend the United States, in this case against the Marxist-Leninist Sandinistas that ruled Nicaragua, you could just picture frustrated conservatives standing and applauding from San Diego to Charleston.

Dick Clark was subpoenaed to testify years before Watergate or Iran-Contra, but after the Army-McCarthy hearings and Richard Nixon's Checkers speech. The power of television in swaying public opinion was not a mystery in 1960, even though the TV-savvy politician was a rarity. Still, the members of the committee probably figured to have their way with Clark and get him to confess his mistakes, after which they would issue a harsh verdict about the widespread use of payola. The result would be a slew of favorable publicity about their efforts to stamp out corruption and clean up rock and roll. Clark's celebrity status would guarantee the necessary press coverage.

They underestimated their prey. Clark earned his living from television, which made all the difference once the hearings began. And the host of *Bandstand* choreographed quite a show. If Clark couldn't expect to charm the committee members like he charmed the kids and performers on *Bandstand*, then he would alternately impress and confuse them instead:

> To aid in his defense, he [Clark] hired a statistician, Bernard Goldstein; while admitting that Clark had a personal interest in records represent-

ing 27 percent of the "spins" on *American Bandstand* over a twenty-eight month period. Goldstein argued that these records had in any case a "popularity" score of 23.9, which "proved" that Clark was playing records because listeners wanted to hear them, not because Clark stood to gain financially. Observers were bewildered by Goldstein's computations and correlations, but Clark himself laid any doubts about the conflict of interest to rest when he testified.[6]

"Speaking in a soft tone, Clark explained how he had given up whole or part of interest in thirty-three businesses since the payola issue had surfaced; he'd become involved in that many businesses, he later said, to take advantage of tax laws."[7] Which member of Congress could argue with that?

In the end, Dick Clark testified to secure a show biz future for himself, but he did little for rock and roll, which to be frank had a more pressing concern in early 1959—lack of good product. Dick Clark could survive rock and roll, and rock and roll could survive Dick Clark. Two decades after the payola scandal, Clark was the television personality's version of Everyman, hosting quiz shows, teaming with Ed McMahon on a variety of specials, and continuing to present *American Bandstand* on a weekly basis. No one else closely associated with rock and roll had as many diverse TV credits to his or her name.

As part of his testimony, Clark agreed with the subcommittee that he made considerable profits from rock and roll, although he repeatedly denied having accepted payola himself. He thus came across as an ambitious yet clean businessman, practicing the time-honored American art of making a buck. The total package satisfied the members of Congress, who were clearly smitten by this charming and seemingly polite young capitalist; a marked contrast to the young ruffians who played rock and roll records and went to rock and roll concerts. Representative Oren Harris of Arkansas, chairman of the subcommittee, proclaimed Clark "a fine young man," which was not something you heard members of Congress saying about Elvis Presley back in 1959.

The subcommittee eventually recommended the adoption of anti-payola amendments to the Federal Communications Act. These amendments, which became law in 1960, prohibited payment of cash or gifts in exchange for airplay. To the extent that payola—or the lack thereof—had prevented the public from hearing records, the new law was good for rock and roll. But the payola scandal also claimed one famous victim—Alan Freed.

If not the darling of rock and roll critics, Freed elicits their considerable sympathy, in part because he's presented as the opposite of Dick Clark. His death on January 20, 1965, at the age of forty-three, from complications of uremia, a disease that affects the kidneys, confirmed his status as a tragic figure. Meanwhile, Clark is still going strong into the twenty-first century.

Freed reveled in the two principal components of rock and roll—sex and race—that infuriated and frightened the guardians of virtue, and were essentially edited out of *American Bandstand*. He claimed to have coined the term *rock and roll*, which has been described as a euphemism used by black people to denote sexual intercourse. The Rock and Roll Hall of Fame is located in Cleveland because from 1951 to early 1954 Freed hosted "The Moon Dog Rock-n-Roll Show" there, playing rhythm and blues for white listeners before or his audience knew they were making musical history. Freed also must be considered one of the people that deliberately aligned rock and roll with the forces of progressive politics in this country.

After he took his act to New York in 1954, Freed began to sponsor live shows at cities in the East and Midwest. Only a few years after President Harry Truman outlawed segregation in the armed forces, Freed was bringing that same message to the dance floor—except in this case girls were involved as well. You couldn't do that in the mid-1950s without making certain people or groups very angry. As Wes Smith wrote in *The Pied Pipers of Rock and Roll*:

(Freed's) outspoken advocacy of black music—he refused to play the more acceptable white "covers" of black tunes by Pat Boone and others— aroused the suspicions of the Klan, the Catholic Church, and J. Edgar Hoover, to name a few, who didn't like the beat or the way teens were dancing to it. Freed became a primary focus for their fears that the country was going to hell in a transistor radio.

Repeated news photos of white teenage girls dancing with black teenage boys or white teens in adulatory poses around black performers at Freed's concerts increased the racial tension.[8]

As it happened, the Klan, the Catholic Church, and the FBI played no apparent role in Freed's unfortunate demise. On May 19, 1960, a New York grand jury investigating the payola scandal charged eight men with receiving more than $10,000 in gratuities. Freed was the sole nationwide celebrity in the group, and the only one subpoenaed. Despite an offer of immunity, he refused to testify. His stance has since made him a hero to rock and roll historians, as opposed to Dick Clark, cast as the careerist who kissed up to Congress and has since become fabulously rich. In the words of the *Rolling Stone Illustrated History of Rock and Roll*, "Freed, the disc jockey most vociferous in support of rock and roll, took the fall for the scandal."[9] In December 1962, Alan Freed pled guilty to two counts of commercial bribery. He received a six-month suspended sentence, and was fined $300.

Less then two years later, another grand jury indicted Freed for income tax evasion. At this point he was living in Palm Springs, his money supply dwindling, and without much chance of ever finding work as a disc jockey again. The bribery charge was part—not all—of the problem. A month earlier the Beatles had come to America, which rendered Freed obsolete and had the unintended effect of dividing the rock and roll audience along racial lines. The "Freed dream" of an integrated dance hall gave way to the Beatles performing in front of lily-white audiences across America. It was not much later that black performers in a new category called soul music started playing before, and to some extent catering to, the black audience exclusively. Even Alan Freed could not have brought the races together under such difficult circumstances.

In 1958, Danny and the Juniors, a Philadelphia-based teenage group aligned with Dick Clark, released an optimistic anthem called "Rock and Roll Is Here to Stay." Like other Philadelphia performers assisted by *Bandstand*, Danny and the Juniors were well-groomed, polite, and purveyors of a cheerful sound. Even parents who didn't want rock and roll to stay would have been hard-pressed to find much to object to in the song. There were even a couple of kids with Italian surnames in the band, a recurring pattern with Clark. (Philadelphia apparently had an inexhaustible supply of Italian American teen idols.) "Rock and Roll Is Here to Stay" peaked at number eleven in March, which was not as high as the Danny and the Juniors' single that proceeded it, "At the Hop," which went all the way to number one. There was, of course, something nervy about a group connected to Dick Clark reassuring the audience that rock and roll was here to stay. Many die-hard fans saw Clark as the problem, not the solution. The song could plausibly be regarded as one more instance of *American Bandstand*'s cynical attitude toward rock and roll and its core audience.

Still, in their own inimitable way, Danny and the Juniors had touched on a legitimate issue; rock and roll was suffering by 1958. Many of the superstars were out of commission, and there were no performers of their caliber waiting on deck. The detractors who from the beginning had predicted that rock and roll was a passing fad might soon be vindicated.

Over the next five years rock and roll managed to stay afloat, partially vindicating Danny and the Juniors. Still, in the 1976 edition of *The Rolling Stone Illustrated History of Rock and Roll*, only two artists— Roy Orbison and Phil Spector—who did their best work in the period from 1958 to 1963 merit a chapter, as opposed to six from the 1950s and nearly twenty from the 1960s. And Spector was a producer and co-writer, so he doesn't really count. There were several memorable songs released during these years, including "Duke of Earl," "Blue Moon," "Runaway," "Lovers Who Wander," instrumentals such as "Green Onions," and several from Duane Eddy. Surf music got started at this time, which some people consider a good thing, while Motown grew to become a bona fide hit factory by 1962 to 1963. But you couldn't put rock and roll and revolution in the same sentence anymore. The requisite hysteria (the young) and shock (their parents) was missing.

It's revealing that politicians and ministers in the early 1960s essentially ignored rock and roll. Gone were the days of fiery sermons about race-mixing and sensual rhythms, as well as city councils threatening or approving punitive measures to ban concerts and dances from towns around America. The sad truth is that most local politicians and community leaders had better things to do then worry about rock and roll in the early 1960s. Having just gone through Elvis, Little Richard, and Jerry Lee Lewis, they knew how insane things could get. This was nowhere close.

In 1961, John F. Kennedy assumed the presidency, and we know what happened next: Camelot, idealism, and "Ask not what you can do for your country. . . ." After the stodgy Eisenhower years, so the story goes, America now had a young, dynamic commander-in-chief who by his very presence inspired young people to make the world better. His administration created the Peace Corps, which sent students around the globe to help the less fortunate and thereby deter communism, and his seeming support for the African American cause provided an additional boost to the civil rights movement.

If youth politics did well by Kennedy, youth culture—rock and roll, to be precise—was not similarly blessed. Kennedy could be of no help here. By the time of his election the president at forty-three was far too old even to feign interest in Elvis Presley or Chuck Berry. The theme song of his 1960 campaign, "High Hopes," was a cheery and lightweight pop tune recorded a year earlier by JFK's then-good friend, Frank Sinatra, whose hatred of early rock and roll has been thoroughly documented. From 1958 to 1963—Dwight Eisenhower's last two years in the White House through the assassination of his successor— rock and roll and politics went their separate ways. That first group of rock and roll stars in the mid-1950s might not have engaged in direct political action, but they were feared and loathed by authority figures both political and religious, which has made them more than a mere footnote to history. Indeed, the music and impact of Elvis Presley, Little Richard, and Chuck Berry tells us something profound about American society in the middle of the 1950s. Yet through no fault of their own, the music and careers of Roy Orbison, Del Shannon, and Duane Eddy tell us virtually nothing about that society in the late 1950s and early 1960s.

While rock and roll remained in a virtual holding pattern, the country lurched from one dangerous situation to the next during Kennedy's time in the White House. It would be more than a stretch to even attempt to correlate political events with hit singles of the period. The best example of the gap between the record charts and reality occurred in October 1962, the month of the Cuban Missile Crisis. For twelve tense days, October 16 to 28, millions of people in Europe and the United States went to sleep wondering if they would live to see the morning. And what was number one in America while John Kennedy and Soviet leader Nikita Khrushchev contemplated actions that could have destroyed the planet? "Monster Mash" by Bobby "Boris" Pickett and the Crypt-Kickers, which in subsequent years became *the* Halloween song much like "White Christmas" will always be *the* Christmas song. "Monster Mash" is rather ridiculous even judged by the lax standards of early 1960s rock and roll.

The gap between rock and roll and politics expanded further in 1963. That year witnessed Martin Luther King's famous "I Have a Dream" speech in Washington; the killing of four black schoolgirls by a terrorist bomb in Birmingham, Alabama; the murder of South Vietnamese president Ngo Dinh Diem; and, three weeks later, JFK's assassination in Dallas. The number one songs in November and December 1963 were "I'm Leaving It Up to You" by Dale and Grace, "Deep Purple" by Nino Tempo and April Stevens, and "Dominique" by the Singing Nun. Not only do these songs stand in stark contrast to the news of the day, they bear no resemblance to real rock and roll. Indeed, they exist in a kind of time warp, as if there had never been an Elvis Presley or a Little Richard. By this point the charts—the single best measure of the musical tastes of the American masses—suggested a return to the days of 1950 and 1951. Forget the free world; the fate of modern music hung in the balance.

Passionate rock and roll fans have suffered through bleak years, with 1960, 1963, and 1974 being among the worst. The only consolation during these grim months has been the knowledge that rock and roll, like the economy, goes through cycles; a recession is invariably followed by a boom, and so on. Sharp observers familiar with the pattern save their money until it's safe to return to the record store.

And yet even in the worst of times a handful of top-notch songs somehow manage to sneak high on to the charts. These minor miracles can be as good as the best songs from any era. Even more surprising, many of the same people who buy the "inferior" product purchase the better stuff as well, almost as if they are unable to tell the difference. In 1960, Maurice Williams and the Zodiacs had a number one hit with "Stay"—doo-wop vocals and a funky beat—while in 1974 the Hues Corporation went to the top with "Rock the Boat," still the best synthesis of disco and pop ever recorded. Unfortunately, there was no single as good as "Stay" or "Rock the Boat" in 1977, which in my opinion qualifies as the worst single year—or worst year for singles—in rock and roll history.

The song that "saved" 1963 only made it to number two on the charts. Nevertheless, the Kingsmen's "Louie Louie" clearly takes the prize for the most discussed, analyzed, and, yes, overplayed single in the history of rock and roll. "Louie Louie" is the subject of its own book—as far as I know no other rock song has been similarly honored—and has spawned an album's worth of cover versions. Finally, "Louie Louie" was the first song in the then seven-year history of rock and roll to trigger a congressional investigation and a wide-ranging FBI inquiry.

During an otherwise uneventful time in rock and roll, "Louie Louie" served as a reminder that some songs could still upset parents and enrage the authorities. In the end, the earnest efforts by the federal government to decipher the supposedly highly sexualized, even obscene lyrics of the song only guaranteed that it would achieve a kind of immortality. We have seen the same thing happen many times, from disco singles that simulate the sounds of an orgasm through the blatant sexuality of Madonna and rap.

Richard Berry, an African American performer from Los Angeles, wrote "Louie Louie" in the spring of 1956. At that point, Berry was singing with a talented group from Orange County, California, called the Rhythm Rockers. The band featured Filipinos, Chicanos, and Berry himself. The founding members of the Rhythm Rockers, Barry and Rick Rillera, had introduced Berry to Latin jazz in 1955. Berry liked the sound so much that he wrote "Louie Louie" in that vein, basing it on a song called "El Loco Cha Cha" by the Latin jazz artist Rene Touzet.

Berry's single of "Louie Louie" did not crack the *Billboard* Top 100, although to this day his version is very popular with older fans in the Latino community of Southern California. It's probably the case that only the more dedicated white rhythm and blues fans had even heard of the song before the Kingsmen, who hailed from the Pacific Northwest, recorded it in the fall of 1963. The teenaged audience at that time, desperate for any signs of life from rock and roll, bought hundreds of thousands of copies of "Louie Louie," although sadly not enough to dislodge "Dominique" from the number one spot. (There is no better example of the quixotic nature of the American record-buying public; the Singing Nun v. the Kingsmen). Judged strictly on its musical qualities, which admittedly is a tad unfair for a garage band, "Louie Louie" gets a passing grade, but nothing more. The song has its moments, especially the world-famous opening riff and the fumbling, stumbling guitar solo, but the whole is never so good as these appealing parts.

Still, "Louie Louie" presaged a major change in the American music scene. Rock and roll would soon be back and, as excitable promoters like to say, better than ever. Within a few months, the Beatles, the Rolling Stones, the Animals, and other bands collectively known as the British Invasion were firmly in control of the charts on both sides of the Atlantic. "Louie Louie" was easily as good as the best rock and roll singles released by the Dave Clark Five and Herman's Hermits, though not at the level of the elite among the early British groups. But the comparison is less important than the fact that the

Kingsmen and many of the Anglo groups chose to record updated cover versions of rock and roll songs from the 1950s, the first great era. Early rock and roll didn't die between 1958 and 1963, it merely went into hiding, only to re-emerge as rich source material for unknown teenage musicians who were set to embark on their own careers. In the end, the respite actually enhanced the reputation of rock and roll from the 1950s.

November 1963 is remembered today for that fateful visit President Kennedy made to Dallas. But how many people also remember that this was the same month when the Federal Bureau of Investigation began to look into the possibility of obscene lyrics in the song "Louie Louie"? The Kingsmen were thus one of the first domestic "enemies" of the 1960s watched closely by the FBI. According to the book *Louie Louie* by longtime rock critic Dave Marsh, the bureau received information that a woman had purchased the single, played it at 33 1/3 RPM rather than the usual 45—and as a result claimed to hear hidden lyrics of an obscene nature. Whether the woman did this deliberately or as the result of an honest mistake has never been determined.

The FBI did not immediately act on this tip; Marsh says the earliest reference to the song from a FBI file is dated March 27, 1964. To be fair, following the events of November 22, 1963, the FBI had more important things to worry about than any "dirty" words or phrases the Kingsmen or Richard Berry may have slipped into "Louie Louie." And besides, it was damn difficult to figure out the words that either Berry or the Kingsmen were actually singing.

Still, the FBI took the investigation quite seriously, spending almost two years gathering information from the field, interviewing concerned parents, and speaking to Richard Berry. In the end, this exhaustive process did not prove beyond a reasonable doubt that "Louie Louie" was, in fact, obscene. By that point, however, the song had become a hit, reaping the benefits that accrue from being pursued by the guardians of public morals, whether they are the government, religious groups, or self-appointed community leaders. Of course, the rumor was better than the truth.

When news traveled that the words to "Louie Louie" might be naughty, it was turned into the rock and roll equivalent of—and accompaniment to—juvenile sex talk. Since the actual lyrics were next to impossible to understand, kids could substitute any that they wanted, providing a unique opportunity for virgin males ages nine to fourteen to show that they knew something about sex, or the sex act.

An elementary school student during the 1960s, I can barely recall any of the sex jokes told to me by friends or acquaintances on the playground. But I vividly remember the rendition of "Louie Louie" I heard one day after class when I was maybe nine or ten. In a high-pitched and off-key voice, the "singer" described body parts and sex acts that made about as much sense to me at the time as advanced calculus. I also had no way of knowing whether this version was true to the original, but it didn't really matter.

Unlike the payola scandal, which has never been replicated on a similar scale, the "Louie Louie" affair bears a close resemblance to the government v. rock and roll controversies that have occurred periodically over the past several decades. At various times since 1963, Congress, the FBI, or both have looked into the question of rock and roll and sex, or rock and roll and violent behavior. Inevitably these inquiries, or if you prefer, witch hunts, generate widespread media attention and result in definitive pronouncements from one side on the decline of civilization and from the other on the unalienable right to free expression. As they like to say in politics, it's a win/win situation.

SATISFACTION

Dick Clark missed his chance to join the Beatles family. He first heard the group in the summer of 1963, six months earlier than probably 90 percent of the American public, when someone played him the single of "She Loves You," the Beatles' latest release in Britain. That summer the number one songs in America were "Easier Said Than Done" by the Essex, "Surf City" by Jan and Dean, "It's My Party" by Lesley Gore, and Little Stevie Wonder's "Fingertips." A black group consisting of two men and a woman, a surf duo made up of two blonde guys, a feisty young lady, and a black adolescent pop genius who was blind—a quintessentially American mix. Who was thinking of England? Certainly not the host of *American Bandstand*. Clark could have owned a piece of the Beatles, but he turned it down. According to later reports, he didn't think "She Loves You" was either original or especially interesting, and that the Beatles' long hair would repel American teenagers.

Throughout the remainder of 1963 it seemed as if Clark's private prediction about the prospects of the Beatles in the United States—"it'll never fly"—was absolutely on target. The group released a couple of singles in America, but they flopped. Whether this was due to poor promotion, insufficient radio airplay, or that most common explanation in the entertainment business for failure, bad timing, has never been firmly established. The English rock writer Philip Norman in his book *Shout! The Beatles in their Generation* offered his own intriguing theory:

"America up to now (early 1964) had regarded the Beatles as it regarded every British pop performer—an inferior substitute for a product which, having been invented in America, could only be manufactured and marketed by Americans."[1] Rock and roll consumers had a penchant for sticking with their own kind. Along with race, national pride can play a role in turning rock fans against a group or solo performer. The Byrds discovered this in 1965 to 1966, during a disastrous tour of England. Members of the band have claimed that English critics resented any actual or potential competitors with the Beatles. I can recall attending a comprehensive school in London in 1972, and being told by classmates that "I had to admit" that English rock bands were far superior to American rock bands during a general discussion about the relative merits of our two countries. I conceded the point only after they acknowledged the superiority of American films.

There is just one problem with Norman's thesis. The English performers that penetrated the American market before 1964 were not very good. Indeed, one can argue the opposite, that U.S. fans were overly generous toward British imports. For example, Lonnie Donegan's silly single "Does Your Chewing Gum Lose Its Flavor (On the Bedpost Overnight)" made it all the way to number five in America in 1961. Cliff Richard—regarded by some as England's answer to Elvis—had a couple of minor hits in the U.S., but his singles were mediocre at best. On the other hand, an instrumental called "Telstar" by an English group called the Tornadoes hit number one in 1962, and deservedly so. A lovely and simple melody filtered through heavy electronic amplification, "Telstar" was technologically and musically ahead of its time. Had England quickly sent a fleet of singles as good as "Telstar" across the Atlantic, America might have succumbed prior to hearing "I Want to Hold Your Hand."

In his chapter on the Beatles in the 1976 edition of *The Rolling Stone Illustrated History of Rock and Roll*, Greil Marcus wrote that at the end of 1963 "Rock and roll—the radio—felt dull and stupid, a dead end."[2] Dull and stupid, yes, but in retrospect, it was no dead end. In 1963 the Beach Boys released "In My Room," a complex melody that points the way toward "God Only Knows," "Heroes and Villains," and other seminal songs from the period 1965 to 1968, while Marvin Gaye, arguably the greatest performer ever on the Motown label, had his first hit singles. Rock and soul music in the 1960s would have been much poorer without the contributions of the Beach Boys or Marvin Gaye.

Then again, the Supremes, like the Beatles, put out a couple of singles in 1963 that went nowhere. Who can honestly recall "Let Me Go the Right Way" or "A Breath Taking Guy"? The biggest boy group and the biggest girl group in the history of pop both burst onto the scene in 1964.

What rose to the top in 1963 might have been crap, but a significant share of the pop audience was also on the prowl for something better. You can see it in the sales for "Louie Louie," "Blowin' in the Wind" by Peter, Paul & Mary (number two), "Heat Wave" by Martha and the Vandellas (number five), and "It's Up to You" by Rick Nelson (number six), a country-rock ballad that sounds at least five years ahead of its time. If you want an example of the swift maturation of a pop performer, compare Nelson's "Young World" from 1962 with "It's Up to You." It's the difference between *17 Magazine* and *Rolling Stone*.

The American president for eleven months of 1963 had made a big deal about the torch being passed to a new generation. He was, of course, referring to politics and public service, but for younger rock and roll fans the phrase could also be applied to their particular interest as well. The Elvis/Chuck Berry/Little Richard group was not going to save rock and roll. They were too old and too far removed. Elvis was about to turn twenty-nine in January 1964, which by the standards of early rock and roll was tantamount to filing for Social Security. Would girls really scream and faint over a guy who was pushing thirty? For young people born between 1948 and 1952, Elvis was what their older siblings listened to. Who or what would be their Elvis? Every generation wants to be witness to and part of The Next Big Thing. It adds a little more pizzazz to those supposedly boring teenage years.

The oldest Beatle, Ringo Starr, was five years younger than Elvis. The youngest Beatle, George Harrison, was almost nine years younger than Elvis, and seventeen years younger than Chuck Berry. The Beatles learned from the masters, but they were too young to be considered their contemporaries. They were representative instead of the first generation of bands that could claim to be "totally knocked out" by 1950s rock and roll. In that sense, the Beatles had more in common with their restless thirteen-year-old fans than they did with the old guard.

Being from England accentuated the difference from Elvis, which had to be considered a plus. After all, the American rock stars were no longer getting the job done. In addition, the Beatles were a group, and they wore suits. They also had their own sound, which mixed the best from before: Buddy Holly, Chuck Berry, Little Richard, Ritchie Valens, and the Everly Brothers. The result might not have impressed Dick Clark, but it was a big improvement over "Dominique" or "Sugar Shack."

An explanation offered many times for the enthusiasm that greeted the arrival of the Beatles in America was a desperate need for young people to shake off the lingering gloom of the Kennedy assassination, which had occurred barely two months before the group arrived in New York. In other words, we have Lee Harvey Oswald to thank for Beatlemania. The same all-encompassing theories were offered in the aftermath of September 11, 2001. Some critics described the resurgence of family-oriented sitcoms in the fall of 2002 as viewers seeking a return to traditional values following the terrorist attacks on New York and Washington. Other theories: A decline in private funding for the arts was due to 9/11. Fewer people would attend films thanks to 9/11. Or maybe more people would attend films because of a desire to escape the lingering effects of 9/11. Having declared that "everything changed" after 9/11, the media had to keep proving it, using pop culture, politics, sexual mores, travel patterns, the economy, education, and so on as examples.

Before the destruction of the World Trade Center, I was skeptical of the JFK assassination/Beatles connection, and I'm even more skeptical now. The record shows that the Beatles had been meticulously planning their "invasion" of the U.S. several months prior to President Kennedy's death, figuring (perhaps naïvely) that their unprecedented success in Britain could be duplicated in the colonies. As early as 1962, the group's manager, Brian Epstein, had predicted that someday the Beatles would be bigger then Elvis. He didn't mean only in Britain. Obviously the Kennedy assassination was not part of his grand strategy. And had Kennedy been alive during the first U.S. tour, one can imagine latter-day rock historians linking the Beatles' wildly successful reception to the youth, vigor, and wit of the sitting president.

But for all the explanations of what happened in early 1964, the most credible one is also the most obvious: the music. Paul McCartney has said that the Beatles decided months earlier that they would not go to America until they had a number one record on the U.S. charts. In February 1964, "I Want to Hold Your Hand" reached that coveted spot, and remained there for seven weeks. "I Want to Hold Your Hand" replaced Bobby Vinton's syrupy "There, I've Said It Again" in the number one position, a resounding victory for rock and roll in the battle against schmaltz.

Since "I Want to Hold Your Hand" was the single that wowed America, it has tended to serve as the quintessential example of the Beatles' songwriting talents in the early (1962–1964) period. But the song Dick Clark dismissed, "She Loves You" is even better.

"She Loves You" is written as one-sided conversation; a male friend telling another male friend that in reality "she loves you." The lyrics could easily be reinterpreted for the stage, and coming from the Beatles, it's a reminder that the English excel at the dramatic arts. Hearing the song, I imagine two men in their early twenties having a serious discussion about a relationship, up until the famous "yeah, yeah, yeah" chorus, which seems clearly designed for pre-teens. The Beatles offer something for everyone in this song—an early indication of their unprecedented appeal. The rock and roll audience in early 1964 was still mostly segregated according to age and education levels. Junior and senior high school kids were the most enthusiastic consumers. Thanks to the Beatles, the fan base would soon expand.

The Beatles had to be heard and seen in order for young America to surrender. Their February 9, 1964, appearance on *The Ed Sullivan Show* is considered V-B day in virtually every book written about the band. A total of sixty million people watched that night, or 60 percent of the American viewing audience. The group sang "I Want to Hold Your Hand" on the Sullivan program, and the song went on to spend a total of seven weeks at number one, until the superior "She Loves You" replaced it in March.

According to legend, after one listen Bob Dylan immediately declared that "I Want to Hold Your Hand" represented the future of pop music. Melissa Etheridge, then three-years old, can still remember where she was when she first heard the song on the radio. The release of "I Want to Hold Your Hand" and the performance on *The Ed Sullivan Show* launched a thousand bands across America. A popular Mexican American rock and roll group from east Los Angeles called Thee Midniters decided in the early spring of 1964 to dress in matching suits and grow their hair like John, Paul, George, and Ringo. Fans of the group started calling them the Mexican Beatles, in tribute to their outfits and the hysteria they generated at gigs in Latino neighborhoods around Southern California.

After the Beatles, rock and roll could never again be dismissed as music just for teenagers. College students embraced the band in short order, having much more in common with four stylish and witty English guys then with their fellow American, Elvis Presley, who could seem vulgar and rather dim by comparison. The Beatles transcended the class and intellectual barriers that had prevented an influential segment of the population from taking rock and roll seriously prior to 1964. The release of the film *A Hard Day's Night* that summer won over such hard-hearted and erudite critics as John Simon and Dwight MacDonald. Writing in *Esquire*, where he reviewed film for many years, MacDonald said of *A Hard Day's Night* that it "is not only a gay, spontaneous, inventive comedy but it is also as good cinema as I have seen for a long time."[3] He gives some credit to the Beatles, and a bit more to the director of the film, Richard Lester. In a short review marking the re-release of *A Hard Day's Night* in 2000, Stanley Kauffmann, an eighty-something film critic for *The New Republic*, wrote: "When the thirty-six-year-old picture finished, the audience applauded. I joined. The picture is a joy. The Beatles were and remain endearingly brash, four Pucks with irresistible songs."[4]

There is no evidence that in the early days the Beatles deliberately sought the approval of the cultural elite. It just turned out that way, compelling evidence of the unique ability of this band to woo every sector of society, with the notable exception of (most) African Americans. By the time that *Revolver* and *Sgt. Pepper's Lonely Hearts Club Band* were released, in 1966 and 1967, respectively, modern-day classical composers Leonard Bernstein and Ned Rorem were praising the music of the Beatles. It would have been unthinkable for Bernstein and Rorem to be as complimentary to the Beatles' precursors from the 1950s.

Intellectuals, college students, and academics were not content to sit around and discuss the cultural significance of the Beatles among themselves. Having "discovered" rock and roll, which by the mid-1960s was being called rock in order to distinguish the new music from the earlier stuff, they were eager to share their impressions with the rest of the world. In February 1966, Paul Williams, a student at Swarthmore College, launched *Crawdaddy*, which took the then radical position that rock was art, and should be analyzed accordingly. Some eighteen months later, Jann Wenner launched *Rolling Stone* in San Francisco, figuring correctly that there were a sufficient number of literate rock fans to justify his investment. For a while rock was as smitten with this audience as it was smitten with rock. The "concept" album, use of instruments such as the sitar and harpsichord, and more elaborate production gave rock an intellectual veneer that it lacked before. By 1967, "Jailhouse Rock" seemed a thousand—not ten—years ago. But playing up to the interests of the college crowd did not only mean making adjustments to the music. With students around the country protesting the war in Vietnam, rock performers were being pulled into politics, whether they liked it or not.

In 1964, England saved rock and roll from the Americans, the people who invented it in the first place. How this happened has never been adequately explained. English performers had played little role in the development of jazz, and contributed even less to country and western. Of the various predictions offered in the 1950s about the future of rock and roll, I know of none that said it would be British bands who would take the lead. Danny and the Juniors didn't write this ending. Indeed, everything about rock and roll in the 1950s goes against what is still considered to be the stereotypical English personality. Many American stars from the 1950s were vain, outrageous, and in some cases, semi-articulate. By contrast, the English are supposed to be self-effacing, modest, well spoken, and in control.

Some of the early British Invasion groups did comport themselves and play music in what Americans would consider to be a "British" fashion, including Gerry and the Pacemakers, Billy J. Kramer and the Dakotas, and Herman's Hermits. Herman's Hermits actually had a number one U.S. hit in 1965 with an old English music hall song, "I'm Henry VIII, I Am." These groups showed few traces of ever having listened to black American performers, let alone having been influenced by them. In that sense, they were not that far removed from the *American Bandstand* roster of white pop acts, although the singles released by Herman, Gerry, and Billy have aged better then any of the hits by Frankie, Bobby, or Fabian. One English band, Freddie and the Dreamers, did uphold their country's reputation for producing friendly eccentrics. In the 1965 hit "Do the Freddie," the lead singer, Freddie Garrity, who wore horn-rimmed glasses, moved in place like some grinning pogo stick. This was one weird dance, which you would not want to try at home, or anywhere else. But Freddie's success—his group had a number one hit in 1965 with "I'm Telling You Now"—sent a message to oddballs and geeks that you too could have a career in rock and roll.

At the other end of the British Invasion is Mick Jagger, who not only listened to more blues and hard-to-find rhythm and blues than most black or white Americans, but also sounded black on record. Until "As Tears Go By" in early 1966, there was nothing about the music of the Rolling Stones that would make a listener think of England. In conversation the band retained their accents and probably drank tea several times a day, but in the recording studio they turned into a blues-based band. And the Stones played the blues their way, which made them more than just another example of Caucasian copycats. There were plenty of those too in the 1960s, from both England and the United States.

The rock and roll audience increasingly divided along lines of taste, age, education, and race during the 1960s. The idea of Woodstock Nation—a new generation united by rock—doesn't stand up to scrutiny. It's another one of those myths from the era that gets repeated so often that even skeptics are finally persuaded. But consumers who bought Tommy Roe's "Dizzy"—number seven record of the year in 1969—the Archies—"Sugar, Sugar"—number four record of the year in 1969—and the long forgotten duo Zager & Evans' "In the Year 2525"—number two record of the year in 1969—probably didn't make the scene at Woodstock. Of course, some would argue that the above-mentioned songs are really pop, not rock, and bubblegum pop at that, unworthy of inclusion in any serious discussion of late 1960s culture. "Bubblegum" was coined at the time to distinguish lightweight juvenile pop acts such as the Lemon Pipers, 1910 Fruitgum Company, Cowsills, and other groups from the more mature, musically sophisticated, and lyrically advanced acts like Jimi Hendrix, the Doors, and Cream. Readers of *Rolling Stone* hated bubblegum, because it gave their beloved art form—soundtrack to the revolution—a bad name. And yet who could honestly say that "Green Tambourine" and "Incense and Peppermints" weren't rock songs? Even semi-legitimate groups such as Tommy James and the Shondells and Three Dog Night were unfairly tainted with the bubblegum label. Still, I'll put "Crimson and Clover" up against "Get Back" any day of the week.

As believers in the Brotherhood of Man—as distinguished from the group of the same name who charted in 1970 with "United We Stand"—you would think that former hippies, former radicals, and forever baby boomers would be troubled that their Woodstock Nation included very few black people. There may have been blacks on the stage—Richie Havens and Sly Stone—but there were few in the crowd. In its racial composition that 300,000-member community didn't seem much different from the typical American suburb. Out with the old and in with new? Well, not exactly.

Indeed, Woodstock continued a trend that began with the British Invasion in 1964: segregation of the rock and roll audience. Black listeners didn't really dig the British groups, even though the best of them frequently credited black American musicians. The response from the black community was thanks, but no thanks. If blacks can be said to own anything in the United States, it is twentieth-century popular music, and with good reason. Shut out just about everywhere else, blacks took the lead in creating and sustaining jazz, rhythm and blues, and rock and roll. The story has been told countless times, in music history courses, cultural studies classes, Black Studies departments, and popular texts. Fair or not, popular music is what black Americans are most famous for around the world, with sports a distant second.

And then in 1964 British rock groups come to the States, influenced by black music, but hailing from a land where at that time there were comparatively few black people. Who did they think they were, coming over here and showing America how to play rock and roll and rhythm and blues? This didn't bother white Americans too much, because they didn't invent rock and roll anyway. Elvis was accused of sounding black, but nobody accused Little Richard of sounding white. A black woman, Willie Mae Thornton, recorded "Hound Dog" before Elvis jumped on it.

But it's not only racial differences that explain why most blacks were cool to the British Invasion. National pride played a part as well. In the 1950s and early 1960s, black consumers purchased many singles recorded by Elvis Presley, a white Mississippian. The *Billboard* rhythm and blues charts, which was the most accurate official survey of the tastes of African American consumers, indicates that four Elvis songs actually made it to number one on the R & B charts. Many of his releases finished in the top twenty. On the other hand, the Beatles *do not even have an entry* in Joel Whitburn's *Top Rhythm & Blues Records 1949–1971*, which lists every record that made the R&B charts during that twenty-two-year period. The Rolling Stones for that matter are represented only by "Satisfaction," which made it to number nineteen, and "19th Nervous Breakdown," which peaked at number thirty-two. Black musicians, however, have not been as dismissive of the music of the Beatles and Stones. Ray Charles covered "Yesterday" in 1967, and Stevie Wonder recorded a version of "We Can Work It Out" four years later. In 1966, Otis Redding's cover of "Satisfaction" reached number thirty-one on the pop charts, and number four on the rhythm and blues charts.

It may have been partly out of spite that black radio stations all but deleted white performers from their program lists in the 1960s. Indeed, a disproportionate number of the few white performers that made the cut were American. Among the singles from white groups that landed on the R & B charts in the 1960s were "Groovin'" by the Rascals, "Mercy, Mercy, Mercy" by the Buckinghams, and "Expressway to Your Heart" by the Soul Survivors. To be sure, fledgling FM stations did the same in reverse after 1967, although these stations labeled themselves "progressive" or "alternative," which primarily meant they programmed the extended album tracks that AM eschewed. But the result was that relatively few black artists were played on FM rock outlets.

The year of the British Invasion, 1964, was a landmark in the history of American race relations. As the rock audience began to split up along racial lines, the United States Congress passed the Civil Rights Act, officially ending Jim Crow laws. The next year Congress approved the Voting Rights Act, which finally gave black people everywhere the opportunity to participate in the American system of government. It was the beginning of the end for the Old South. "The great change in Washington began in the late 1960s," wrote Meg Greenfield in her memoir *Washing-ton*. "It started with the defeat of the southern coalition in Congress on the Civil Rights Bill of 1964. People were startled to find that they could vi-olate old cultural and political rules and the world wouldn't end."[5] In the 1950s, rock and roll was ahead of the larger society in the field of race re-lations. Unlike President Eisenhower, who did not move with all deliber-ate speed in bringing the races together, the rock and roll shows featured black and white performers playing to mixed audiences. But by the mid-1960s, the roles had reversed. Johnson's Great Society was the catalyst for integration, while black and white listeners started to go their separate ways. That trend continued for the rest of the decade, culminating in the Woodstock Festival in August 1969.

Woodstock was not planned as a political rally—Who guitarist Pete Townshend kicked Abbie Hoffman off the stage at Woodstock when he attempted to advance his own agenda—but this and other similar events were later analyzed in terms of their political importance. The common view is that Woodstock represented the "good" side of the 1960s and the Rolling Stones' free concert at Altamont in December of that year its dark, evil strain. Woodstock is "Make Love, Not War," Al-tamont is Charles Manson.

Black music festivals of this magnitude did not occur as often. But in 1972, the Wattstax concert at the Los Angeles Coliseum, which drew an audience of 100,000—nearly all of them black—openly mixed music and politics. The concert was held to commemorate the 1965 Watts riots, and it featured performances by every artist signed to the Stax label, such as Isaac Hayes and Sam and Dave. The Reverend Jesse Jackson led the crowd in chanting, "I am somebody" and raising their fists in the black power salute. "It was a symbol of black self-suf-ficiency," wrote critic Nelson George. "Wattstax became a film—shot by a predominantly black crew—and a six-sided album."[6]

It's fairly typical for historians and journalists writing about modern America to define the 1960s as the period from the assassination of

John F. Kennedy in November 1963 through the resignation of President Richard Nixon in August 1974. According to this assessment, Camelot is considered an era unto itself, certainly not the 1950s, but not really the 1960s, either. These accounts tend to underplay the role of the Kennedy administration in expanding the American commitment in Vietnam, virtually ensuring that the war would escalate for a number of years. Some have even suggested that had he lived, Kennedy would have extracted the U.S. from Vietnam after the 1964 presidential election. Whether this view is based on sound analysis or wishful thinking is hard to discern. Those intent on preserving the JFK legacy primarily make the case by arguing that he was preparing to turn the conflict in Vietnam over to the South Vietnamese.

In terms of rock and roll and politics, the year 1964 marks the end of one era and the beginning of another, although this was not apparent at the time. The Beatles during this early period in their American career were not inclined to talk about the issues—either in songs or interviews—and politicians in either party had more important things to worry about than the resurgence of rock and roll. "Right-wingers disliked but could ignore rock and roll, men's long hair, and love beads."[7] How different this sounds from today, the post–Cold War era, in which monitoring and/or condemning rock or rap is one of the "wedge issues" that ranks high on the conservative agenda. But in 1964, the Republican presidential candidate, Arizona senator Barry Goldwater, talked instead about the threat of communism, the danger of civil rights, and the bloated size of government. Probably his most controversial position was in support of the privatization of Social Security. The so-called culture wars had no substantive role in the 1964 campaign. Indeed, in his later years Goldwater spoke out against the growing influence of the religious right over the GOP. His remarks made him something of a hero to Republicans and Democrats alike distressed by this change in American politics.

On August 4, 1964, in the early stages of the presidential contest between Johnson and Goldwater, and as "A Hard Day's Night" reached number one on the charts, an American destroyer exchanged fire with North Vietnamese PT-boats in the Gulf of Tonkin. As a result, the U.S.

bombed North Vietnamese PT-boat bases. On August 6, the U.S. Senate voted 98-2 in favor of the Tonkin Gulf Resolution.

The Resolution gave the president the power to "take all necessary measures to repel any armed attack against the forces of the United States and to prevent further aggression." Since it provided a pretext for increasing the level of American commitment to Southeast Asia, historians have cited the Tonkin Resolution as the closest thing to a declaration of war in what turned out to be an undeclared war.

From August 1964 through April 1975, when the last Americans desperately departed Saigon just ahead of the victorious North Vietnamese and Vietcong, the war in Vietnam exerted tremendous influence on American politics and popular culture. It was possible to escape the draft, but there was no escaping Vietnam. No issue since has consumed the American public over such a long period of time. As we enter the twenty-first century, the State Department and the Pentagon are still dealing with the effects of the Vietnam Syndrome, which sees every foreign entanglement in terms of the trauma of Vietnam. As a result of having lost in Vietnam, the United States presumably didn't want to fight another war unless it could be finished quickly, preferably without the use of ground forces. It has been noted that the various conflicts and wars involving U.S. forces in the 1980s, 1990s, and early twenty-first century were launched in part to expunge the humiliation of Vietnam.

While the Johnson administration debated its next moves in Vietnam, the Beatles were touring America, playing to thousands of screaming girls, and churning out quality song after quality song to meet rising audience demand. At that moment, rock and roll and politics could not have seemed further removed from one another. Then again, no one in 1964 expected rock and roll to tackle the vexing issues of the time. We had folk music for that.

⌒⌒

Like any healthy industry, rock and roll has always thrived on competition, real or imagined. Over the years these duels included punk

v. heavy metal, rock v. disco, soul music v. funk, and the most famous of them all, the Beatles v. the Rolling Stones. It rarely escalated to fists and knives, except on occasion when punk and heavy metal fans met in the alley behind some club, or in the parking lot of some convenience store in Orange County, California. Since punkers and head-bangers inhabited the same part of town, these battles were as much over territory as over music. Punk rockers and heavy metal fans were united in hatred of disco, but they rarely got the chance to duke it out with that crowd. Disco was played in sleek uptown establishments; punk and heavy metal was performed in neighborhoods and clubs that were not quite so fabulous. The war of words was conducted from a safe distance. Still, in most cases arguments about genres and sub-genres of rock music are settled, if at all, in someone's living room. I try to convince you and you try to convince me by playing particular songs.

The longest-lasting and most significant dispute took place between 1958 and 1964, and it involved rock and roll and folk. The conflict was not limited to differing styles of music. It had other elements as well: The educated elite (folk) v. the public high school masses (rock and roll); acoustic guitar (folk) v. electric guitar (rock and roll); maturity (folk) v. immaturity (rock and roll); social responsibility (folk) v. teen romance and juvenile sexuality (rock and roll); feelings (folk) v. raw emotion (rock and roll); and femininity (folk) v. masculinity (rock and roll). Rock and roll v. folk was hilariously depicted in the 1978 film *Animal House*, set in 1962, when John Belushi's character, a lover of loud music and beer, smashed Stephen Bishop's acoustic guitar while Bishop was singing a soft song to a couple of entranced coeds.

If sales are the determining factor, rock and roll has to be declared the winner, although folk partisans would be willing to finish second in that category; *their* music was never intended to be gobbled up by the masses. Still, there was a brief period when folk actually topped the *Billboard* pop charts. Not coincidentally, this occurred during rock and roll's first major slump, when Elvis, Little Richard, and Jerry Lee Lewis were all out of commission. In 1958, the Kingston

Trio had a number one hit with "Tom Dooley," the song that many music writers and scholars credit for sparking the modern folk revival in the United States.

In the end, folk music produced only a few hits, although the biggest of these remain popular with fledgling acoustic guitar players some four decades after their release. In 1961, the Highwaymen had a number one song with "Michael," and one year later, the Kingston Trio returned to the Top 20 with "Where Have All the Flowers Gone?" which has been a staple of beginning guitar classes ever since. In October 1962, the month of the Cuban Missile Crisis, Peter, Paul, & Mary reached number ten with "If I Had a Hammer." Trini Lopez's semi-rocking version of the same song made it all the way to number three on the charts the following summer.

Both versions of "If I Had a Hammer," "Where Have All the Flowers Gone?" "Michael," and "Tom Dooley" have been added to the playlists of rock and roll oldies stations through the years, proof of their crossover appeal. It may simply be nostalgia, but folk music doesn't sound out of place programmed in conjunction with the hits of Little Richard or Chuck Berry.

For decades, folk music had been inconceivable without politics. "Folk music was a living bridge between the protest culture of the New Left and the genuinely populist elements of the Old Left of the 1930s and after."[8]

The entire first disc of Rhino Records' three-CD anthology of the songs of the folksinger Phil Ochs features song titles that can truly be called the soundtrack of an era. These include "The Power and the Glory," "Love Me, I'm a Liberal," "In the Heat of the Summer," "Here's to the State of Mississippi," and "We Seek No Wider War," a riff on LBJ's speech after the Tonkin incident. Ochs started by singing about the Civil Rights Movement and then turned his attention to Vietnam, as did Students for a Democratic Society and other activist groups in the 1960s.

Folk musicians from the late 1950s and early 1960s did not take "I" as their prime subject, but "us," young and old, student and worker, black and white, etc. Pete Seeger wrote a song called "We Shall Overcome," rather than "I Shall Overcome." By contrast, "I" meant everything in early rock and roll, which focused almost exclusively on the frustrations and desires of teenagers. It's the rare teenager who cares about anybody's life but his or her own. To be sixteen is to be self-absorbed. Rock would need to grow up before it could start to ponder the fate of "us." Folk helped with that maturation process.

Not all folk songs were as explicit as "Love Me, I'm a Liberal"—a very funny exposé of the hypocrisy of that particular group, still relevant today. Neither "If I Had a Hammer" nor "Where Have All the Flowers Gone?" is so obvious in its politics that the listener could exclaim: "Aha! I know what they are talking about." These songs deliberately stay away from specific cases, and instead deal in concepts. "Where Have All the Flowers Gone?" opposes all war, rather than a specific war; at that point in time it would have been too early to make the connection with Vietnam, still a mere "trouble spot." "Where Have All the Flowers Gone?" does not recite the names of battlefields or figures from history. Yet this in the end is the source of its emotional power; the listener can fill in the blanks with the Civil War, World War I, World War II, or the Korean War, among others.

"If I Had a Hammer" offers a vision of utopia wherein the singer expresses a desire to transform the world, using a blunt instrument (metaphorically speaking) to impose love, justice, and freedom on an imperfect and often cruel society. Both versions of the song were released during the heyday of the Freedom Riders, and even today they invoke images of students from northern colleges and universities traveling to the Deep South on behalf of what was then called "the Negro Cause." But here again, the lyrics of "If I Had a Hammer" did not make reference to Alabama, Mississippi, "Bull" Connor, the Klan, Martin Luther King, the Southern Christian Leadership Conference, or any other person, place, or thing from the front lines of the struggle.

Bob Dylan's early songs were more politically specific. "Oxford Town" was a condemnation of anti-black riots at the University of Mississippi in Oxford, and "Talking John Birch Society Blues," ridiculed the paranoid anti-communism of that particular representative of the American Right. In the early 1960s, however, Dylan had not achieved the commercial success of Peter, Paul, & Mary or other folk acts. (Indeed, he became better known only when P, P, & M recorded two of his songs, "Don't Think Twice, It's All Right" and "Blowin' in the Wind" in 1963. Neither of these songs, however, were in the explicit style of "Oxford Town" or "Talkin' John Birch Society Blues.") By the time Dylan surpassed P, P, & M in popularity and influence in the mid-1960s, he had cut back on writing songs about politics and social justice and instead turned his creative powers to love and relationships. He successfully re-entered the political arena with "Hurricane" from 1976, about the murder conviction of the boxer Reuben "Hurricane" Carter, which was much later made into a movie starring Denzel Washington.

The popularity and influence of folk had waned by the mid-1960s, but Peter Yarrow from Peter, Paul, & Mary never stopped being an activist. He has offered his talent and donated his time to issues ranging from world hunger and homelessness in America to education, equal rights, and the prevention of nuclear war. In 1969, Yarrow served as one of the organizers of the famous 1969 anti-war march in Washington, which attracted some 500,000 participants. Rock stars have followed Yarrow's lead. Along with John Lennon, Bono, and Bruce Springsteen, Yarrow has for thirty years been among the most politically active musicians in the world.

One of his colleagues in the folk movement, the estimable Pete Seeger, composer of "Where Have All the Flowers Gone?" among many, was a member of the Community Party until 1951. In 1955, Seeger was indicted for contempt as a consequence of his refusal to testify before the House Un-American Activities Committee in Washington.

Imagine for a moment if Johnny Rotten, Marilyn Manson, or other so-called threats to the American Way of Life from the world of rock and roll had joined the Communist Party—they would never work in this country again. Civil libertarians—some of them self-proclaimed— that inhabit the executive suites of record companies have no problem defending sex or violence on First Amendment grounds, because it creates controversy, and therefore generates sales. The execs can simultaneously meet their business obligations and advance their political agenda. Yet if one of the musicians signed to their label was a member of the Communist Party, a communist sympathizer, or merely a self-avowed socialist, it's a good bet he or she would be cut loose. Even record industry moguls that fancy themselves tolerant and open-minded will in the end choose profits over principles. Still, whatever one thinks of the Communist Party, Seeger was a true rebel, as opposed to the latter-day showoffs that pull down their pants in public or vomit on those lucky fans seated in the front two rows.

On rare occasions in the early 1960s when rock and roll or rhythm and blues performers strove for social relevance, the result could sound like a folk song. Folk provided the prototype for weaving messages into a two or three-minute single. Take "Uptown" by the Crystals, which reached number thirteen on the charts in May 1962. A girl group produced by Phil Spector, the Crystals recorded "He's a Rebel," "Da Doo Ron Ron," and "Then He Kissed Me," three memorable rock and roll songs released during the Kennedy years. These cuts featured Spector's trademark ingredients—booming drums, heavy sax, loud guitar, and joyous vocals. By contrast, "Uptown," written by the Brill Building team of Barry Mann and Cynthia Weil, sounds restrained and serious, an appropriate mood for a song about a man that works at a dead-end job, and under difficult circumstances. For all his labors he can only afford a place on the poorer side of town for he and his family.

> He gets up each morning and he goes downtown
> Where everyone's his boss and he's lost in an angry land
> He's a little man
> But then he comes uptown each evening to my tenement
> Uptown where folks don't have to pay much rent
> And when he's there with me he can see that he's everything
> He's tall, he don't crawl, he's a king

"Uptown" is social criticism, but only to a point. After all, the hero is celebrated for keeping his dignity; he is no union organizer or workplace agitator. What keeps him sane is the love of the woman waiting "uptown" who makes sure to treat him well when he comes home. Slightly daring for its time, "Uptown" would never have been taken seriously in the "We Want the World and We Want It Now" climate of the latter part of the decade.

Despite employing elements of folk, there was little doubt that "Uptown" was geared toward the rock and roll and rhythm and blues audience. Folk in those days meant acoustic guitars and gentle harmonies. Rock and roll wanted little to do with the folk style, and vice versa. There was no compelling commercial or artistic reason to share ideas or work together. Mutual respect among rock and roll and folk musicians did not mean that they would start jamming in the studio. Besides, why risk incurring the wrath of fans for the sake of experimentation? The folkies wanted nothing to do with rock and roll and its adolescent obsessions, and the rock and roll crowd thought folk music was for pretentious old fogies.

But then the Beatles came to the United States. Bob Dylan heard "I Want to Hold Your Hand" and paid it the ultimate compliment: "Their chords were outrageous, just outrageous, and their harmonies made it all valid." When Dylan met the Beatles in New York City, August 1964, he turned them on to pot, perhaps as his way of saying thank you for saving rock and roll. In pop music history, the summit with Dylan and the Beatles was like the first meeting between Nixon and Mao, or Reagan and Gorbachev; i.e., an end to superpower estrangement, and the building of a new relationship.

Within a year, Dylan went electric at Newport and the Beatles started preparing for *Rubber Soul*, an album filled with introspective lyrics, adult situations, and the sound of acoustic guitar. A mere two years after its release, "I Want to Hold Your Hand" was a fading memory. Only the Beatles and Dylan, leaders in their respective categories, could have pulled this off. What they did mattered across the industry. The rock and roll audience was more agreeable to the change than the folk crowd:

"When Dylan and his makeshift rock band shambled onto the stage at Newport (Rhode Island) on the night of July 25, 1965, they launched into 'Maggie's Farm,' one of the electric blues pieces that Dylan had recorded for *Bringing It All Back Home*.

"Jeers floated from the crowd: 'Play folk music!' 'Sellout!' . . . After singing two more songs, Dylan abruptly left the stage, as did his band. The jeering intensified."[9] In 1965, John Lennon wrote the song "You've Got to Hide Your Love Away" for the *Help!* soundtrack, and "Norwegian Wood" on the *Rubber Soul* album. Both feature acoustic guitar, and have a bittersweet quality to the lyrics that is reminiscent of songs Dylan was writing at the time. Dylan was a strong influence during the Beatles' middle period, *Help!* to *Yesterday and Today*. The Beatles "dropped" him from *Revolver* through *Magical Mystery Tour*, and then returned to an acoustic, folk-rock sound for a number of songs (written mainly by John) that appeared on the *White Album* in 1968.

Once the Beatles and Dylan had exchanged pleasantries, brokered a truce, and shared ideas, it was amazing how quickly the seemingly insurmountable barriers between rock and roll and folk music came crashing down. While many fans were still stuck in the old way of thinking—folk v. rock—Dylan and the Beatles had met each other half way. Within the space of a year, folk-rock came into existence, still the most significant of all the 1960s subcategories, such as raga-rock, acid rock, classical rock, and country rock.

This musical merger brought rock and roll and folk music into the modern era. Dylan's own "experiments" provided folk performers the cover to add drums, electric guitars, and organ to their sound and not consider themselves—or be considered by others—as sell-outs to the cause. Soon even critics were acknowledging that folk music and the Big Beat were not incompatible. On the other hand, the aforementioned *Rubber Soul* album, released in December 1965, replaced the unbridled joy of *Meet the Beatles* with a sound more biting, gritty, quiet, and mature. The song titles on *Rubber Soul* are revealing: "Run for Your Life," "You Won't See Me," "I'm Looking through You." For the first time in their career, the Beatles had broken free from their 1950s influences. (They would return to them later.) On *Rubber Soul* the group sang about awkward affairs, sexual jealousy, and declining passion. Could social commentary and politics be far behind?

Where would rock and roll be without the addition of folk? Some of the best groups and solo performers of the mid-1960s fit neatly into the category of folk-rock, including the Byrds, the Turtles, the Lovin' Spoonful, the Association, the Beau Brummels, and Donovan. Folk-rock is one of the few pop music forms from that golden decade that has never gone out of style. A contemporary audience can relate better to the Byrds' jangling guitars and exquisite harmonies than it can to *Sgt. Pepper's Lonely Hearts Club Band*, which will never be able to shake off the memories of the summer of 1967. Tom Petty and the Heartbreakers from the 1970s until today, and the Gin Blossoms in the 1990s are just two of the many examples of rock groups that success-fully emulated and updated the sound of the Byrds. Other than the Bea-tles, and maybe the Rolling Stones, the Byrds sit atop the biggest fam-ily tree in rock and roll history.

Their first hit single, a cover of Bob Dylan's "Mr. Tambourine Man" in 1965, replaced the acoustic simplicity of the original with a multi-layered, electric version, featuring the then-unfamiliar jingle/jangle guitar riff and a booming bass line. From Dylan, the Byrds moved on to another folkie, Pete Seeger, and recorded their unique take on "Turn! Turn! Turn! (To Everything There Is a Season)," a song that Seeger had adapted to words from the Book of Ecclesiastes. "Turn! Turn! Turn!" stayed in the number one spot for three weeks in the fall of 1965, box office confirmation that folk-rock was the new big thing. The song reaches an emotional conclusion with the singer's plea for peace on earth. By that point, the United States had committed hun-dreds of thousands of troops to the defense of South Vietnam, making "Turn! Turn! Turn!" as relevant as the evening news, even though it had been written long before Da Nang.

Around the same time as "Turn! Turn! Turn!" the Byrds recorded an album track called "He Was a Friend of Mine," the first and one of the only rock and roll songs to make overt reference to the assassination of President Kennedy. "He Was a Friend of Mine" is an example of rock and roll contributing to the myth of JFK. Andrew Loog Oldham's reference to the "Soldier of Peace" is another, along with the 1968 hit by Dion "Abraham, Martin, and John," which credits the president with "freeing a lot of people," a claim that has never even been made by Arthur Schlesinger Jr. The torch *had* been passed to a new generation of pop music performers, for whom politics and contemporary history were legitimate subjects.

A paradox of the 1960s is that a decade filled with so many awful events—riots, assassinations, sensational crimes, urban decay and, above all, the war in Vietnam—also gave us the Beatles, the Rolling Stones, Bob Dylan, James Brown, Motown, Cream, and so much more. Of course, those who despise rock and roll might very well discern a causal relationship between an epidemic of violence and the popularity of the Rolling Stones, or an increase in the use of dangerous drugs and the astronomical sales of *Sgt. Pepper's Lonely Hearts Club Band*. But, as they used to say in the 1950s and 1960s, this is a free country.

Still, it would be as difficult to prove the proposition that acts of violence have an effect on rock and roll as it has been to prove the exact opposite. However, it can be said with reasonable certainty that the popularity of folk-rock has some connection to the escalation of the war in Vietnam. In 1965, the year folk-rock was formally identified as a separate category, the United States sent 200,000 additional soldiers to Vietnam, and launched an intensified bombing campaign in the north and the south. From this point until the end of the decade, folk-rock performers wrote and recorded the more explicit songs about the war.

Donovan, originally from Scotland, and Country Joe and the Fish, from Berkeley, each put out songs that mentioned Vietnam by name, a not-too-common occurrence in the 1960s, despite the decade's reputation for risk-taking in the popular arts. Radio programmers, and for

that matter record labels, were not especially comfortable about performers writing songs in opposition to the war, no matter how unpopular U.S. policies seemed to be with the American public. They knew
that all it would take was for one powerful politician or pro-American
lobbying group to raise questions of loyalty and patriotism for advertisers to move their business elsewhere. Criticizing a war while that
war is in progress could have been considered by Middle America to
be a much more serious offense—maybe even treasonous—than writing songs that extol the virtues of casual sex or recreational drugs.

At the same time, however, teenagers and college students, the two
age groups that purchased the vast majority of rock and roll singles and
albums in the U.S, could consider a song that praised the American effort a sell-out. The challenge for those performers who simply couldn't
or wouldn't remain silent was to criticize the war in Vietnam while not
openly condemning the American side—unless you happened to be
Country Joe McDonald, or a member of his band the Fish.

A group that still invokes fond memories in ex-hippies, Country Joe
and the Fish group started performing a funny, sarcastic, and kind of
spooky song in the mid-1960s called "I-Feel-Like-I'm-Fixin'-to-Die
Rag," which combined the clarity and precision of folk lyrics with the
irreverence and mischief of rock and roll. The song demanded to be
taken seriously even as it made the listener laugh out loud.

Somehow "I-Feel-Like-I'm-Fixin'-to-Die Rag" escaped the notice
of Washington. Usually J. Edgar Hoover and his wide network in and
outside the FBI were pretty effective about tagging actual or potential
"threats" to the safety and security of the United States of America, including those that could be found on albums or singles. Just four years
earlier, "Louie, Louie" had been analyzed in the FBI listening lab for
evidence of obscene content. Then again, by the late 1960s the FBI
was obsessed with gathering information on the Black Panthers and
Students for a Democratic Society, both of which were on the front-
lines of the "revolution." Country Joe and the Fish did not pose a similar threat to the American way of life.

"Rag" survived intact, although the song never even made it onto
the Hot 100. This is one song where you had to be there. Country Joe's

performance of "Rag" at Woodstock was one of the highlights of the entire festival.

Donovan's contribution, "To Susan on the West Coast Waiting" did make the charts (number thirty-five in 1969), but it's not nearly so well known today as the County Joe and the Fish song. To be sure, "I Feel-Like-I'm-Fixin'-to-Die Rag" is more in line with the way the left has chosen to recall the movements of the 1960s — fearless, boisterous, and full of conviction. The song appears in numerous documentaries about anti-war protests, and politics and rock and roll.

On the other hand, "To Susan on the West Coast Waiting" is a quiet, acoustic number that would probably not have excited the throngs at Woodstock. This recording was something of a departure for mid-period Donovan, who released a series of singles from 1966 through 1969 more in the style of rock than folk, which included deliberately cryptic lyrics. To this day, I am still not certain what point is being made in "Goo Goo Barabajagal" or "Hurdy Gurdy Man."

The essence of "To Susan on the West Coast Waiting" can be grasped in a single listen. Donovan sings in a clear voice, and the instrumental accompaniment is kept at a low volume. The song's anti-war sentiment is conveyed through a series of letters from, "Susan on the West Coast Waiting to Andy in Vietnam Fighting," and vice versa. It's somewhat unusual that Donovan would use the traditional motif of letters to and from the front to tell a story centered on a war brought to us in living color everyday. But it gives the song an almost poignant quality, which is more than could be expected from most AM singles at that time.

～～

"Eve of Destruction" was released toward the end of the Civil Rights Movement but the beginning of the anti-war protests. It casts one eye on the South, and the other on South Vietnam, which is never mentioned. The song was written by P .F. Sloan and Steve Barri at the suggestion of legendary L.A. producer Lou Adler, who heard Bob Dylan's "Like a Rolling Stone" and wanted to release a record in the same vein as quickly as possible. In one of those miracles of mid-60s rock, "Eve of Destruction" was a blatant imitation that succeeded on its own terms. It also earned a place in rock history as one of the early examples of a song that included lines about actual events or people. "Eve of Destruction" made reference to Red China three years before John Lennon included Chairman Mao in the lyrics to "Revolution." In 1968 as well Mick Jagger offered a quick history of Western civilization—complete with names and places—in "Sympathy for the Devil." Simon and Garfunkel, the Temptations, and Crosby, Stills, Nash, & Young are among the many other performers who tried this technique through the years, with varying degrees of success.

"Eve of Destruction" was not typical fare on AM radio in the summer of 1965; and some stations actually banned the song due to its political content and dark message. The song's politics bend to the left, although not so far that it could be considered anti-American, or anything close. Nevertheless, that didn't stop a long-forgotten group called the Spokesmen from recording a right-wing response to "Eve of Destruction" entitled "Dawn of Correction," which didn't even crack the Top 100. Apparently pessimism was un-American in 1965.

But if not for Adler's usual sterling production, along with a catchy melody—a must for AM—"Eve of Destruction" would not have done much better than "Dawn of Correction." For commercial purposes, beat, melody, and vocals are always more important than words. And if you owned a major record label and was forced to choose between the two, music would have to trump lyrics every time.

⌒

It was suggested earlier that in the history of pop music, 1956 is as significant as was 1914 in European history. To carry this analogy to a later date, in the history of rock and roll and politics, 1965 is the equivalent of 1945—i.e., the dawn of the modern era. There are three reasons why this particular year was so crucial to the evolution of rock and roll and politics.

The first of these is the birth of folk-rock, which gave rock and roll performers the freedom to sing about something other than teen love, teen lust, and the joys of the American automobile. The second is the escalation of the war in Vietnam and its attendant impact on the anti-war movement, which in turn prompted rock groups to start paying attention. And the third is the release of "Satisfaction," the number one song for the entire year, plus the subsequent rise to prominence of the Rolling Stones.

The Rolling Stones were not the first superstars in rock and roll to assume the role of "bad boys"; Elvis Presley and Jerry Lee Lewis did the same in the 1950s. But the Stones were the first that neglected to say "please" and "thank you," "yes ma'am" and "yes sir," and that did not appear to have made any room in their lives for Jesus Christ.

The Stones desired nothing from the middle class, except of course its money, which they happily accepted as they continued to heap abuse on its morality and traditions. Along with their manager, Andrew Loog Oldham, the Stones brilliantly exploited the masochism, self-loathing, and sense of boredom prevalent among young bourgeois in England and America. After all, the Stones had once been in a similar predicament, until they heard Chuck Berry, Muddy Waters, Slim Harpo, Howlin' Wolf, and Bo Diddley, which solved the problem of what to do with the rest of their lives.

A number of other British bands in the early 1960s began their careers covering rhythm and blues and blues songs. These included the Animals, the Who, the Pretty Things, and, for that matter, the Beatles. But the Stones were not only better than the others—their version of "Around and Around" is the single best cover from the mid-1960s of a Chuck Berry song—they also were the first rock and roll group to embrace scorn and contempt as marketing tools. This is not meant to doubt their sincerity, which would be difficult if not impossible to assess, but only to suggest that there existed an audience ready and willing to follow a band that trashed polite society. And while the Stones were consistently and indeed carefully apolitical, which later ticked off some people in the anti-war movement, their disdain for middle-class mores was actually a political act, even if it also helped them sell millions of records.

To a contemporary observer, accustomed to seeing Mick Jagger in the role of fashion plate, it must seem strange that at the beginning of their careers the Stones were widely reviled by middle-aged and old people for their lack of hygiene. The members of this particular rock and roll band apparently did not wash their hands before every meal. In his 1984 biography, *The Stones*, the English rock writer Philip Norman recounted how tabloid newspapers around the world commonly referred to the band as "dirty," "shaggy," "crude," or, my personal favorite, which appeared in the headline of a British publication, "Longhaired Monsters." While one must make allowances for the excesses of tabloids, these descriptions were not all that wide off the mark. And by using these colorful descriptions, the tabloids were presuming to speak for hard-working, socially conservative readers outraged by the antics of these spoiled brats. Yes, the Stones could be exploited to sell papers.

But even unwashed long hair, dirty clothes, and boorish behavior can get old after awhile. In early 1965, the Stones' were already faced with the inevitable question of what to do for an encore. The last thing the band needed to hear was "just ignore them and they'll go away." What could they think of next to piss off parents?

How about actually pissing? During the month of March 1965, they pulled a stunt that it's safe to say would never have occurred to Elvis Presley or his crafty manager. During a stop at a gas station in England, three members of the Stones asked to use the restroom. The proprietor said the public lavatory was out of order, and he prohibited them from using the one reserved for employees. In standing his ground, this man became an unwitting player in one of the better-known sideshows in rock and roll history.

The underlying assumption here is that had the Stones been a group of well-dressed businessmen they would not have been denied use of that other restroom. But "long-haired monsters" could not expect, and did not deserve, special consideration. Still, as any college kid at a fraternity party can attest, when you gotta go, you gotta go. The three

Stones with full bladders—Mick Jagger, Brian Jones, and Bill Wyman—simply relieved themselves in a line against a wall at the garage. Jagger, who is as media-savvy as any politician, was alleged to have pushed the proprietor to the side, telling him "We piss anywhere, man." In short order, it became the quote heard around the world.

In the days before pot busts and public admission of LSD use, urinating in public constituted a scandal in rock and roll, even though the consequences were minor. Jagger, Jones, and Wyman appeared in court, where they paid a small fine as penalty for what was officially deemed "insulting behavior." Of course, the attendant publicity more then compensated for the financial "loss" incurred in court. Pissing on a wall was not about to bring down a band that could write hit singles with such apparent ease.

I don't recall if incidents of this kind made headlines before 1965, but I know crude and vulgar public behavior has been commonplace since that time. Maybe this is the chief difference between the 1950s and the decades that came later. Several months after the Stones' antics, the British drama critic Kenneth Tynan—sixteen years older than Mick Jagger—used the word "fuck" on a late-night program called "BBC-3," the first time that word had ever been heard on television. According to an aside in the 1994 collection of Tynan's letters, as a result of the renowned critic having uttered "fuck" on live television, "for a few days the scandal eclipsed all other news."[10]

By the end of the decade, "fuck" was everywhere. Country Joe and the Fish led 300,000 fans at Woodstock in an F-U-C-K cheer that has become almost as famous as Jimi Hendrix's version of the National Anthem on the final day of the festival. Pictures of demonstrators flipping off cops ran in so-called respectable magazines during the late 1960s and early in 1970. For a number of years, boys and girls have said that word in the presence of teachers and parents. And with the growth of cable television, "fuck" can now be heard in American living rooms every night of the week.

Beginning in the 1980s, Howard Stern's radio program, which garnered big ratings across the United States, traded heavily on crude bathroom humor and the host posing embarrassing questions to the famous, ordinary, and desperate people booked as guests. A particular favorite of his was to inquire whether a female star or wannabe had ever experienced "anal." Out of necessity, Stern avoided naughty words, but with the excess of raunchy subject matter, the loss of a "fuck" or a "shit" here and there was hardly noticed.

A distinction should be made between Tynan, who offended the establishment in part for the sheer pleasure of doing so and the Stones and Howard Stern, who saw this as a means to an end. Polite society—or the myth of polite society—has buckled under the strain of all these assaults. Some conservatives blame over thirty-five years of public crudity and nudity on the counterculture, which if true, would make the Stones one of its founders.

But their music is more interesting, such as the groundbreaking "Satisfaction," or, as it's officially known, "(I Can't Get No) Satisfaction." Johnny Rotten, lead singer of the 1970s punk band the Sex Pistols, once said the Stones should have retired after "Satisfaction." Rotten was half-right; the Stones released many excellent singles and a few great albums in the years after "Satisfaction," but none that were as important. "Satisfaction" represented nothing less than a new kind of rock and roll song.

In July 1958, the Coasters had a number one hit with "Yakety Yak," which in a humorous way depicted the modern teenagers' worst nightmare—domineering and nagging parents. Here mom and dad are in complete control, and all the kid can do is obey orders, unless he wishes to be severely punished. This is not teen rebellion, but teen compliance, albeit with great reluctance. Rock and roll can provide respite from an "oppressive" home life, but only for a short while.

"Satisfaction" considers the same situation but from a different angle. This time consumer culture, lack of sex, and assorted hassles are the problems, not parents. The song is a litany of complaints, with the singer filling in the details. This guy is bored, not to mention frustrated. It would take several pages to list all the rock and roll songs since "Satisfaction" that have exploited this combination of moods. Indeed, the entire punk movement of the late 1970s was to a large extent a treatise on boredom and rage, each of them feeding off the other. And at least since the 1950s, politicians and law enforcement have regarded frustrated teens with seemingly nothing to do and nowhere to go as a potential public menace. The still unresolved question is whether the addition of rock and roll defuses that anger, thereby providing a social service, or reinforces it, and in so doing makes a bad situation even worse.

"(I Can't Get No) Satisfaction" was number one in America for four weeks in the summer of 1965. Several months later, the Rolling Stones recorded "I'm Free"—the "B" side of the number one hit "Get Off My Cloud"—which conveyed the opposite message. In the latter song, nothing stands in the way of the singer achieving much sought after satisfaction because he is, in fact, free, and content as well. Apparently the Stones had trouble making up their minds back then.

⌐⌐

By the summer of 1965, rock and roll was seeking to capture a share of the adult market, namely men and women between the ages of twenty-one and thirty-five. This was due in part to demographics; the audience that first went crazy for Elvis Presley was now reaching their mid-twenties. Some of them had outgrown the early stuff, but most remained loyal to rock and roll. For this group of fans, going steady was no longer the biggest event in their lives. How to reach and keep this aging audience was the next challenge for rock and roll, whether the practitioners wanted to admit it or not.

Fortunately for the future of rock and roll, the performers were aging as well. John Lennon turned twenty-five in the fall of 1965, which was two years older then Elvis when he "retired" and went into the U.S. Army. A month before Lennon's birthday, the Beatles' released the single of "Help!" which Lennon wrote. "Help!" was above all about growing older, specifically the doubts and insecurities that come with the territory. The song was Lennon's most personal to date, and he would write many more in this vein right up to his death in 1980.

Millions of "aging" rock and roll fans recognized their own predicament in "Help!"

Several months layer, the Beatles released "Nowhere Man" (number three in 1966), also a Lennon composition. This song amounted to a half-hearted indictment of a do-nothing suburban dweller. There is a kind of Pied Piper quality to the lyrics, with the narrator reminding the "nowhere man" that he has the power to change his life. It's the kind of advice that usually comes from counselors or therapists, not rock and roll songs. At the same time, the typical Beatles' fan can be thankful that he or she does not live under such dismal conditions. It's nice to feel superior to one's parents and their middle-class friends.

A similar theme was pursued in "A Well-Respected Man" by the Kinks, which went as high as number thirteen on the charts in 1966. The title was meant to be ironic. The song exposes the hypocrisy and secret passions of a certain kind of Englishman who on the surface appears utterly in command of his life. This poor chap was regularly ridiculed in films, plays, and novels, but until that point, he had avoided similar treatment at the hands of rock and roll. "A Well-Respected Man" was just the kind of smart song to appeal to smug college students and trendy intellectuals.

Both "Nowhere Man" and "Well-Respected Man" applied the traditional arrogance of rock and roll to new situations. In the old days, rock and roll celebrated sexual conquests, fast cars, dancing, and the glory of the music itself. These songs by the Beatles, Kinks, and others suggested that a new audience, turned on to a new kind of rock and roll, was more open-minded, happy, and free than either the idle rich or the entrepreneurial class. Best of all, they weren't slaves to their careers. Some of them didn't have careers, or jobs for that matter, which left them with a lot of time to listen to records put out by the Beatles and the Stones.

Another song in this vein is "My Generation" by the Who, which only made it to number seventy-four in 1966, proving yet again that while the charts don't lie, neither do they tell the whole truth. Describing the song in the 1976 edition of *The Rolling Stone Illustrated History of Rock and*

Roll, veteran rock critic Dave Marsh wrote: "The pandemonium continued for three minutes, unrelieved, until it suddenly grew wilder, and the song finished in a burst of feedback, shouts, chants and clanging instruments. No one had ever heard anything like it, and no one ever would again."[11] Marsh goes on in the same article to call "My Generation" a "three-minute revolution." And yet unlike "Satisfaction," whose impact was immediate, few people recognized the importance of "My Generation" at the time because few people bothered to purchase the single. In later years, however, "My Generation" became rock's equivalent of the sparsely attended no-hitter that millions of people claim to have witnessed. What baby boomer would dare admit today that he didn't instantly acknowledge the brilliance of "My Generation," not to mention the Who?

"My Generation" is aimed at "their" generation, which as the song makes very clear, are people older than the Who and its audience. The song is not a plea for understanding or the beginning of a dialogue, but a declaration of independence. Pete Townshend, the band's chief songwriter, is telling outsiders "you are either with us or against us." The decision is up to you; we will go on as we please. And there was nothing that the parents, the government, or Dick Clark could do to reverse the trend. The remainder of the 1960s proved Townshend to be perceptive on this count.

It's somehow appropriate that bands based in and around Los Angeles recorded two of the early rock and roll songs based on actual events. L.A. played a big role in the 1960s; the Watts Riots of 1965, the assassination of Robert Kennedy, and the Manson Family murders all occurred in the City of Angels. The first of these resulted in a brilliant song by Frank Zappa and the Mothers of Invention, a group known mainly for its extraordinary musical experimentation—within a rock and roll idiom—sarcasm, and wit.

In 1966, the Mothers of Invention included a song called "Trouble

Every Day" on its debut album, entitled *Freak Out!* Zappa, who died in 1993, later emerged as one of the most politically astute of all rock musicians, single-handedly taking on Congress when it attempted to regulate so-called offensive lyrics in the 1980s. As a teenager, Zappa lived and breathed doo-wop and rhythm and blues, spending much of his time during the 1950s in the company of Chicano and black groups.

"Trouble Every Day" makes it clear that Zappa was not simply another white musician hanging out with the black guys. The song addresses two profound themes—media coverage of the Watts riots and the state of race relations in America—which few musicians of any genre have ever had the courage or intelligence to tackle. Zappa's trenchant criticisms of the way the press reported the riots could be applied to various wars, protests, or sensational crimes that have occurred since the dawn of TV.

> And if another women driver gets machine-gunned in her seat
> They'll send some joker with a Brownie
> And you'll see it all complete.

Like other whites, hip or square, Zappa had to rely on television and newspapers to follow events in Watts: A number of Caucasians that had the misfortune of being caught in the riot were pulled from their cars and beaten. The rest stayed far away, and indeed many of them kept guns and ammo close at hand after hearing a barrage of media-fueled rumors that "a black mob" would soon be on the move across Southern California.

Zappa delivered the song in a quasi-blues vocal, backed by a no-holds-barred instrumental assault from the Mothers of Invention. The powerful opening riff and pounding drums heralded the arrival of a new sound—hard rock. Of course, there was no chance that "Trouble Every Day" would be a hit single: the song was too controversial, and, at five minutes and forty-nine seconds, much too long for AM. Still, no rock and roll song has so successfully captured the political drama of the 1960s.

The other song worth special mention, "For What It's Worth" by Buffalo Springfield (number seven in 1967), was written about an L.A.

disturbance that received far less local or national attention then did Watts. In this case, the combatants were white longhairs and cops, and the confrontation occurred along the Sunset Strip in Hollywood, in the neighborhood of the beautiful people. For a number of years, lyrics from "For What It's Worth" were quoted in *Time* and other establishment publications seeking to understand the current generation—a mixed blessing to be sure for Buffalo Springfield.

True to its nonpartisan title, "For What It's Worth" neither preaches nor offers solutions. The song is actually a report from the front, with the singer registering confusion as events unfold before his eyes. As it happened, the song has outlived the event, which almost no one remembers anymore. In time, Stephen Stills and Neil Young, leaders of Buffalo Springfield, would be widely regarded as among the more politically astute performers in rock and roll. "For What It's Worth" is an early example of their predilection.

"Trouble Every Day" and "For What It's Worth" reported on domestic events. Soon the war in Vietnam would preoccupy rock and roll, as it would the rest of the country. "During 1966 alone, according to an official Pentagon tabulation, the United States staged seven thousand air raids against roads, five thousand against vehicles, and more than a thousand against railway lines and yards in North Vietnam, hitting many of the targets several times."[12] By late 1966, the U.S. had nearly 300,000 troops based in Vietnam as well. "With the war there was no sense of not being involved (in the anti-war movement)," said Wayne Kramer of the MC5, which is one of the most politically committed groups in the history of rock and roll. "You had to be involved, especially if you were a young male of 'cannon fodder' age."

"There have been a few times when rock and roll was involved with issues," said music executive and political activist Danny Goldberg. "The most notable of these was during the Vietnam War."

7

LET'S LIVE FOR TODAY

Robert Hodierne dropped out of college in 1966, the end of his junior year, and purchased a one-way ticket to Saigon. Hodierne had been intrigued by an advertisement in a photography magazine directed at those who were "young and hungry and wanted to be rich and famous." Although the notice read like a Hollywood casting call, the company that placed it was actually looking for aspiring reporters and photographers to cover the war in Vietnam. It worked for Hodierne. He wrote a detailed letter in response, sent it to the given address, and then waited in vain for his assignment.

Disappointed yet undeterred, he decided to try a different approach. If the company wouldn't get back to him, well then he would go to them.

Hodierne bought that one-way ticket to Saigon, and when he arrived there he headed straight for the office of the photo editor for United Press International. He placed his original letter on the table, and demanded an explanation for UPI's failure to respond. The photo editor claimed ignorance, but he liked Hodierne's attitude, and offered him a job on the spot. It was the beginning of a long career in journalism for Hodierne, including many years as national editor and deputy bureau chief for Newhouse News Service. Today he is senior managing editor of Army Times Publishing Company.

Reflecting thirty years later on his hastily arranged trip to Saigon, Hodierne said he must have been "fuckin' nuts." But it sure seemed like a good idea at the time.

He worked in Vietnam as photographer and reporter for UPI and its chief rival, Associated Press. He recalled that in 1966 the American ground forces primarily consisted of enlisted men, both older and more seasoned than the typical draftee. Hodierne recalled that at the time the American side seemed confident of victory and well prepared. "It was a time of relative innocence over there," he said. "We still thought we were going to win. America was going to go in there and kick some Vietnamese butt, and that was going to be it." The war effort had not yet disintegrated into the chaotic, freaked-out scene depicted vividly in the 1979 film *Apocalypse Now*. "Drugs were not in widespread use among the soldiers," he said. "If there were any drugs being used at all, it was pot."

When they were not out in the field, the troops went in search of diversions, as troops have probably done since the beginning of warfare. They partied in Saigon's clubs and took short trips to safe areas around the country. They also listened to rock and roll at every available opportunity. In those days, the local U.S. Army PXs sold top-of-the-line Japanese stereo equipment at incredibly cheap prices. The soldiers bought as much of it as they could afford, thereby earning the distinction of being among the first groups of American consumers to satisfy a voracious appetite for Japanese-made electronic goods. "You'd go into these tents and there would be these huge speakers, reel-to-reel tape decks, pretty good systems," said Hodierne. A lot better then hearing the Beatles on that old AM radio back in Ohio.

The troops and young officers loved rock and roll because they had grown up loving rock and roll. It was the music of their youth. But stationed in Vietnam, 10,000 miles from home, the typical GI *craved* rock and roll, because like a letter from his parents or a picture of his girlfriend, it reminded him of good times back in the States. "I can remember the time I was out on an aircraft carrier, and they had just gotten in a bunch of new music," said Hodierne. "I was sitting there in the public affairs office on the *U.S.S. Enterprise* with headsets on listening to the Mamas and the Papas. It brought tears to my eyes, it just made me so homesick."

He covered the war for UPI and AP for fourteen months, returning to America in the middle of 1967 to complete his college education. But it was not yet time to settle down. Within a year, Hodierne enlisted in the army. He completed basic training in 1969 and went back to Vietnam, where he now covered the war as a reporter/photographer for *Stars and Stripes*, the authorized but unofficial publication of the Department of Defense.

Hodierne returned to a very different war and a very different army. The vast majority of the American troops in the field in 1969 had been drafted, and many of them were bitter about having to leave their neighborhoods to go fight in Vietnam. Hodierne heard no more cocky predictions about how the U.S. was going to "kick Vietnamese butt," or dreams of how it would be to ride in a victory parade. The Tet Offensive in the spring of 1968 had destroyed any lingering illusions among the troops in Vietnam—and much of the American public for that matter—that this war would be won soon, or even that it would be won at all.

But what the draftees in 1969 had in common with the enlisted men in 1966 was an overwhelming desire, an all-consuming need, to hear rock and roll. When Hodierne received a copy of the Beatles' White Album from friends in the U.S., he filled requests from *500* soldiers who wanted the entire two sides on tape. Hodierne estimated that most of the troops he encountered during his second tour were between eighteen and twenty-three, and they loved the music of Jimi Hendrix and the Doors, as well as the Rolling Stones and the Beatles. The Byrds' number one anti-war hit from 1965 "Turn, Turn, Turn" was one of the most requested songs over there.

But by 1969 rock and roll served a dual purpose in Vietnam, both as a reminder of the States and accompaniment to the use of drugs, which was more widespread among the troops than had been the case three years earlier. This time, acid and heroin were popular as well as pot. "It could be a very surreal experience to be some place fairly far forward, stoned, listening to Jimi Hendrix, and watching flares going off in the horizon and listening to artillery rounds," said Hodierne.

And even if the commanders at the base and in the field thought rock and roll was a pernicious influence on the young troops, they were not about to ban it, either in the barracks or on Armed Forces Radio. "There was no way they could stop it," said Hodierne. "When Armed Forces Radio wanted to program bland music, it pissed the soldiers off. And you didn't want to piss them off, because they were all heavily armed."

⌐⌐

Despite the impact on the troops, in fact not one song on the *Billboard* charts during the late 1960s and early 1970s—the peak period for American casualties and anti-war demonstrations—had the name Vietnam in its title. There were songs recorded about Vietnam in the sense that they conveyed an anti-war message, but not specifically in reference to the war going on at the time. It fell on the listener to make the connection. In May 1969, Tommy James and the Shondells had a number seven hit with "Sweet Cherry Wine," which throws in the stock line about how "we" aren't going to march off to war. The song didn't reference Hue or Da Nang or Saigon. Rock and roll groups walked the line between showing solidarity with the protesters and staying in good with radio programmers. Play it cool, but play it safe. Of the sixteen selections on the Rhino Records' CD *Songs of Protest*, which only includes material released in the 1960s, no songs have the word "Vietnam" in the title. While anti-war demonstrators of the period carried signs supporting Ho Chi Minh or the National Liberation Front, anti-war rock or soul songs steered clear of the specific conflict, instead offering universal themes and letting listeners draw their own conclusions. For example, Freda Payne's "Bring the Boys Home" (number twelve in 1971) could be applied to any lengthy and controversial military engagement—although a contemporary cover version would need to add "and Girls" to the title. And "Ruby Don't Take Your Love to Town" (number six in 1969) by Kenny Rogers & the First Edition makes reference to "that crazy Asian war" without specifying which one.

Of course, it would be disingenuous to pretend that either of these songs, and others of their type, weren't "about" Vietnam. The vast majority of the rock audience could have no other frame of reference; the Korean War ended in 1953. So if that's the case, why not just come right out and say it? Isn't rock and roll, in the opinion of its fans, supposed to be brutally honest and direct?

The best answer is not exactly. Even when talking about sex, the single most common subject of rock and roll songs for fifty years, euphemisms and double-entendres are frequently substituted for the language of the street, or the gutter, depending on your point of view. In all the talk about the "idealism" of rock bands, especially those from the 1960s, it sometimes gets forgotten that rock and roll is above all a career, and a potentially lucrative one at that. The Beatles were willing to wear suits and the Stones were willing to act like spoiled children because it was good for their careers. The same principle is true of Madonna, Marilyn Manson, and Eminem, each of whom has at various times made asses of themselves to sell more records. You can't make money if your music doesn't sell.

Beginning with "Sixty Minute Man" by the Dominoes in 1951, rock and roll and rhythm and blues have come up with creative ways of referring to sexual intercourse, sexual performance, and sex in general. In that sense, rap music, which throws out more four-letter words than a hot-headed football coach berating his team at halftime, goes against the tradition of rock and roll and R&B, which is positively genteel by comparison. Can you imagine the rap group 2 Live Crew using the term "parking lot" to refer to female genitalia, which is what the Rolling Stones did in their 1969 song "Let It Bleed"?

It's not that rock lyricists have been prudish through history, merely cautious— some might say *too* cautious. Radio programmers would never have played—and record labels would never have released—

songs in the 1950s, 1960s, and 1970s that used the language of a typical high school locker room to describe heterosexual relations. And
what went for sex went double for the war in Vietnam, where charges
of disloyalty and anti-Americanism presumably awaited any rock band
that attacked U.S. policy in unambiguous terms. And if that seems like
an exaggeration, remember that in 1969 Richard Nixon became president, Spiro Agnew became vice president, and J. Edgar Hoover was
still director of the FBI. Harassing dissenters—real or imagined—was
a full-time occupation in the Nixon White House. As a matter of fact,
Nixon's predecessor, Lyndon Johnson, wasn't especially fond of the
anti-war movement either.

Indeed, the most popular rock bands of the 1960s even stayed away
from discussing the war in Vietnam in interviews. The Beatles, to take
the best example, spoke openly about their involvement with drugs,
and John Lennon in 1966 famously proclaimed that the group was
"more popular than Jesus Christ" (infuriating Southern Baptists, who
burned Beatles' albums in protest). But for the most part they kept their
opinions about Vietnam to themselves, even as their fans grew more
vocal and demonstrative in opposition to the war.

At a time when seemingly everyone had an opinion about the war,
pro or con, rock and roll spokespeople were rare, which is something
veterans of that era may regret today. In a published interview, Paul
McCartney told Chrissie Hynde of the rock group the Pretenders: "I remember when we first came to America and all the publicists said,
'Don't mention the Vietnam War.' So of course, the first question we
got, we mentioned it."[1] Whatever the group said has apparently been
lost to posterity; in the many collections of interviews with the Beatles, or with individual members of the band, there are almost no references to Vietnam. After John Lennon slipped away from the band and
formed a musical duo with his new wife, Yoko Ono, he wrote and
recorded the first unmistakably anti-war song from a member of the
Beatle family, "Give Peace a Chance" (number fourteen in 1969). Yet
here again, neither the title nor the lyrics specifically refer to Vietnam,
although "Give Peace a Chance" quickly became an anthem for anti-

war demonstrators, in much the same way as did "We Shall Overcome" during the civil rights marches of the 1950s and early 1960s. In fact, "Give Peace a Chance"—the phrase and the song—has been recycled by activists whenever military conflicts have occurred, or threaten to do so.

Ironically, the single biggest-selling song about the war in Vietnam was written to please Hawks and not Doves. "The Ballad of the Green Berets" by Sgt. Barry Sadler, released in March 1966, spent five weeks at number one, and was actually the number one single for the entire year. In truth, "The Ballad of the Green Berets" had about as much to do with rock and roll as did "Doggie in the Window." But "Ballad" seemingly brought older, more conservative record-buyers out of the closet, the people who rejected the Beatles, the Stones, and Dylan, as they had rejected them. The counterculture didn't always win in the 1960s.

The song was also timed perfectly, as are most number one hits. In March 1966, a majority of American people still believed the war could be won, and as a consequence were willing to listen to and embrace simple patriotic appeals. If a record label had released "The Ballad of the Green Berets" in 1968, the year of the Tet offensive, the Eugene McCarthy and Bobby Kennedy anti-war presidential campaigns, and Walter Cronkite's public questioning of U.S. policy in Vietnam, it would have seemed like a sick joke. "Ballad" is another "victim" of the war; the song is almost never heard today on oldies' radio stations, which will gladly play Frankie Avalon or Pat Boone before they play Sgt. Barry Sadler.

In light of the scarcity of rock and roll songs written about Vietnam, it's not easy to understand or assess the impact of the war on the music, and vice versa. Yet Vietnam has been called the "rock and roll war" almost as often as it has been referred to as the first televised war. Just don't take that to mean rock and roll played a part in ending American involvement, or goading demonstrators to action. Rock and roll was very effective background music.

Apocalypse Now and *Platoon*, two of the very best films about the war in Vietnam, rely heavily on rock songs to establish the proper mood. In *Apocalypse Now*, a napalm strike occurs to the accompaniment of the Doors' song "The End," and in the case of *Platoon*, the troops stage an impromptu party that includes a group sing-along to "The Tracks of My Tears" by Smokey Robinson and the Miracles. A third film—not in their league—*Good Morning, Vietnam* is the story of a Saigon-based DJ who played rock and roll and rhythm and blues records for U.S. forces.

As Robert Hodierne indicated, rock and roll served as a source of aid and comfort to the troops based in Southeast Asia. But this had happened before with American popular music; recordings by Benny Goodman and Glenn Miller helped lift the spirits of the soldiers stationed in Europe and Asia during World War II. Miller actually joined the U.S. Army in 1942 and formed an all-star service personnel band. In 1944, his plane disappeared over the English Channel while he was en route to France to entertain Allied troops.

But Hodierne also recalled being stoned, miles away from army headquarters, and listening to Jimi Hendrix. I think we can safely say that there was no close approximation to this experience for soldiers who fought in either World War II or Korea. On the one hand, rock and roll cheered up the troops stationed in Vietnam, and reinforced their pride in being American, while on the other it assumed a dark and subversive role, especially with draftees toward the end of the 1960s. As the insanity and futility of the continuing war effort became all-too-evident on the ground, the combination of rock and roll and drugs formed a kind of alternative universe, much as they had within the counterculture back home. While Hodierne smoked pot in the field and listened to "Foxy Lady" or "All Along the Watchtower," students were doing the same in their dorm rooms at Ann Arbor, Madison, Cambridge, and Berkeley, albeit under less threatening circumstances. The troops and the protesters had more in common then they may have admitted at the time, although the anti-war movement often treated vets with disdain, neglect, or hostility after they had returned to the States. But in fact the draftees were as much a part of "My Generation" as were the Chicago Seven.

It is in this way that rock and roll will forever be connected to the war in Vietnam and that to some extent justifies the "radical" label that has been applied to the music from that era. In addition, during a period of rapid political, social, and cultural change—not progress, necessarily, but change—rock managed to keep pace. In less then four years, the Beatles had moved from "She Loves You" to "Day in the Life," a transformation so absolute and swift that it's hard to imagine the same group wrote and performed both of these songs. The contrast with film—rock's closest competitor for the youth entertainment dollar—is striking:

> The old men who ran the studios were increasingly out of touch with the vast baby boom audience that was coming of age in the '60s, an audience that was rapidly becoming radicalized and disaffected from its elders. The studios were still churning out formulaic genre pictures, an endless stream of Doris Day and Rock Hudson vehicles; big-budget epics like *Hawaii, The Bible, and Krakatoa, East of Java*, war films like *Tora! Tora! Tora!* and *D-Day the Sixth of June.*[2]

Prior to the escalation of the war, and the rise of the anti-war movement, there was no reason to presume that rock and roll or rock and roll performers would be more closely aligned with the Left than the Right in America. Given that many of the early stars were God-fearing white southern males, it would have been perfectly logical to arrive at the opposite conclusion. And in fact, Elvis Presley sought the friendship and approval of President Nixon at their famous meeting in 1970, even if Nixon kept referring to the King as "Mr. Presley," and was not in awe of his guest, unlike some younger White House staff.

When rock became identified with the anti-war movement, it also became identified in the minds of many with the New Left. That association continues to this day, even though there is no longer a New Left to speak of in American politics. But rock is generally linked to causes from that end of the political spectrum, including abortion rights, gun control, and freedom from censorship. There are notable exceptions; the guitarist Ted Nugent loves guns, and one would assume Christian rock groups are not fond of abortion. Still, it would seem that most rock stars—like most movie stars—back liberal causes and the Democratic Party. Since a lot of the powerful figures in Hollywood are Jewish, gay, or both, and Jews and gays tend to vote Democratic, the political leanings of the entertainment industry are rather predictable. It's not as immediately clear why rock musicians tend to go this way— Jews and gays are certainly not overrepresented in their ranks—but one can speculate. Perhaps they are rebelling against parents who are either Republicans or working-class Reagan Democrats. Perhaps they feel guilty because they make so much money, and they want to be aligned with the party that does more for the poor and the disadvantaged. Whatever the explanation, Democratic politicians and party operatives are just happy to have the support, especially if it includes endorsements, contributions, and benefit concerts. "The Republicans don't really have very good rock stars," said Jon Wiener, a columnist for *The Nation* magazine and the author of *Come Together: John Lennon in His Time*, during a 1998 interview. "They've got a few country stars, and they've got Arnold Schwarzenegger, but pop music starts with Clinton/Gore and then goes to environmental causes, feminist causes, and on out to the Left."

The situation is actually not quite as grim as that for the Republican Party. One notable exception to the rock star equals Democratic Party rule is the very same Ted Nugent, an excellent rock guitarist as well as unabashed conservative. Nugent is sex and rock and roll, but he strongly condemns drugs. In 1996, Nugent shared a podium with GOP presidential candidate Bob Dole in Detroit. And the first and still the only pop music star of the 1960s elected to Congress, the late Sonny Bono, was a staunch Republican.

ॱᲚ

I don't usually laugh out loud at hearing rock lyrics, unless they are unintentionally awful, such as the chorus of "Afternoon Delight," the

number one hit from 1976 by the Starland Vocal Band. But I can remember to this day driving in my car on a Southern California freeway
and breaking into hysterics when I first heard the late Ian Dury's "Sex
and Drugs and Rock and Roll" in the summer of 1978. The life of a
typical eighteen-year-old reduced to the basics. To be more precise, the
life of a typical eighteen-year-old on a Friday and Saturday night reduced to the basics. On Monday morning, it was back in class again,
as Chuck Berry would say, or off to work.

Dury's song was a refreshing antidote to those highfalutin' claims
from the 1960s about rock and roll and its relationship to the revolution, social justice, and artistic integrity—take that *Rolling Stone*. Ian
Dury is having fun with that part of the audience that believes "sex and
drugs and rock and roll" is all a body needs. Well, maybe not all the
time, but you get the idea. In my informal research, no one before this
singer had the insight to string these three popular "vices" together in
a single phrase. In the last twenty-five years, the phrase has been used
more than any other popular saying from rock's glorious past, including "You can't always get what you want, but if you try some time, you
get what you need." And to think Dury's song never even cracked the
Top 100!

In the 1950s, it would have been accurate to limit the title to "sex
and rock and roll," drugs not yet having made any more than a token
appearance in middle-class society. The mainstream media discovered
widespread drug use at some point in the middle of the 1960s, and immediately linked it to rock and roll, not without reason. In his book,
Flowers in the Dustbin: The Rise of Rock and Roll, 1947–1977, James
Miller wrote that Bob Dylan introduced the Beatles to pot on August
28, 1964, when they met backstage after the group's performance in
Forest Hills, New York. By the end of 1965 the Beatles' had become
so enamored of pot, or so dependent upon it, that they smoked a joint
in the bathroom at Buckingham Palace prior to being made Members
of the British Empire at a royal ceremony in October. At the end of that
year, the Beatles released the album *Rubber Soul*, and I swear you can
hear one of them taking a hit off of a joint during the song "Girl."

From 1965 to 1970, drugs played as crucial a role as did sex a decade earlier in polishing rock and roll's rebellious image. The timing could not have been better. Drugs came along just as the image of the rock musician as sexual outlaw had become passé. Most of the British Invasion bands of 1964 to 1965, including the Beatles, aimed for the opposite effect, and it worked. It was risky enough for these bands to come to America and play "American" music; projecting raw sex appeal would have been asking too much of a Yankee audience. The Brits smiled a lot, dressed in stylish suits, and sang songs about young love, crushes, and wholesome fun. Of course, the Stones were an exception, but they didn't break out of the pack until "Satisfaction." Even parents with a visceral hatred of rock and roll could not have been *that* offended by Gerry and the Pacemakers, Herman's Hermits, and Billy J. Kramer and the Dakotas

Still, rock and roll must at some point return to rebellion, or some facsimile of rebellion. It's *the* rule of the game. "(Rock and roll) is the pageantry of teenage rebellion," said Jeff Ayreoff, former president of Virgin Records, who also served as a consultant on the Beatles *1* release in 2000. "It's a way of losing the family, declaring your space, and sort of saying 'you're dead and alive, this is my world, and not yours.'" When rebellion runs its course, you get Dick Clark or friendly lads with charming accents. But those who are drawn to rock and roll out of anger, boredom, or love of the music, will eventually reclaim the playing field in the name of integrity and truth. The musicians rarely use those exact words—sympathetic and sycophantic critics have provided the intellectual justification for rock over the years.

Drugs, or the drug culture, served to restart rebellion in the mid-1960s. In this case, both British and American performers played leading roles. It would be preposterous to claim that drugs "saved" rock and roll, especially since so many people both in- and outside the music business have been harmed or have died since the 1960s as a consequence of using them. But acid in particular brought back the old and not entirely unwelcome—on either side—conflicts over the effect of rock music on young people. The area of concern this time was not below thc waist, but above the shoulders. The connection to drugs hastened the return of outraged parents, exploitative politicians, and concerned pundits to the ranks of the anti-rock army. If you were trying to sell records, you couldn't ask for a better opponent. That is, unless your record got banned.

It was 1956 all over again, only to Middle America widespread drug use was more shocking then teen sex. After all, even sexually repressed parents have "done it" at least once in their lives, but smoking pot or taking acid was probably not part of mom and dad's social circle in the 1940s. With the exception of jazz musicians (pot and heroin) and the victims of CIA-sponsored experiments (LSD), the use of hard drugs was rare in America—and rarer still in Middle America—prior to the 1960s. Easy availability of pot and acid enabled white teenagers from 1966 through the middle of the next decade to act like bad boys and girls in a way that their parents had never considered. It's hard to top that kind of thrill when you're seventeen.

Widespread drug use resulted in drug-influenced songs—or was it the other way around? And what exactly constituted a drug song, any way? AM radio programmers thought they had the answer: the words "high," "Mary" or "trip" were prominently featured. The establishment got hip to the new lingo pretty fast. Whenever programmers decided to remove a song from rotation, they sent a message to rock bands and their fans that in effect said: "You can't fool us. We know what you're up to."

The Byrds got hassled over "Eight Miles High," the brilliant single that reached number fourteen in May 1966, a year before the media discovered Haight-Ashbury and the Beatles released *Sgt. Pepper's.* The song was actually banned from many radio stations around the country, which was a contributing factor in its surprisingly weak showing on the charts; "Eight Miles High" is the most ingenious and innovative single from the 1960s that never made it into the Top 10.

Roger McGuinn, the leader of the Byrds and writer of "Eight Miles High," protested that the song was actually about an airplane flight the group took to London. It seemed to be a plausible explanation, and if this had been 1964, that probably would have mollified the critics. But in 1966, there was no chance McGuinn and the Byrds could get off so easy, especially since a growing segment of the public was convinced that rock and roll was aiding and abetting drug use among the young. McGuinn could say whatever he wanted; radio programmers knew darn well what the Byrds were up to.

The Association, another folk-rock group from Southern California, ran into trouble with the title of its number seven hit from 1966, "Along Comes Mary," which opponents claimed did not refer to a common name for a girl, but was actually short for marijuana. The Association responded that, in fact, the "Mary" in this case *was* a girl. Not everyone was convinced. The song was banned in a few places, although it still managed to do well on the charts.

And then there was the case of Godfrey Kerr, an amiable white DJ who had a large following within the Mexican American community of Southern California. Godfrey (he went by his first name on the air) mainly played soul ballads and slow rhythm and blues numbers, the style of music that appealed to this particular audience. These songs dealt in romance, love, and heartbreak, subject matter that even priests and right-wing republicans could find perfectly acceptable.

But in 1966, that watershed year in the history of drug references and rock and roll, Godfrey decided he wanted to make his own hit record, instead of merely promoting others. His inspiration, if you want to call it that, was Sonny Bono, who had proven that you don't need a good voice to have a successful career in rock and roll. Thanks to Sonny's example, Godfrey, who couldn't sing either, confidently entered the recording studio.

Godfrey's small record label was willing to overlook his inadequate vocals, but it was not as forgiving of the lyrics of this song, which carried the then ominous title of "The Trip." It's not that Godfrey was advocating the use of drugs, or anything close, but still the producers worried that the words could be misconstrued. And with a small label, there is little room to maneuver. Godfrey meekly protested, but in the end, he rewrote the lyrics. The new version of "The Trip"—the title remained the same—openly celebrated the joys of going on summer vacation with the family. So much for being a good soldier; the song sold only about 300 copies.

Drug references—actual or presumed—gave hard-line conservatives a reason to listen to rock. The hunt for telltale lyrics wasn't as sexy as rooting out suspected communists in the early 1950s, but it could still garner publicity, especially if the "guilty" party was a big name. In 1967 and 1968 several songs were viewed with suspicion, including the Beatles' "Lucy in the Sky with Diamonds" (the initials spelled LSD) and the Who's "I Can See for Miles"—a feat apparently possible only in the imagination of someone on acid. The lyricists, John Lennon and Pete Townshend respectively, labeled these interpretations absurd, but that didn't phase the establishment one bit. To be sure, the rock groups in this dispute tended to play it very coy, like politicians trying to distance themselves from a controversial election campaign being run on their behalf. John Lennon protested that the title "Lucy in the Sky with Diamonds" was the name his five-year-old son, Julian, gave to a picture that he made at school. "Equally vainly did discerning critics point out that the song was worth more, as music and poetry, then the undoubtedly intended coincidence of its title."[3] When charged with aiding the drug culture, rock groups would claim that lyrics such as "high" or "trip" were not hidden or not-so-hidden references to illegal substances, even though these were the exact words they used among themselves to denote the use of drugs. In the end, they trusted that the youth of America would sort out the differences—and buy the records. But above all, they hoped to avoid being banned from the airwaves, which could not only doom the prospects of a particular single, but also those of the group that recorded it.

It should never be forgotten that even in the swinging, do your own thing 1960s, rock stars had no qualms about getting rich from their labor. In the spring of 1968, Frank Zappa and the Mothers of Invention released an album entitled *We're Only in It for the Money*, which included a spoof of the cover of *Sgt. Pepper's*. Never a big fan of hippies, Zappa was blissfully free of the self-delusion that was common among his generation in the late 1960s. For all its musical brilliance, *Sgt. Pep-*

per's was also a marketing and promotion success story. People are still making money today from exploiting psychedelia and the Summer of Love.

It's been quite a number of years since suggestive lyrics about drugs have generated much controversy. Since the early 1980s, sex, obscene language, threats against the police, and alleged anti-Americanism have been the prime suspects. But the consequences of getting high with a little help from a friend or friends lives on in American political campaigns. Since Bill Clinton first ran for president in 1992, there has been concern among younger politicians, who were in college at the time of "Lucy in the Sky with Diamonds," that they will be damaged by revelations of past indulgences. Richard Nixon first put the Democrats on the defensive with his "Acid, Amnesty, and Abortion" description of the 1972 George McGovern campaign and its supporters. There was no hint from the Nixon people that McGovern, a World War II veteran, smoked pot or dropped acid, only that he could claim a greater share of voters who were "experienced," in the Jimi Hendrix sense of the word. Hard to disagree with that, although there must have been some acid freaks that were also closet Nixon-lovers. Still, it's been more than thirty years since McGovern ran for president, and the perception remains that the Democratic Party is more sympathetic to the use of drugs and the drug culture than are the Republicans. Once again, it's not so easy to shake the legacy of the 1960s.

The political repercussions of this are serious. "Soft on drugs" is indistinguishable from "soft on crime," a charge that Republicans have successfully leveled at Democrats for more than three decades. Not true, say Democrats, pointing to positions in favor of more police, the death penalty, and the war on drugs. Indeed, the Clinton administration enthusiastically continued the so-called drug war that had been waged under Reagan and Bush. On this issue, President Clinton behaved not like a New Democrat, but an old Republican.

Just as politically perilous is the issue of how baby boomer Democrats running for office choose to handle questions about their own experiences with drugs. As was his wont, Bill Clinton proposed a third

way, otherwise known as "I smoked, but I didn't inhale," which translated means, "I tried pot, but not really." Presumably he was hoping to
make the pot smokers and the pot haters happy by this answer, but he
only ended up looking ridiculous to everybody. Along with "I did not
have sex with that woman," "I smoked, but I didn't inhale" will go
down in history as one of the most memorable quotes from Bill Clinton, another shining example of his audacious political persona.

In 2000, Al Gore admitted at the outset of his campaign that he tried
marijuana on a number of occasions—inhaling included. His seeming
candor and directness resulted in generally favorable press coverage
on the issue. By contrast, the Republican nominee, George W. Bush
proclaimed his "young and foolish" days off-limits to reporters, which
aroused their curiosity and anger. "Young and foolish" was presumed
to mean consumption of illegal substances, but that was just speculation. Nothing had been proven, and no one was talking. If Bush got
high with a little help from his friends, his friends were keeping their
mouths shut. In terms of press coverage, the lesson from the 2000 campaign would suggest that openness is preferable to being evasive. And
yet George W. Bush defeated Al Gore in the election. It will be interesting in 2004 to see how Democratic and Republican presidential contenders choose to address the question of past drug use.

The Summer of Love was also a summer of riots: Detroit, Newark, and
other cities. The top rock groups were too busy trying to duplicate *Sgt.
Pepper's* or come up with something to say about Vietnam to release a
1967 version of "Trouble Coming Every Day." But with art rock and
the San Francisco scene as the dominant influences, it was a time when
white and black music was headed in very different directions. James
Brown released "Cold Sweat" in August, the song that invented modern funk and rendered the sweet soul sound of vocal groups like the
Temptations and the Supremes immediately retro. In its own field,
"Cold Sweat" was as influential as *Sgt. Pepper's*, released a mere two

months earlier. "Cold Sweat" was one giant step for mankind. You can hear its influence in dozens of funk singles from the late 1960s and early 1970s. In his book, *Funk: The Music, the People, and the Rhythm of the One*, Rickey Vincent wrote that "Cold Sweat" is "often acknowledged as the closest thing to the first funk groove."[4]

Brown's standing was at its highest among black audiences during the late 1960s. When he came to a major urban area, everything stopped, including a potential riot in Boston on the night Martin Luther King was assassinated.

The white groups meanwhile had gone tripping, whether or not they actually dropped acid. In the fall of 1967, the Strawberry Alarm Clock had a number one hit with "Incense and Peppermints"—the group would never again crack the Top 100—a slice of bubble gum/psychedelia for the masses. Though members of the Strawberry Alarm Clock looked like real hippies, a line in the song makes reference to "beatniks" which indicates that somebody wasn't paying attention. Still, the intended pre-teen/young teen audience was not concerned with historical accuracy.

Sitars seemed to be used as often as electric organs on album cuts and singles from that period. Both lyrically and musically much of rock took a hiatus from its blues and R&B base in 1967. In December, the Stones released *Their Satanic Majesties Request*, an album almost completely devoid of anything to do with sex, but filled with references to drugs and the mysteries of the universe. Not your typical Stones' LP, and yet not a complete failure, even when popped into a CD player three decades later. Like the cover of *We're Only in It for the Money*, the cover of *Their Satanic Majesties Request* is a rip-off of a certain Beatles album, although the Stones were loath to admit it.

It was two singers that the majority of the rock audience probably considered rednecks—Mac Davis and Elvis Presley—who wrote and recorded a hit song about life in the inner city at the end of the 1960s. As social commentary, "In the Ghetto" was pretty tame, but at least they made the attempt. According to Davis, the composer, he originally wanted to call the 1969 song "Vicious Circle," and set the story of a tragic confrontation between a cop and a teenager in Anytown, U.S.A. Born in Lubbock, Texas, in 1942, Davis was not exactly on familiar terms with urban America. But the various ghetto riots of the 1960s prompted him to change the venue of the song, even though he didn't really know the lay of the land. Of course, neither did the members of most rock bands, for that matter, or at least not since Watts exploded and it was regarded as risky for white people to take a stroll through what we now call "the hood."

Elvis Presley could never have recorded a song about the condition of black people—poor or middle class, north or south of the Mason-Dixon Line—during the 1950s. His white fans would have been confused, and the southern religious and political establishment would have done everything possible to force him into early retirement. And besides, issue-oriented rock and roll songs would not appear for another decade.

So was *In the Ghetto* a marketing decision or a political awakening? Speaking on behalf of the late singer, Mac Davis suggested both. "Elvis was looking to change his image," said Davis in a 1998 interview. "I also think he realized it was a hit song."

SIGNS OF THE TIMES

Danny Goldberg, current president of Sheridan Square Entertainment and Artemis Records, entered the music business in 1973, when he became the press agent for Led Zeppelin's massive American tour that year, an event that served as a subplot in the 2000 film *Almost Famous*. Goldberg has since held several executive positions in the industry, and he served for a number of years as the manager of Bonnie Raitt.

Although Raitt is one of the most politically active musicians in the business, Goldberg, long involved with the American Civil Liberties Union, can match her issue for issue and cause for cause. No one on the corporate side has been as active in speaking out publicly against censorship and in favor of freedom of expression for performers. While there is no denying the element of self-interest in Goldberg's stance, he nonetheless is willing to debate the issue, which gives him much more credibility then his colleagues, who prefer to hide behind the First Amendment. At times in the late 1980s and early 1990s it seemed as if Goldberg was an army of one standing up against William Bennett and the other right-wing crusaders.

Danny Goldberg turned eighteen in 1968. If you turned eighteen in 1968, you didn't have to lie in later life about having been caught up in the excitement of the 1960s. For Goldberg and his peers, 1968 meant Eugene McCarthy, Bobby Kennedy, the Chicago Convention, the Chicano Movement, Columbia, Martin Luther King, the Tet Offensive, "Jumpin' Jack Flash," Cream, "Hair," "Electric Ladyland," and "Say It Loud (I'm Black and I'm Proud)." Goldberg witnessed firsthand the sometimes constructive, sometimes tenuous alliance between rock and radical politics, manifested in anti-war rallies and concerts, particular lyrics, and interviews in the more sophisticated fan magazines. "The Baby Boomer generation that peaked in the 1960s gave power to the teen voice and power to rock and roll artists," said Goldberg. The power was financial, cultural, and to some extent, political.

What follows is sketches of three *musicians* whose careers flourished in the late 1960s, each of whom is consigned by the history books to different categories of rock and yet each of whom also is politically astute. The section concludes with the brief portrait of a Los Angeles-based disc jockey who for years has made politics central to his on-air rap, and some thoughts on John Lennon, Yoko Ono, and their own political battles in the 1970s.

⌒

Peter Tork of the Monkees participated in several protest marches during his lifetime, but none in opposition to the war in Vietnam. It was, one might say, a case of bad timing. The big anti-war demonstrations of the late 1960s—the Pentagon in 1967, the Chicago Democratic Convention in 1968, and New York City in 1969—roughly coincided with the massive fame of the Monkees. A group so controlled by its managers and handlers that they weren't allowed to play their own instruments for two albums could hardly be granted permission to demonstrate against the war, even on their own time. Tork's sympathies were with the protesters, but he had to admire them from afar. He couldn't be both a Monkee and publicly oppose the war. Indeed, the Beatles steered clear of anti-war demonstrations—at least until John and Yoko got married at the end of the decade—and the Beatles could seemingly get away with a lot more than could the Monkees.

The Monkees were the first rock and roll band chosen by committee. "What happened was that a group of California businessmen set up a series about a pop group, 1966. They didn't want to use any established group, they wanted no public hassles, and they decided to create a phenomenon out of nowhere. Accordingly, they advertised for four young men."[1]

Tork was one of the fortunate four, along with Davy Jones, Mickey Dolenz, and Mike Nesmith. The television program debuted less than three years after the Beatles appeared on *The Ed Sullivan Show*, and yet enough time had elapsed that a new generation of preteens was poised to follow the Next Big Thing. An eight-year-old who wasn't quite ready for the Beatles in the winter of 1964 had grown into a ten or eleven-year-old ripe for the Monkees in the fall of 1966. That the new band claimed American citizenship probably didn't hurt either. Once singles and albums started to be released—instrumental backing courtesy of skilled session musicians—the Monkees actually rivaled the popularity of the Beatles. From January 1967 through March 1968, the Monkees had six Top 10 singles, including three that reached number one. The group's single "I'm a Believer" was *Billboard's* top song for the entire year in 1967.

Some people prepare themselves, or are prepared by others, for pop music stardom from an early age. Michael Jackson is one example, Donny Osmond is another. Not so Peter Tork. Prior to being selected for the Monkees at the age of twenty-one, Tork's musical career had gone in a very different direction, one in which hit singles and screaming girls were symbols of artistic failure, and commercial success was considered selling out. In other words, he played folk music.

"When I was a kid, before the Monkees, I was not primarily a rock and roller," said Tork during a 1998 interview. "I was primarily an acoustic folkie. For us, as acoustic folkies, the politics were very clear. We were strongly liberal, in the Pete Seeger mold. We certainly had a strong sense of right and wrong, and we certainly believed a lot that was wrong with society was the fault of the moneyed class. I think all of us to some extent believed ourselves to be socialists."

Tork's earliest musical heroes were the Weavers, the folk group formed in 1948 by Pete Seeger, Lee Hays, Fred Hellerman, and Ronnie Gilbert. In the 1990 edition of the *Penguin Encyclopedia of Popular Music* it's written that the Weavers "campaigned for left-wing political candidates."[2] The Weavers recorded many songs that even contemporary fans may know, including "Kisses Sweeter than Wine," "Guantanamera," and "If I Had a Hammer," co-written by Seeger. The group's biggest hit, Leadbelly's "Goodnight Irene" (1950), sold two million copies in the same year that Senator McCarthy launched his aggressive hunt for suspected communists and the Korean War began. These events are related insofar as the Weavers were blacklisted in the 1950s, which not surprisingly hampered their career. Indeed, Tork believes the group could have been as big as the Platters or the Four Freshmen—two hugely popular, nonrock and roll groups from the mid-1950s—had it not been for the blacklist. Still, the Weavers recorded several well-received albums in the late 1950s and the 1960s.

In addition to enjoying their songs, Tork considered the Weavers the model of how to successfully combine politics and music. "I think they had their priorities in order," he said. "They were musicians who put their music at the service of some political thought. There is nothing more boring than someone who sets themselves up as a musician, but who is primarily about politics, and whose music is entirely subservient."

The young Tork was a folkie, but not a folk purist. He readily admits to switching sides several times in the folk v. rock and roll battles of the 1950s and 1960s. He started in folk, and fully intended to remain there, except that one day he heard Elvis Presley on the radio singing the emotional ballad "I Want You, I Need You, I Love You," which went to number one in 1956. He put his banjo away, picked up the guitar, and became "a total Elvis fan." He moved on to Little Richard, astonished by the performer's vocal abilities and "manic energy."

By the early 1960s, however, Tork retrieved his banjo, because rock and roll had in his view become boring and repetitive. It was not a difficult decision. Like Ray Manzarek, Tork didn't need rock and roll. When the music was good, they paid attention, and when not, there were always other pursuits. Tork returned to folk—in the midst of a revival—vowing never again to stray from his true musical home. And he might have kept his promise if the Beatles hadn't come to America. But who could have predicted music like that? "I loved the early Beatles," said Tork, "They started out devoid of politics, but musically they were so adventurous for a pop group." It was once again time for Tork to plug in his electric guitar.

Three years later, Tork won a coveted spot in a new group that was conceived as America's answer to the Beatles, albeit one put together by artificial means. The inside story of the Monkees is pretty familiar by now, especially the fact that Davy, Peter, Mike, and Mickey were barred by management from playing their own instruments until the release of their third album, *Headquarters*, in the late spring of 1967. Seeing limited action, Tork still managed to contribute one of the great musical moments in Monkees and rock and roll history—the harpsichord solo on the single of "The Girl I Knew Somewhere" (1967).

It could not have been easy for someone who grew up listening to the Weavers and folk music to remain on the sidelines during such a fertile period in American politics as the late 1960s. Had Tork not strayed a second time from folk, perhaps he would have written a memorable protest song himself. But doing something like that was out of the question while a member of the Monkees. Still, Tork tried at one point to break free of his "captors." "I thought that we had no business being in Vietnam, and I said so to the *New York Times*," Tork recalled. "I was asked (by Monkees' management) to retract the statement. I called the *Times* and did that." It was, said Tork, a question of honor; he had signed a contract, and he would abide by its terms.

Tork is under no illusions that the music of the Monkees contained strong political messages, with the partial exception of "Pleasant Valley Sunday" (number three in 1967, and written by the famous team of Carole King and Gerry Goffin). That song indicted suburbia on charges of boredom, conformity, and repression, hardly a daring theme

for a rock and roll song, let alone a novel, play, or film. No program-
mer, even in the heartland, would pull a record that slammed the soulless existence of the nouveau riche. This was perfectly acceptable political commentary during a time of body counts over there and riots
over here. Yet Tork insists that the Monkees had a political agenda, although not one that named a specific enemy. The clue, said Tork, was
in the television shows. The singles and albums rarely contained any
messages—hidden or otherwise—pertaining to the state of the world.
But television offered Peter, Davy, Mike, and Mickey more freedom to
experiment, one of the few cases in the decade when TV held its own
with rock and roll. "We were the only group on television to be young
adults without an authority figure. We didn't need authority figures.
Until then, it (television) was *My Three Sons* and *Father Knows Best*,
the kindly and wise parental figures. We were the avatars of the 1960s
through television."

After twelve years of Ronald Reagan and George Bush, eight years of
that New Democrat, Bill Clinton, and at least another four of George
W. Bush, it is quite difficult to recall a time when labor unions were a
major player in the American economy. The "New Economy," so proclaimed by Alan Greenspan, purred along during the 1990s without so
much as acknowledging the role of the American worker. We were in
an Information Age, which dispensed with traditional modes of production. And when this new economy seemed to implode in 2001 to
2002, labor unions were considered neither part of the problem nor the
solution. Other than walking precincts and getting out the vote, unions
were viewed as irrelevant, except in professional sports. Even conservative commentators and right-wing talk radio hosts all but ignored
them, which may have been the unkindest cut of all.

   To people born after, say, 1965, it must therefore seem very weird
that unions once played a pivotal role in the American economy. It
must also seem weird that the unions were especially powerful in De-

troit, a city that since the riots of 1967 and the oil embargo of the early 1970s has, fairly or not, epitomized urban decline. You would have trouble locating stories in the 1980s and 1990s about the revival of Detroit, although many other major American cities were making or had made a miraculous comeback from the misery and blight of the 1970s.

Wayne Kramer remembers the glory days of Detroit, and the glory days of the United Auto Workers (UAW). Kramer grew up in Detroit in the 1950s, the son of a single mother who worked as a beautician and a labor organizer. The vast majority of her customers were the wives of working-class employees of the big auto companies, and much of the casual conversation in the beauty shop centered around prevailing wages, working conditions, and the state of relations between labor and management. Just a kid at the time, Kramer today doesn't recall paying much attention to these discussions, although from the perspective of over forty years later he believes that simply being in the vicinity helped to form his political consciousness. "One of my fundamental beliefs is that it's [politics is] all about jobs, working, and having meaningful work," said Kramer in a 1998 interview.

When he was in grade school, Kramer spent a lot of his free time at the Boys Club in Detroit. He remembers one night when he left the club for home, and decided along the way to stop at a popular hot dog stand to grab a quick dinner. Not only did this establishment serve good food—in the judgment of this ten-year-old junk food expert—it also featured a jukebox with an eighteen-inch speaker. Kramer walked through the door on this particular evening and immediately heard the deep, rich sound of a Duane Eddy guitar riff, quite possibly the opening of the song "Forty Miles of Bad Road." And yes, it did change his life.

"What I heard in that electric guitar was liberation," said Kramer. "The sound spoke to me directly. Then when I heard my first Chuck Berry guitar solo, I knew that was what I wanted to do."

Kramer started playing in bands in 1960, when he turned twelve. Although he came from a proud union family, he had no interest in folk music. Indeed, he regarded rock and roll as the more "political" of the two, because it just might free your soul—and when that happens, everything else follows. One more thing; Kramer liked his music loud, very loud. The acoustic stuff just couldn't deliver the goods.

In 1967, the Summer of Love year, Kramer joined MC5 (MC for Motor City), a rock group that had apparently not been reading *Time* or the *New York Times*. While George Harrison put on his heart-shaped sunglasses and went strolling in Golden Gate Park, and hippies even began to camp out in suburban neighborhoods, MC5 played aggressive rock and roll that owed everything to its Midwest working-class roots. The band's debut single, "I Can Only Give You Everything," released in March 1967, sounds like the Stones of a year earlier, but more menacing, distorted, and loud. These guys were in no mood to be happy, and of no mind to get happy. Their friends were the ones being sent to fight and die in Vietnam, and the parents of their friends were fighting to keep their jobs and benefits. Peace and love might have been nice ideas in theory, but when did they ever stop a war or put food on the table? In his frequently misunderstood song from 1967, "All You Need Is Love," John Lennon mockingly notes how easy it is to learn to play the game, and then repeats the title for emphasis. The members of the MC5 were more skeptical then Lennon—who owed it to his fellow Beatles not to be too much of a contrarian—while at the same they developed a plan of action. They deliberately placed themselves at the center of events; the leaders of the movement didn't have to come get them.

"Vietnam politicized everybody real quick," said Kramer. "Once you had to start thinking about those questions, then you started to question the whole program. How does it end up that somebody sits in Washington and decides whether I live or die?" While some of the self-appointed leaders in the "hippie community" were extolling the virtues of dropping out, not to mention turning on, the MC5 argued precisely the opposite, namely the necessity of taking a stand and perhaps provoking a response. "We had this band, and we could really affect people," said Kramer. "We were trying to report on what was going on around us."

The MC5 could actually make a strong case that they were too radical for the 1960s, which is saying something. For example, they were the only band with the courage and dedication to perform for the demonstrators that attended the Democratic National Convention (DNC) in 1968; according to Kramer, other invitees stayed away out of fear for their own safety. Given what happened in Chicago during the DNC, one can sympathize. Still, there's something inherently phony about groups or people, who talk about revolution but keep a safe distance from the front lines. To some people this is precisely why the 1960s "failed." When the time came to make a stand, the rebels opted for the comforts of middle-class society, and then tried to pretend that they were still committed to change.

The MC5, on the other hand, had nothing to be ashamed of on this score. And it says something about society and the band that they were too hot to handle in 1968. None of the presidential candidates that year, including the Peace and Freedom nominee, approached the MC5 for an endorsement. You would think they were communists or something. Not quite, and yet, "We were crazy, we were militant, we endorsed the Black Panther Party, and we fought the drug laws," Kramer said. "We were way too far to the left to be endorsing any political candidates."

But surely the Beatles, comrades in rock and roll if not in politics, would have no qualms about associating with the MC5. That thought prompted Kramer and his band mates to send tapes, clippings, books of poetry, and original art to the London headquarters of Apple, the Beatles' newly formed record label, in an all-out effort to get a deal. "They had advertised that they were looking for artists that didn't fit the mainstream," recalled Kramer. "We said, 'we are just what you are looking for.'"

Well, not exactly. Within a few weeks of mailing their hefty application, the MC5 received a response from Neil Aspinall, Apple's managing director, containing one of those irksome rejection notices, along the lines of "you don't fit in with what we are trying to do." Kramer and the rest of the band were peeved, to put it mildly. Meanwhile, Apple released product such as "Those Were the Days" by Mary Hopkin and "Come and Get It" by Badfinger.

It's certainly possible that there are rock fans who remember where they were when they first heard "Kick Out the Jams," the most famous song by the MC5, but for most, the group is known more by reputation then direct exposure. After all, their albums were never big sellers, and none of the singles from the 1960s and early 1970s landed on the charts. But a mansion, a Rolls Royce, a personal trainer, and an accountant are not the only measures of success in rock and roll. The MC5 are still the first and one of the only groups for whom politics and political change was as important as the music, and a segment of the rock public continues to revere the band for its earnest efforts to combine the two. The MC5 didn't merely mouth revolutionary slogans from the stage; they spent time with the participants, such as Jerry Rubin, the Black Panthers, and John Sinclair, founder of the White Panthers.

Its association with the radical left garnered the group more attention from J. Edgar Hoover's FBI then they ever received from Apple. Kramer said that in the early 1970s, following the election of Richard Nixon, the FBI placed wiretaps on phones in the group's home in Ann Arbor, Michigan. He also said the local police, perhaps on orders from Washington, would regularly pull up to the house at night, flash their lights, and turn on their sirens. Even for a rock band accustomed to performing concerts at painful noise levels, this form of harassment was not appreciated. Still, it could have been worse, as other political targets of the FBI can attest.

It was one thing for the Nixon administration and its friends to try to make the band go insane. The members could live with that, if only just barely. But it was quite a different matter to take away their issue. When Nixon initiated Vietnamization in 1970, gradually turning the prosecution of the war over to the South Vietnamese army, the antiwar movement was deprived of its main selling point. And when Nixon abolished the draft in 1973, the movement had nowhere to go and nothing to do. As much as protesters despised American policy in Southeast Asia, they hated *and feared* the possibility that they might be sent into battle over there. Without that threat, students discovered other issues to pursue, or simply drifted away from politics altogether.

The new apathy, or indifference, was not a good thing for the MC5, a band that thrived on political turmoil. "We were part of a mass movement," said Kramer. "In the 1970s, there was no mass movement." The MC5 gave its last performance on New Year's Eve in 1972, a few weeks after Richard Nixon defeated George McGovern in a landslide.

Ex-rock stars, like ex-politicians, have a lot of difficulty contending with the sudden loss of power and prestige. Kramer's ill-advised solution was crime and drugs, in part as an attempt to recapture the thrill of being in a band at the end of the 1960s. "We had gone through the fire together; the riots in Chicago, the riots in Detroit, the touring, the music business, the war in Vietnam, the White Panther Party, the sex orgies, and great, great accomplishments and failures," said Kramer. To have all this come to an end was a "tremendous loss."

But a nice, quiet retirement certainly would have been preferable to jail, Kramer's "home" for several years after being convicted on drug charges. After his release, Kramer left Detroit for New York, where he spent the better part of the 1980s. He went back to rock and roll, producing several bands, playing in others, and writing a rhythm and blues musical that he and his writing partner took on the road for a few months. His state of mind oscillated between contented and resentful. He was happy to be working, but angry about what he considered to be a veritable plethora of bands ripping off the MC5 package, especially the aggressive sound and tough-minded politics. Kramer spent perhaps too much time sitting around the house, watching MTV stoned or drunk, and loudly cursing these bands every time their videos appeared.

Eventually Kramer gave up alcohol and drugs, an effort spurred by the entreaties of his wife. His sobriety may help to explain his renewed desire to get out there and tell the story of the MC5 to as many rock journalists and disc jockeys as possible. "I kind of look at it as my responsibility," he said. In 1998, Kramer wrote a vivid first-person article on the band's performance at the Grande Ballroom in Detroit on Halloween night in 1968.

In 1994, he signed with Epitaph, a local Los Angeles label, and returned to the business of making rock records. He continued to stress the rock and politics connection, writing songs with apt titles such as

"Revolution in Apt. 29," "Dope for Democracy," and "Something Broken in the Promised Land." In 2002, Kramer released *Adult World* on the MuscleTone label, which included songs such as "Love, Fidel," "Sundays in Saigon," and "Brought a Knife to the Gunfight."

In 2000, Rhino released *The Big Bang: The Best of the MC5*, with liner notes and commentary from Wayne Kramer. "It's too bad, in a way, that we didn't have the support of the music-business establishment," wrote Kramer, "because when the story of the '60s and the counterculture is told, you rarely hear about the MC5's part in it."

Still, Kramer is not bitter; he's far too busy for that. He also has a new audience to satisfy. Those who vividly remember Kramer's contributions to the MC5 are the easiest to please. "They know my history," he explained, "and they appreciate what I'm trying to say."

And there will always be another demonstration to attend. In 1998, Kramer joined Zack De Le Rocha from the band Rage Against the Machine and 100 or so others at a busy intersection in the Westwood section of Los Angeles to protest the Mexican government's treatment of rebels in the state of Chiapas. In addition to pressing the rebels' case, Kramer enjoyed temporarily disrupting the lives of neurotic, materialistic young executives darting to and from appointments. "What was great was all those yuppies on their cell phones and in their Porsches while we've got Aztec dancers in the middle of Wilshire Boulevard, and everyone's pissed off because they can't make their meetings," said Kramer, smiling at the memory.

⌒

Ray Manzarek was a hippie; Ray Manzarek is a hippie. Unlike many of his peers who long ago expunged "hippie" from their personal histories, Manzarek, former keyboard player of the Doors, is proud of his past. In his definition, the word *hippie* does not connote a way of life, but rather a philosophy of life. He rejects the popular stereotype of a hippie as someone who wears his hear long, is indifferent or hostile to the basic rules of grooming, prefers panhandling to getting a job, and,

If the arrival of Elvis Presley didn't herald the arrival of the New South, it suggested that the days of the Old South were numbered. With a white boy from Mississippi making millions performing songs written by blacks, how much longer could segregation last? (*Library of Congress*)

Rock and roll was not all that great during the Kennedy years. But the Johnson years have never been surpassed. (*Library of Congress*)

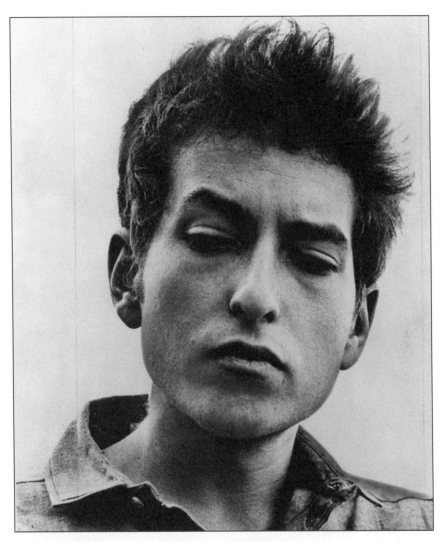

The young Bob Dylan oozed politics in his songs. Then he heard the Beatles and picked up an electric guitar. (*Library of Congress*)

Coincidence? The escalation of the war in Vietnam in 1965 is the same year that folk-rock crashed the charts. (*Library of Congress*)

With songs such as "To Susan on the West Coast Waiting" Donovan registered his pointed criticism of American foreign policy. (*Library of Congress*)

Officially apolitical, the Rolling Stones are one of the founding members of the counterculture. By the late 1990s Republican congressmen were just dying to meet them. (*Library of Congress*)

Yippie/hippie nirvania: Country Joe and the Fish and the Doors on the same bill in San Francisco in 1967. (*Library of Congress*)

Nineteen sixty-eight was the year of riots, student demonstrations, revolution, free love, acid, and the election of Richard Nixon as president and Spiro Agnew as vice-president. Go figure. (*Library of Congress*)

After *Sgt. Pepper's Lonely Hearts Club Band*, they dabbled in politics. "All You Need Is Love," "Baby, You're a Rich Man," and "Revolution" have held up very well—words and music. (*Library of Congress*)

John moved to the Left after he met Yoko. As long as there are wars, people will be singing "Give Peace a Chance." (*Library of Congress*)

Were they or weren't they? The songs, the hair, and the glitter kept us guessing in the early 1970s. (*Frank Moriarty*)

Bruce Springsteen has been singing and talking about politics since Watergate.
(*Frank Moriarty*)

Joe Strummer of the Clash, the band that dissed Elvis and the Beatles in 1977 and in 2003 was elected to the Rock and Roll Hall of Fame. Who says rock and roll never forgets? (*Frank Moriarty*)

The Reagan/Bush team tried to claim "Born in the USA" for the campaign in1984. But they couldn't win the consent of its creator. (*Library of Congress*)

IT'S REVEILLE IN AMERICA!

Who can forget where they were the night in 1992 when presidential candidate Bill Clinton brought along his sax to the *Arsenio Hall Show*. (*Library of Congress*)

President Bill Clinton (*center*), Robert Dole (*left*), and Newt Gingrich (*right*) here discuss politics, not rock and roll. (*Library of Congress*)

Newt Gingrich thought Too Much Joy were his allies in the 1994 Republican revolution. Boy, was he surprised! (*Warner Brothers Records*)

of course, lives for sex, drugs, and rock and roll. One more thing: hippies—according to the stereotype—use the words "peace" and "love" without a clue as to how to attain either. But not one of these stereotypes fits Ray Manzarek, who stopped wearing his hair long sometime during the Carter administration.

Where Manzarek and other hippies would seemingly find common ground is in their questioning of societal norms, whether in 1968 or in 2008, because, as he noted, how much have things really changed? The Doors did not reject particular government policies per se, but the underlying belief system that spawned those policies. In contrast to folk performers of the 1950s and early 1960s, the Doors did not peruse the headlines in search of ideas for songs. "Our job was not to register a daily protest, but to *be* a protest against the prevailing religious sanctions and religious authorities of our times," said Manzarek in a 1998 interview. "The two went hand in hand." Or as he put it later in the same interview: "We were fighting the basic religious foundation of the warmongers. That was our protest."

Warmongers were probably not paying attention; whether other people got the message is anyone's guess. Lead singer Jim Morrison, a poet who became a rock star, wrote most of the group's lyrics, and poets don't often make it easy on their audience. You had to listen to the Doors, and listen closely, which is rarely the case in rock and roll. The transition from albums to CDs was a blessing for Doors' fans—the technology has made it easier to return again and again to the same song. By the end of twenty repeat plays, even Morrison's most obscure lyrics can begin to make a semblance of sense.

The group's one obvious anti-war song, "The Unknown Soldier" (1968) was no more about Vietnam than it was about any other war in the twentieth century, and maybe the nineteenth as well. Of course, this didn't stop a contemporary audience from staking its own claim: "The Unknown Soldier" must have been written as *their* song about *their* war. "We played it at the Fillmore (in San Francisco)," recalled Manzarek. "As soon as they heard the opening notes, people knew it was the 'Unknown Soldier.' And when Jim finally sang the line 'Make a

grave for the Unknown Soldier,' people just loved it, there was screaming and hollering."

The Doors didn't discourage equating the song with Vietnam, but
they didn't encourage it either. Indeed, a film the band released to accompany "The Unknown Soldier" contained no scenes of napalm, hel-
icopters, or jungles. Morrison is cast as a deserter who is tied up and
shot for having abandoned his fellow soldiers, played by the other
three members of the Doors. Manzarek said the brief story line has always reminded him of *Paths of Glory*, the late Stanley Kubrick's masterful film about soldiers serving during World War I. In addition, the
joyous clips at the end of the promotional film are based on the famous
scenes of couples kissing in Times Square after the signing of the
armistice agreement at the end of World War II.

As was true for the MC5, and probably many other rock groups at
that time as well, not a single presidential candidate approached the
Doors for an endorsement or support during the 1968 campaign. Given
that the Doors were the crème de la crème of American bands at the
time, this would not have been such a ridiculous request. The Doors
could seemingly help deliver the youth (ages twenty-one to twenty-
five) vote, which was critical during the 1968 Democratic primary. But
the days of candidates courting rock stars were in the future. Not even
Gene McCarthy or Bobby Kennedy—the leaders of a new youth movement in the Democratic Party—sought their help. "We were the dirty
Doors; who the hell would want the Doors," Manzarek explained. "The
Doors were strictly a counterculture pothead band." Which must mean
that many people in America answered to that description in 1968, considering that the Doors had a number one single in 1967 with "Light My
Fire" and a number one single in 1968, "Hello, I Love You."

The last two or three decades have demonstrated how very different
the Doors were from most of their contemporaries. Their sound has successfully traveled across several rock and roll time zones. For example,
punk rock fans of the late 1970s hated all that hippie stuff, especially the
San Francisco scene epitomized by Jefferson Airplane and the Grateful
Dead, but they liked and, even more important, respected the Doors. In-

deed, Manzarek produced *Los Angeles*, the seminal album released by the L.A. band X in 1980. Like Jimi Hendrix, the Doors succeeded on their own terms, and have never really gone out of style.

Manzarek exemplifies an independent streak in his own political views, which are not what you might expect from a hippie rock musician. "I was very disappointed in the Peace and Freedom Party in 1968," he said. "Whom did they put up for president but Eldridge Cleaver, a convicted rapist? I didn't care what his policies were, this guy was a loser." Manzarek broke completely with the radicals after some within the movement manufactured bombs, brandished guns, and advocated violent revolution. He sincerely does put his faith in peace and love.

To this day, Manzarek remains skeptical regarding rock and roll's ability to affect politics. At best, he believes rock can function as a kind of sideshow. "I think the only vehicle for political change is going out to vote," he said. "I don't see how rock can affect the propositions on the ballot, or the list of candidates in the national election."

Take away the Christian Coalition, reduce the power and influence of the National Rifle Association, and cut out the inflammatory rhetoric of some of its members, and Manzarek would be reasonably content within the Republican Party. "In my heart of hearts I am a Republican," he said in 1998. "I'm for as little welfare as possible—except for those who really need it—as little government interference as possible, and as little taxes as possible. A Republican with a good heart can really turn this country around."

⌣⌐

Against those who argue that the 1960s ended with a bang—Altamont, the Manson murders, Kent State—I would like to offer that it ended with a whimper. How about the day that the first FM rock radio station abandoned its free-form style in pursuit of the big bucks and major advertisers? It probably happened sometime in 1972 or 1973, and there are those who say it changed us all.

Jim Ladd can tell you about it. In 1969, Ladd got his first job in radio at KNAC, a small FM station based in Long Beach, California. At
that time, KNAC featured extended album cuts and music by lesser-
known bands: the stuff that you could never hear over on the AM side
of the dial. The new stations were in some ways pretentious and elit-
ist, but also a much-needed alternative to the rank commercialism of
the rock business at the end of the 1960s. The FM DJs—often called
"jocks" for short—didn't scream and shout, or promise a trip for two
to Disneyland to caller number three. What you got instead was hip
patter, including occasional potshots at the government, and the total-
ity of serious white rock. Post-*Pepper's* rock had grown too big to be
covered by five adrenaline-filled stations with a similar musical
agenda. FM asked its listeners to do just that: listen. Dance rock was
out; contemplative rock was in. The parodies of this mode of rock music appreciation would be devastating, but that would not happen for
several more years. If the Beatles in 1964 had influenced thousands of
young people to dream of making hit singles, the Beatles in 1967
caused them to dream about making the perfect concept album. In addition, the success of the Yardbirds and Cream was key to developing
a new crop of dedicated blues musicians, guitarists, vocalists, and har-
monica players.

As groups whiled away in studios in London, New York, and Los
Angeles on their works of art, the FM stations were just getting started.
They needed each other desperately. Savoy Brown, Pink Floyd, the
Nice, the Moody Blues, the Electric Flag, and Matthew's Southern
Comfort depended on this new medium to reach the public. At the
same time, KNAC and similar stations eschewed the notion that rock
and roll radio should only program All the Hits All the Time. They coveted lengthy solos—on guitar, bass, keyboards, or drums—extended
jams, and obscure lyrics, preferably steeped in mysticism or ancient
history. "When it started out, it was a bunch of hippies playing this
weird music," said Ladd, of FM rock back in the day.

And talking about politics—which you would also never hear on
AM—Ladd was a longhaired, left-wing version of Paul Harvey, using

radio to dispense opinions on myriad issues. He talked about anti-drug laws, civil rights, the environment, class warfare, upcoming elections, and, of course, the war in Vietnam. There was never any question in Ladd's mind that politics and rock were closely connected. He has always maintained that FM radio was "the third piece of the puzzle," along with rock and roll and protests that fueled youth politics during the latter part of the 1960s. If he's correct, then FM could be regarded as an instrument of left-wing propaganda, albeit one that reached a comparatively small audience. You can be sure that Jim Ladd was not calling for the re-election of Ronald Reagan as governor of California in 1970, or throwing his support behind President Nixon's decision to mine Haiphong Harbor in 1972. Ladd would spend hours each day searching for songs to play during his shift that contained either overt or subtle political messages. "The kind of radio we did was very set-oriented, because the lyrics were very important," he said. "We were aware of how to put songs together from a musical and a lyrical standpoint." A DJ selecting his own music, sometimes on the spur of the moment? It seems impossible in this age of computerized playlists and by-the-book program directors.

The eventual fate of FM radio gives credence to the notion that the 1970s stands for the commercialization of the 1960s. American forces withdrew from Vietnam, Nixon resigned in disgrace, but the universe of FM stations kept expanding. Turned out that FM was not dependent on political turmoil or the presence of the New Left to survive. It was dependent on a particular kind of audience that craved a particular kind of rock. The hatred of hit singles was not confined to the late 1960s. Groups from the early 1970s such as Yes, Emerson, Lake and Palmer, and Genesis, exponents of so-called art rock, wrote and recorded songs that in length were the pop music equivalent of *War and Peace*, and their fans loved them for it. At the same time, college students enrolled in elite private and public institutions in the 1970s would have rather flunked out of school then get caught listening to an oldies station, or buying a stack of 45s. On these campuses you could be gay, bi, lesbian, or confused, but you didn't dare sing along with "Brandy" by the

Looking Glass. The choices were FM rock and jazz; otherwise transfer to a "party" school.

As the number of listeners increased, profit-minded station managers aggressively pursued advertisers, including those that hocked "conventional" products. Out with head shops or free clinics, and in with cars, furniture, and department store bargains.

Ladd stuck it out, although he was not pleased to see his "baby" kidnapped by corporate America. He continued to combine rock and politics, even as the audience became more apathetic. In the early 1970s, Ladd created a syndicated radio program called *Innerview*, a series of weekly hour-long conversations with the biggest names in rock, including John Lennon, Pink Floyd, Stevie Nicks, and the Eagles. In addition to discussing music, "I would definitely ask them about current issues," said Ladd. Over the course of eleven years, he recorded almost 600 interviews for the program.

Today Ladd is a DJ at Los Angeles radio station KLOS, where he mixes observations about contemporary politics with rock music—most of it recorded from 1966 to 1982. He cannot stand to hear people trash the 1960s, much as a proud military veteran cannot stand to hear some snotty kid trash the United States of America. Ladd one time nearly went berserk over the air when a well-known musician didn't pay proper respect to a couple of rock icons from his favorite decade. "I was once interviewing (the rock group) the Police, and I almost came to blows with the drummer (Stewart Copeland), because I made the 'radical suggestion' that they might owe something to bands like the Grateful Dead and the Jefferson Airplane," said Ladd. "He answered; 'Oh nothing. We don't like them.'" More than fifteen years later, Ladd still seethed over Copeland's seemingly impertinent remark.

⌐⌐

John Lennon is the political iconoclast of late 1960s rock. While many of his peers were embracing the counterculture and radical politics, John had the temerity, indeed the courage, to doubt the seriousness of hippies at the height of Flower Power, and the ethics of student revolutionaries during 1968, the year of Columbia and Paris. Unlike an artist such as Albert Camus, who was ostracized for challenging the tenets of the French left, John paid a small price for challenging the New Left. After all, the protesters were also Beatles fans. "Revolution" received criticism from some quarters, but the song was the flip side of "Hey, Jude," which spent nine weeks at number one. And "All You Need Is Love" is misunderstood to this day, with many people still regarding it as a hippie anthem. John was being ironic with an audience that couldn't even recognize irony when it was directed at them. Along with "Imagine," "All You Need Is Love" has been turned into a memorial to Lennon in the decades since his tragic murder: two songs that (we are told by those in the know) encapsulate his personal philosophy and hope for the world.

This interpretation of the Beatles hit does Lennon a disservice. In a career dedicated to blowing away convention, nothing is more laudatory then Lennon's refusal to hew the youth party line when rock musicians were under considerable pressure to not only go along, but also join the fight. Here is the rare rock star unwilling to let others chart his own political course. His second wife, Yoko Ono, has been credited or blamed for turning her husband into a political animal, but Lennon obviously paid close attention before they officially became a team. Indeed, she may have intentionally or unintentionally curbed his independent streak, which would be unfortunate. John became more politically predictable after he married Yoko.

In the summer of 1967, Scott MacKenzie sang about going to San Francisco with "flowers in your hair," and hippie convert Eric Burdon told the people of San Francisco—as if they needed to be told—that "you are beautiful" in the song "San Franciscan Nights." But "All You Need Is Love" didn't follow the crowd to Haight-Ashbury. In the Beatles song, the hippies have trivialized love, turned it into a game, with easy rules that we can all follow. As if the words weren't sufficient, George Harrison's hilarious guitar solo bends the notes into a kind of sarcastic whine. And yet rather than engage Lennon's barbs, or perhaps concede his points, hippies simply claimed "All You Need Is Love" as their own.

"All You Need Is Love" is cleverer than "Revolution," which somewhat awkwardly rhymes "how" with "Mao," and "hate" with "wait." And yet while "All You Need Is Love" is no longer controversial, "Revolution" can still generate passion, even if we are two generations removed from the events that inspired it. Peter Tork, a huge fan of the Beatles to this day, thought "Revolution" was a terrible song. "Lennon managed to say 'no' to revolutions," observed Tork, "that since you must do it with hate, you can't do it all." On the other hand, Jim Ladd felt Lennon was searching for a spiritual meaning that transcended the pure politics of rebellion. "It (the song) is about a much deeper revolution," said Ladd. "I was hearing that while it's all well and good to march, the real revolution is inside. That's what the message is, and that's the revolutionary message of the 1960s."

Danny Goldberg comes down somewhere in the middle: "'Revolution' is not a call for revolution. It truly represented the sensibilities of the larger audience."

Lennon himself was not entirely at ease with "Revolution." He recorded an acoustic version for the *White Album* that suggested he was ready to man the barricades. Was this political confusion or wanting to have it both ways? The reason for the second take has never been entirely clear. But it's the electric "Revolution" that most people remember, and which is still played on classic rock stations. Both in terms of music and lyrics, the song has aged extremely well. We now know that the radicals did not achieve their particular utopia, and that Chairman Mao was among the one of the most murderous dictators of the twentieth century. As he got older, I suspect Lennon would have been increasingly proud of "Revolution," as well as relieved that he didn't embarrass himself back in '68 with grandiose pronouncements about The Revolution.

Lennon became a 1960s radical in the 1970s, which could be seen in some sense as another example of his unorthodox political style. He and Yoko were among the earliest rock and roll performers to champion the cause of a particular individual being persecuted by the American justice system. In December 1971, the couple participated in a rally to free John Sinclair, the leader of a radical group called the White Panthers. Sinclair had been sentenced to ten years in a Michigan prison for selling two joints to an undercover officer. It doesn't take an unrepentant leftist to recognize this sentence as an injustice and Sinclair as nothing less then a political prisoner. The government obviously wanted to make an example of Mr. Sinclair.

The event included music, speeches, and the distribution of political literature. A few days later, an amazing thing happened; Sinclair was freed from jail.

Buoyed by this success, the couple then turned their attention to a rather more daunting task, the electoral defeat of President Richard Nixon in 1972. Despite conservative rhetoric to the contrary, the Left in the United States rarely achieves victory at the expense of the all-powerful federal government. And yet the outcome of the Sinclair case left John and Yoko feeling very optimistic about winning other "hopeless" fights. According to the writer Jon Wiener, Lennon actually thought that he and his fellow peace activists could take down Nixon, with a little help from millions of their friends.

"Lennon wanted to use his own star power to organize a concert tour that would travel around the country coinciding with primary elections in the different states," said Wiener. The objective was to combine radical politics with a voter registration drive aimed at eighteen to twenty-year-olds, who for the first time would be eligible to cast their ballots in a presidential election.

What John and Yoko could not have anticipated, even from a close reading of *Six Crises*, was the extreme paranoia that Nixon was feeling during the 1972 campaign. Nixon was not going to allow some long-haired, pot-smoking guitarist and his weird Japanese wife to stand in the way of a great triumph at the polls. When South Carolina Republican senator Strom Thurmond, then a sprightly sixty-nine, brought the benefit concert/registration drive strategy to the attention of Nixon, the president's response was to order the Immigration and

Naturalization Service to begin deportation proceedings against Lennon. On the advice of his attorneys, Lennon cancelled the tour. It would be another several years before he gained his U.S. citizenship.

Despite his personal travails, Lennon firmly believed that George McGovern would soundly defeat Richard Nixon in the 1972 presidential election. He was confident that in the end the American electorate would display wisdom and common sense and dump the incumbent. As a result, Lennon took Nixon's landslide victory hard. "He had a total loss of faith in the (antiwar) movement at that point," said Wiener.

John and Yoko continued to be active on behalf of political causes until his death in 1980, although they didn't plan anything on the scale of the proposed 1972 tour. Over the years Yoko has given hundreds of thousands of dollars to a variety of community-oriented groups through the Spirit Foundation, which she and her husband started in the 1970s.

In his final years, John Lennon became an advocate for making ours a better world, rather than concentrating on specific issues, a change of direction reflected in his 1971 song "Imagine." On the one hand, it's hard to criticize a political philosophy that in the end just wants us all to get along. But on the other hand, John and Yoko could at times come across to the public as hopelessly naïve, and even politically unsophisticated. Though the song is blessed with a lovely melody, "Imagine" is ripe for satire, principally because the lyrics are so far removed from the realities of governments and nations as to seem almost laughable. A song that suggests throwing away the last 5,000 years of recorded history and starting over again cannot be taken seriously.

But through no fault of the composer, "Imagine" has become the Great White Hope of love and peace songs, referenced often by those who want the rest of us to stop and think about how we might improve the human condition. Yet unlike "All You Need Is Love," there is nothing ironic about "Imagine"; Lennon meant exactly what he said.

"John and Yoko believed in utopia," said Elliot Mintz, a publicist for, and close friend of, John and Yoko's. "They wanted a cessation of war, and hungry people to be fed."

9

EVERYBODY IS A STAR

One night in 1969 Richard Nixon and his wife, Pat, departed Washington, D.C., to spend the weekend in Florida. They left the care of the White House in charge of their daughter, Tricia, along with maids, cooks, the Secret Service, and assorted others. Tricia decided to throw a party, as young people often do when their parents conveniently go out of town for the weekend. To provide entertainment she invited a folk-rock group, the Turtles, which had had a number one hit in 1967 called "Happy Together." As it happened, the Turtles were a favorite band of Tricia's.

If Tricia had voted for the Grateful Dead or Jimi Hendrix, the White House concert would not have occurred. But the Turtles were a safe choice for the daughter of a Republican who despised the antiwar movement and, presumably, most of late 1960s rock as well. The Turtles were a happy-go-lucky Southern California band with no discernible ties to the drug culture, and they were silent on the big issues of the day, including the Vietnam War. Mark Volman, one of the founding members of the Turtles, even said that the group turned down "Eve of Destruction" because "we didn't understand the politics." The song was then passed on to Barry McGuire, who needless to say was quite delighted by the turn of events.

As Volman recalls, the Turtles performed in the East Room of the White House for an audience that included the children of the members of the House of Representatives and the Senate. "It was just kids having a good time," he said. In the years since, the White House has been the site of several rock and roll "concerts," especially during the Clinton years. But it all began with an invitation from the daughter of Richard Milhous Nixon.

A couple of nights after the East Room gig, the Turtles played at the Fillmore East in New York, before an audience that must have included hippies, freaks, radicals, and maybe some anarchists as well.

~~

On April 30, 1970, President Nixon went on television to announce that the United States had invaded Cambodia—the precise word he used was "incursion"—in order to rout enemy forces that been staging attacks on American troops stationed inside neighboring Vietnam. "An allied force of twenty thousand men, supported by American aircraft, was attacking the two main North Vietnamese and Vietcong bases in Cambodia as Nixon spoke."[1]

The invasion of Cambodia prompted a new wave of campus protests across the nation. Of all these demonstrations, the one that is still recalled occurred on Monday, May 4, 1970, at Kent State University in Ohio, where the Ohio National Guard fired on a group of protesters, killing four and wounding nine. For five years prior to Kent State, the antiwar movement had coordinated hundreds, if not thousands, of demonstrations and none of them had resulted in the death of a single participant. Even the 1968 Democratic Convention in Chicago— bloody though it was—ended without a fatality.

Although demonstrators were the victims and not the perpetrators at Kent State, the killings traumatized movement organizers, and in a kind of perverse way might have contributed to a decline in the number and size of antiwar demonstrations from that point forward. College protesters were by and large not terrorists or martyrs. If death was the price to pay for hurling rocks or screaming obscenities, then perhaps it was time to retrench. Unless, of course, one was willing to kill, in which case both the Weather Underground and later the Symbionese Liberation Army were viable options.

Kent State hardly registered among rock and roll bands. The shootings took place as the audience was contending with the breakup of the Beatles, the aftermath of Altamont, revelations that mass murderer Charles Manson was inspired by the Beatles' song "Helter Skelter," and a sinking feeling that the end of the 1960s meant that the good times were over. Kent State was just one more bummer in a long list of bummers.

Crosby, Stills, Nash, and Young, however, refused to join the rush to the exits. Soon after the event, the group recorded a song called "Ohio," the lyrics of which blamed President Nixon for the killings, a view shared by many on the Left. This would not be the only time that CSNY mined daily newspapers for ideas. Over the next few years the group recorded songs about political events that especially resonated with the hippie/anti-war demonstrator contingent, such as Kent State, Woodstock, and the 1968 Democratic Convention, which was the topic of "Chicago" (1971), a song that Graham Nash released on his own. Neil Young's "Southern Man"—the title sounds like something out of the Phil Ochs school of songwriting—inspired a kind of rock and roll version of "Crossfire." In 1974, Lynyrd Skynyrd put out "Sweet Home Alabama," which referenced Young and his ignorance of southern ways. Eventually Neil Young and the guys from Lynyrd Skynyrd made their peace, like retired Democratic and Republican senators who once battled over issues that had since diminished in importance.

"Ohio" was one of the last Vietnam, or Vietnam-related, rock and roll songs from the late 1960s and early 1970s. The few rock groups that wanted to say something about the war followed the agenda of the antiwar movement. When the size and amount of demonstrations against the war in Vietnam began to decrease, so did the number of songs about the war, or its cumulative effects on society. By 1971, President Nixon was bringing the boys home, as well as seeming to avoid any more "incursions" that could ignite a new round of protests. In the spring of 1972, Nixon ordered the mining of Haiphong Harbor to prevent Soviet matériel from reaching the North Vietnamese army. But the accompanying protests were small in comparison with those from the period 1967 to 1970, no doubt in part because this action didn't involve using American forces in combat.

Leaving the fate of Vietnam to the Vietnamese drastically reduced the power and prestige of the antiwar movement and the New Left. And to the regret of its founders, the New Left has been unable to re-claim its past glory. Various attempts have resembled once-retired rock bands reuniting to make a new album. The results are invariably either a tired retread or a misguided attempt to sound contemporary. There re-main pockets of the New Left, mainly on college campuses, but they have come up with nothing tangible to oppose, such as Vietnam or seg-regation in Mississippi. Instead, they fulminate against racism, sexism, heterosexism, patriarchal culture, and American influence around the world. Having set out thirty-five years earlier to change the world, and achieve a revolution of the mind, body, and soul, there is nowhere to go but down. The irony is that the remnants of the New Left have sul-lied if not destroyed the reputation of the actual movement, as it ex-isted in the 1960s.

The splintering of the Left into many component parts, which at times work at cross-purposes, has had a residual effect on rock. Cate-gories within rock are now akin to the course listing at a typical liberal arts college. You have feminist rock, Chicano rock, gay rock (a small sample), and black rock, which is necessary only because blacks in the 1960s and 1970s derided rock as "white boy music." Jimi Hendrix, brilliant guitarist though he was, had to deal with criticism from African Americans for having gone over to the other side.

Not surprisingly, in the last two decades rock has been transformed into an all-purpose political tool, with individual performers or groups lending their name or musical talents to numerous causes, most of them associated with liberals and the Democratic Party. These have included abortion rights, feminism, the environment, economic justice, gay rights, the needs of People of Color, the fight against world hunger, and the battle against AIDS. The character of rock's political activism today resembles that of Hollywood, which to a diehard fan is rather appalling. Hollywood stands for glamour, glitzy premiers, happy endings, tearjerkers, artifice, and air kisses. Rock doesn't. Everyone knows actors really want to be rock stars and that rock stars consider acting a joke, even after they have been in a film or two. Look what happened to Elvis once he started making movies: his music turned to crap. For rock to emulate Hollywood on any level is an admission of defeat.

But if you thought benefit concerts a bore, were indifferent toward the fate of the whales, believed rock should steer clear of liberal causes, a foe of Women's Liberation, and born between 1952 and 1957, what option did you have in the early 1970s? Why not heavy metal? As female rock groups made some gains, and the Rolling Stones toned down egregiously anti-women lyrics (no more songs in the vein of "Under My Thumb"), there arrived the most blatantly macho movement in the history of the genre. To young boys who desperately needed fantasies of male dominance and control, especially at a time when even their dads felt threatened by the rise of the New Woman, heavy metal was an absolute godsend. This music was intended for teenage boys first and foremost; girls were allowed to hang around as long as they played by the rules, which essentially meant making themselves available to "party" with the guys. The heavy metal rockers came on like barbarians from the fifth century A.D., wielding their guitars like swords, stomping across the stage, and swinging their long and probably unwashed hair from side to side. You can bet that the Goths, Visigoths, and Huns didn't have to put up with women's lib. Black Sabbath and Deep Purple were the prototypical heavy metal bands of the early 1970s. Led Zeppelin had their moments, but Robert Plant's flower power lyrics made the group suspect. And then "Stairway to Heaven" came out in late 1971, which was adored by girls for godsakes! Many nonmetal fans bought the album *Zeppelin IV* just to hear that song. After "Stairway," Led Zeppelin was effectively banished from the ranks of true heavy metal.

Radical chic, the practice of precious politics, and the legacy of the 1960s have at various times inspired counter-reactions within rock and roll. The identification of some rock performers with left-wing causes smacked of elitism, a sense that they had the moral authority to tell the rest of us how and what to think. Sting is a contemporary example of this, particularly his preoccupation with the fate of the rain forest. And despite rock's having been accepted if not embraced by professors, corporate America, and increasingly, mainstream politicians, a segment of the audience has been disgusted by this development. These fans have been for the most part middle-class teenagers that look to rock—as their elders did—to provide an alternative to polite society. By the mid-1970s, trendy events on behalf of trendy causes fit the definition. When you include the rules of political correctness, strictly observed on such occasions, then the environment becomes almost unbearable.

Heavy metal, and later punk, seemed to rebel against this side of rock life. Of course, punk was deliberately provocative in its politics, whereas heavy metal was merely suggestive. Indeed, I can't recall the best-selling heavy metal performers of the 1970s—Black Sabbath, Deep Purple, Alice Cooper, Grand Funk Railroad, KISS—saying much of anything about feminism, except perhaps to answer critics. The one exception is Ted Nugent—who had his breakthrough in the late 1960s. Through the years Nugent has embraced a range of conservative positions, of which opposition to the feminist worldview is but one. Above all, it's the stud image, pyrotechnics, and guitar heroics (a holdover from the 1960s) that for three decades have captured the hearts and minds of teenaged white guys from Chelsea, Massachusetts, to West Covina, California.

Let college kids groove on the concept of rock as a force for social and political change; there were other fans that would rather get wasted and rowdy at a Sabbath concert. They listened to escape the "real world," and not to have their own politics validated by a rock star with a good heart. Rock and pop in the 1970s offered something for everybody: the highly educated, the academically challenged, right-wingers, left-wingers, sexists, and the New Man.

⌒

And now, equal time for the other side. There is no universal theory that can adequately explain why rock absorbed to varying degrees the personality of the Left in the 1970s and 1980s. It's not as if rock and pop deliberately sought to curry favor with the youth of America by waiving the flag of post–Vietnam liberalism. And as the example of heavy metal indicates, it could be good for business to move to the right. Still, left-wing politics provides a framework to understand some of the trends that took hold in the early and mid-1970s.

FEMINISM AND ROCK

In an article on the 2000 Republican presidential campaign of Elizabeth Dole—who was elected to the U.S. Senate from North Carolina in 2002—a GOP consultant named Alex Castellanos told a reporter that, "she has to have a message beyond 'I am woman, hear me roar.'"[2] Where would we be without Helen Reddy's number hit from 1972, "I Am Woman," which begins with the line quoted above? How many times over the past three decades have stories about powerful or ambitious women found a way to work the opening of "I Am Woman" into the narrative? Like *Ms. Magazine*, the song has survived the transition from women's liberation to feminism, and from feminism to postfeminism. "I Am Woman" has had a shelf life longer than *Our Bodies, Our Selves*. Talk about a classic.

Even men have been known to go around singing the lyrics, which is tantamount to an anti-war protester taking a stab at "Ballad of the Green Berets." But before you start saying "Alan Alda," it should be noted that the song has a superb hook and strong vocal. The "I am strong, I am invincible" coda is like the grand finale of a Broadway musical, except that upon hearing it, you feel like marching instead of dancing.

"I Am Woman" was released the same year that the Equal Rights Amendment passed the Senate and Shirley Chisholm ran for president.

A month after it reached number one in December 1972, the Supreme Court rendered its decision in *Roe v. Wade*. It had been a very good year indeed for the women's movement. Never in the history of rock and roll has a political song been so brilliantly timed. "'I Am Woman' was a statement of female pride and solidarity articulated with a directness that had never before reached the pop Top 10."[3]

The words certainly don't stand close inspection, as either poetry or a profound statement of the position of women in society. How many females do you know who can say the line "I am woman, hear me roar," with a straight face? But the song has been destined to serve a higher purpose—the political rather than the personal. It is not just a hit, but an anthem. For three decades women have sung "I Am Woman" at pro-choice demonstrations and other politically appropriate gatherings.

Alas, Helen Reddy did not go on to become the Gloria Steinem of the *Billboard* charts. Her subsequent hit records were apolitical, and often country-tinged, including "Delta Dawn" and "Angie Baby." She even had a song that cracked the Top 10 in 1975 called "Ain't No Way to Treat a Lady," a title that conjures up the bygone days when wives were subjugated by sexist husbands, and women on the fast track were scorned by the boy's club at the top.

"I Am Woman" notwithstanding, few hit singles from the 1970s and 1980s directly addressed either feminism as a political philosophy, the condition of women in American society, or eradicating male chauvinism. As rock groups discovered during the height of the Vietnam War, it's no easy task to write a three or four-minute song about a complicated and controversial issue. The difficulty lies less in figuring out what to say as in how to say it, especially given that apprehensive radio programmers are ready to pounce on anything that smacks of controversy. If a performer wants to placate or even enroll in the Left, the wisest course is probably to declare his or her solidarity with this or that movement, and readily agree to play at a rally or two.

As with heavy metal, however, there were some mainstream singles released in the mid-1970s that could be construed a response to feminism and changing women's roles. Pop music is in danger if it overdoses on traditional values, but done in moderation, the results can be pure gold. In the summer of 1974, Paul Anka, who had not had a Top 10 record since 1960, recorded "(You're) Having My Baby." The song went to number one, and became after "Lonely Boy" the second biggest hit in Anka's career. Had Anka released the song in the late 1950s, it would have survived without a scratch. But a decade later he received flack from feminists, offended by the suggestion giving birth is the most valuable service that a woman can perform, and the real reason she is here on God's earth. In the long run, feminists would have been better off leaving the song alone. The perception that feminism ridiculed women having children and choosing to stay at home with them did the movement irreparable harm, and contributed in no small way to the right-wing's successful attack on the legacy of the 1960s. Indeed, women were probably the main consumers of "(You're) Having My Baby." Somehow I can't see many men buying a song with that title, except as a gift.

Still, progress was made on other fronts. It can't be simple coincidence that a confident crop of female rockers happened on the scene in the 1970s, 1980s, and 1990s. We are no longer talking girl groups—who usually came across as talented, friendly, and approachable—but women that acted tough and strong, and played their own instruments. In other words, they were now more like their male counterparts. The new female performers were reincarnations of the Shangri-Las, those take-no-shit girls from the middle of the 1960s, only louder and more assertive. These women didn't want to date the leader of the pack, but lead the pack themselves.

Until the 1970s, Janis Joplin was the lone female superstar in the virtually all-male worlds of hard rock, acid rock, and blues/rock. She completely overshadowed the all-male band playing behind her, known otherwise as Big Brother and the Holding Company. Only rock and roll trivia buffs can break down Big Brother into its individual parts, while everybody has heard of Janis Joplin.

Janis left the band in 1968 and embarked on a solo career that included the album *Pearl*, which reached number one on the LP charts.

A single taken from that album, "Me and Bobby McGee," made it to number one in 1971. Unfortunately, Janis was not around to enjoy the success of either the album or the single. She died of a heroin overdose in Los Angeles on October 4, 1970, the kind of tragic end usually associated with men in rock.

Still, Janis, like Grace Slick of the Jefferson Airplane, was a vocalist. Even sexist fans could accept the notion if not the reality of a woman as lead singer. But it would take much more to convince them and other fans—male and female—that a woman could play lead guitar, bass, or drums. A woman who did more than hold a microphone threatened rock and roll's stereotypical male/female divide. Besides, it just looked weird.

In the 1960s, female guitar players gravitated toward acoustic folk, including Janis Ian, Joan Baez, Mary Travers, and Joni Mitchell. These performers sold many records—by the standards of that genre—and were better known than many rock and roll bands. On occasion, they had crossover hits on the pop charts; Janis Ian's 1967 song "Society's Child" about a white girl/black boy romance reached number fourteen, and aroused the ire of some conservative groups. Judy Collins' beautiful rendition of "Both Sides Now," a song written by Joni Mitchell, went as high as number eight in 1968.

The other famous women in pop music in the 1960s were vocalists, including Mama Cass, Marianne Faithfull, Aretha Franklin, Linda Ronstadt, Dionne Warwick, and the Supremes. The Supremes in particular sold more records than all but a few of the all-male rock and roll bands, and during the 1960s and 1970s they had twenty Top 10 hits. But none of the all-female groups played instruments in public.

You had to be paying close attention to find women that did anything other then provide vocals in the 1960s. Several years ago I was looking through *Rock Explosion: The British Invasion in Photos 1962–1967*, which was published by Rhino Books in 1984. On page 45 is a picture of the Honeycombs—a five-member band that had a big hit with "Have I the Right" in November 1964. I remembered the song, could even sing most of the words, but I didn't know that the drummer was a woman named Honey Lantree, described in the accompanying caption as the "first female rock drummer." This was not a case of tokenism. Ms. Lantree doesn't just keep time on "Have I the Right," she pounds the skins in the style of Dave Clark, leader of the Dave Clark Five, on that group's 1964 hit "Bits and Pieces." If the Honeycombs had been more than a one-hit wonder, we would have read about Honey Lantree. At the same time, "Have I the Right" was released only a year after publication of *The Feminine Mystique*, and a full four years before the women's movement garnered widespread media attention. We weren't yet celebrating examples of women breaking the glass ceiling.

Karen Carpenter played drums for the Carpenters, which had their first massive hit in the summer of 1970 with "(They Long to Be) Close to You," the number four song for the entire year. By this point women's lib had been "discovered" by the mainstream media, and yet I can't recall Karen Carpenter receiving kudos for tackling a traditional male role. In her 1992 book, *She's a Rebel: The History of Women in Rock and Roll*, author Gillian G. Garr barely mentions that Karen played drums, and instead devotes much more copy to the singer's battle with anorexia. Of course, Karen poses a bit of a problem for feminist writers or writers with feminist leanings. Although she may have broken new ground—female drummer in a hugely successful group—the music of the Carpenters was geared toward middle America, President Nixon's Silent Majority. Nixon—Richard not Tricia—invited the group to perform at the White House in 1973, and according to Garr he said they represented "young America at its very best." This was not the sort of praise that would count with Germaine Greer or Gloria Steinem.

In the period from 1970 to 1975, the all-female groups Fancy and Fanny, along with the solo performer and ass-kicking guitarist Suzi Quatro, demonstrated that old barriers had started to crumble. None of these bands had big hits, although Fancy released a cover of the Troggs' "Wild Thing" that made it to number fourteen in 1974, but neither were they laughed off the stage. Quatro parlayed her name identification into a role as Leather Tuscadero on the hit television show about the 1950s, *Happy Days*, which made its debut in 1974. On the show, Quatro played a rock and roll star (naturally), and among other songs performed a cover of Elvis Presley's "All Shook Up," which she had actually released a year or so before joining the series.

The producers of *Happy Days* had a recurring habit of mining the 1970s for ideas and plots that could be applied to a program ostensibly about the 1950s. It's doubtful—though not impossible—that kids in suburban Milwaukee would have been treated to the likes of Leather Tuscadero/Suzi Quatro around 1958. But since when should authenticity get in the way of the never-ending quest for ratings?

Rock and roll does not practice affirmative action or a quota system. In a billion-dollar business that tries, with varying success, to predict the fickle tastes of teens, college students, and baby boomers, it would be bad policy for companies to stipulate that a certain percentage of bands had to be Asian, Latino, gay, female, vertically challenged, or disabled. (For obvious reasons, African American is not included in this mix). The many record executives and producers that profess to be good Democrats might well support affirmative action—just as long as it's practiced somewhere else.

By the same token, record labels have no qualms whatsoever about signing gay, Asian, or female bands if they perceive the chance to make lots of money. That's the goal, after all, and everything else is subordinate to it. Over the past ten years some record executives have acted like the producers of slasher films, promoting violent material— specifically rap songs about killing cops, or having one's way with "bitches" and "hoes"—and then citing the First Amendment when others raise questions about marketing the stuff to teenagers. The record business has tangled with self-appointed arbiters of taste that hail from both ends of the political spectrum. At the same time, lowering of standards has rarely if ever presented a moral dilemma for any branch of the entertainment business.

But there are times when the quest for new hot acts runs parallel to political developments, thereby making everyone happy. During the six years from 1975 to 1981, Heart, Pat Benatar, the Pretenders (Chrissie Hynde and the guys), Joan Jett, the Bangles, Cyndi Lauper, and the Go-Gos recorded and released a series of excellent singles. In late 1983, Madonna released "Holiday," and a major female star was born, although not one who played an instrument. In the 1990s, Hole—led by Courtney Love—and Melissa Etheridge were among a number of female performers who contributed to the advancement of rock and roll. Today the notion of women playing electric guitar, drums, keyboard, and bass is no more exotic or surprising than the existence of the Women's National Basketball Association—an ingrained part of American life at the dawn of the twenty-first century.

JEWS, GAYS, AND ROCK

Rock and roll has always been reasonably hospitable to Jews and gays, those two "groups" without whom the American musical theater could never have achieved such prominence. Jewish contributors are numerous, including Phil Spector, Simon and Garfunkel, Mike Bloomfield, and, of course, Bob Dylan. If early rock and roll or folk/music is not your preference, there is always Gene Simmons of KISS, who was raised in a family of Hasidic rabbis only to grow up to become one of rock's most sexually promiscuous performers ever—and that's saying something.

As for gays, one need look no further than Little Richard, who was as flamboyant for his time as anyone on Broadway, which was and probably is the best environment for a gay male or lesbian performer to achieve sexual orientation nirvana. And compared with the movie business, which is notably hypocritical on the subject of who is and who isn't gay, rock and roll has for decades evinced a healthy disregard for sexual preference. The rumors and innuendo involving various big-name actors—a kind of Hollywood tradition—has no parallel in rock. This is not to suggest that drummers, lead singers, or guitar players are no more or no less homo/heterosexual than movie stars, only that it doesn't seem to matter much to *their* public what they do and whom they do it with. When Elton John revealed his homosexuality in the mid-1970s, for example, it not only didn't hurt his career, but he also continued to play to sold-out audiences across Europe and the United States. And David Bowie, one of the pioneers of modern-day androgynous rock, may well be the only performer in the entire history of the entertainment business to have come out of the closet as a heterosexual. During the early and mid-1970s, when Bowie was either sexually experimental, gay, or presumed to be gay, he sold millions of records in England and America. Admitting to a preference for women could have been a career-breaker for him.

In the 1960s, redneck enemies of post-Beatles rock and roll would yell such choice insults as "fag" or "queer" at musicians who wore their hair long, but this hardly caused the band members to run to their local barbershop. If anything, rock musicians took these snide comments to mean they were doing something right, considering the source. In the last three decades, homosexual or effeminate stereotypes (mincing, prancing, eye shadow, cross-dressing . . .) have served rock and roll quite well, especially when employed by straight or bisexual performers who wish to offend—yet again—the sensibilities of middle-class parents.

By the same token, homophobia has never been a big problem in rock and roll. In the last two decades, as gay politics have become more visible, vocal, and assertive, there has been occasional controversy, usually due to stupid comments from some musician regarding AIDS, the supposed sexual practices of gays, or same-sex couples in general. But this happens on a case-by-case basis, and it not typical of the entire scene. The same cannot be said of rap, which has had several run-ins with homosexual rights groups due to offensive lyrics or degrading comments.

I have read the argument that the Rolling Stones' "Let's Spend the Night Together" from early 1967 is about the desire of the lead singer to spend the night with a man. After hearing the song probably a hundred times, I still can't arrive at a definitive conclusion. Perhaps you had to be there. In any event, there is as far as I can tell no gay equivalent of "I Am Woman," or certainly not one that went as high on the charts. More common are songs such as "He's the Greatest Dancer," a 1979 disco hit for Sister Sledge, which could be all things to all sexual preferences. Straight women and gay men can lust after the hero, who is being checked out while dancing at a "disco in Frisco" (how much more obvious can you get then that?), while a straight man can imagine a hot babe is looking at him. I suppose there is little here for lesbians, but you can't please all the people all the time.

Openly gay groups are rare in rock, and generally confined to the margins, whether by choice or realities of the market. In 1978, the Tom Robinson Band, from England, released "Glad to Be Gay," which garnered considerable attention on the strength of its unusually blunt title. This was not the kind of song a young man in a suburban high school could sing out loud unless he had a strong sense of self. Still, the Tom Robinson Band never sold a sufficient number of copies of this or any other record to make much of an impact: "Glad to Be Gay" did not lead to a spate of gay power rock and roll songs.

Which is probably a good thing for Tom Robinson, because later in life he married a woman with whom he had a child. The turn of events reportedly upset some in the gay community, which can be both fiercely protective of its own and extremely hostile to "turncoats." Gay leaders can take some comfort, however, that Robinson will likely never record a song called "Glad to Be Straight."

When historians rattle off the names of key events in the 1960s, one of the least known to the general public is called Stonewall, in actuality the name of a gay pub in Greenwich Village. On June 27, 1969, Stonewall clientele, depressed by the death of Judy Garland and sick and tired of being harassed by the police, this time fought back when officers entered the establishment. "Stonewall sparked a nationwide liberation struggle; it also led to more open, assertive statements of homosexuality."[4] The Stonewall riot happened to roughly coincide with the breakup of the Beatles, which represented liberation of a different sort, although despondent rock fans would not have dared to suggest any such thing in the summer and fall of 1969. But for the first time in more than five years, rock and roll groups did not have to worry about what the Beatles might be planning next. This was especially advantageous to the Rolling Stones, who made their finest albums when they stopped chasing the Beatles and went back to being themselves. The four albums the Stones released between 1968 and 1972—*Beggar's Banquet, Let It Bleed, Sticky Fingers,* and *Exile on Main Street*—are as good as any quartet of LPs by any group in rock and roll history, including the Beatles. The end of the Beatles was also good news for Brian Wilson of the Beach Boys—or it should have been—but by then he had turned into such an emotional wreck trying to top Lennon and McCartney that nothing could restore his damaged psyche to health.

With the Beatles essentially out of the picture, pop music branched out in several different directions, including heavy metal, singer/songwriter (Jackson Browne, James Taylor, Cat Stevens), and something called glam (short for glamour), which originated in England. While the connection between glam and Stonewall is tenuous at best, glam in many ways did for rock and roll what Stonewall did for gay politics. Before glam, you had Little Richard and, on occasion, Mick Jagger, but theirs were individual displays of effeminacy, and not precursors of a genuine subculture within rock and roll.

The unofficial founder of glam was David Bowie, virtually unknown to Americans in the 1960s, and a minor figure at best in his native Britain. Barney Hoskyns, author of a book on glam, actually identified the month, year, and event that brought glam into the world—a concert by Bowie in London in February 1970. On that night, Bowie "wore a glittery 'Rainbowman' costume and blue hair."[5]

The title of Hoskyns' book is *Glam! Bowie, Bolan and the Glitter Rock Revolution.* "Bolan" is Marc Bolan, the leader of the group T. Rex, which was huge in Britain from 1971 to 1974, although less successful with American fans, who showed poor judgment in this case. T. Rex painted odd, and at times enchanting, lyrics on a Chuck Berry canvas. The band played beautifully executed basic rock and roll, in songs with such offbeat titles as "Bang a Gong," "Telegram Sam," "The Slider," and "Jeepster." The band's massive British hit from 1972, "Metal Guru," is the *Rocky Horror Picture Show* soundtrack with power chords. Bolan, the vocalist, was like an actor who is adept at comedy, drama, and love scenes. He could sound funny on one song, shy on another, and sly and sexy on a third. Lennon could pull this off, McCartney couldn't, and Jagger had a mixed record.

Glitter clinched the deal for T. Rex in Britain. Bolan employed lots of it, plus makeup and nail polish, as did the other members of the group. The combination of pounding rock, macho lyrics, and a feminine touch excited teenage girls. Perhaps some of the girls thought they could "convert" the pretty lead singer. Perhaps they liked looking at images of themselves—from the neck up. Of course, if the girls were turned on, the boys had to pay attention. But was Bolan gay or not? And what about Bowie? Did it matter?

In his music, Bowie swung both ways, recording songs about boy/girl situations, boy/boy situations, and others where you needed a listener's guide to sort it all out. For example, "John, I'm Only Dancing" from 1973 tells the story of a man dancing with a woman while his ostensible boyfriend ("John") fumes on the sidelines. A year later, Bowie released the blatantly heterosexual "Suffragette City," which either dispelled doubters or further clouded the issue of his own preferences. One thing was clear after Bowie: a bisexual songwriter, or a songwriter assuming the persona of a bisexual, had twice the possibilities as did his gay or straight peers.

Before Will and Grace, Ellen and Anne, or Ian McKellen and whomever, there was Lou and Marilyn. You don't remember Lou and Marilyn? Check out the back cover of Lou Reed's 1972 album, *Transformer*. Reed, a couple of years removed from the Velvet Underground, put out a solo album that included the song "Walk on the Wild Side," which did for transvestite/straight guy sex what "Louie Louie" did for the boy/girl variety. Like that earlier song, the listener could not quite believe what he or she was hearing in "Walk on the Wild Side."

Did Lou Reed really say that? Yes he did, and he meant it too. In 1970, the Kinks released "Lola," which was about a man having a dance with a gorgeous woman who turns out to be a man. That song broke new ground, but in "Walk on the Wild Side" the lead character does much more than dance.

At sixteen, when I first laid eyes on *Transformer,* I figured Marilyn was a woman in the traditional sense of the word. She looked quite beautiful, and I remember thinking to myself that Lou Reed was one lucky guy. It was a bit of a surprise to learn the true story about his friend a year or so later.

In the mid-1970s, Queen broke through in England and America, and over the next decade they would become one of the biggest bands in the world. Like "Velvet Underground," the name "Queen" was suggestive, but that didn't prevent kids in the suburbs from buying millions of their albums. Girls developed crushes on the lead singer, Freddie Mercury, who spent his nights cruising for men. In the early 1980s, Boy George became a star, although his music and image was far removed from the aggressive sexuality of Bowie, Bolan, and Reed. Boy George committed the unpardonable sin—in the eyes of straight rock fans—of being both gay and a wimp. Still, for those who track such things, his was another name to add to the list of homosexual rock stars. It's now accepted that a man or a woman can come out and rock out at the same time.

LATINOS AND ROCK

Around the time Negroes officially changed their name to blacks, let's say 1968, young Mexican American activists insisted that they be called Chicanos. The media duly complied, and a new noun was born, although not one with which all Mexican Americans were comfortable by any means. The Chicano movement and the rise of 1960s-style ethnic pride among Hispanics had a strong influence over the music performed by Mexican American bands. Yet this was not the first time American audiences were treated to a variety of Latin music. Long before the advent of Chicano politics, the rhumba, samba, mambo, and salsa had been both successful and influential in the States. "Virtually all of the popular (American) forms—Tin Pan Alley, stage and film music, jazz, rhythm-and-blues, country blues, and rock—have been affected throughout their development by the idioms of Brazil, Cuba, or Mexico."[6] Desi Arnaz, Xavier Cugat, Perez Prado, Tito Puente, and other Latin artists did very well with Anglo and black audiences in America.

Latin rock is a direct result of the political and musical environment of the period from 1967 to 1970, especially in Southern California. The changeover from rock and roll to rock caught East L.A.—the hub of the Mexican American community—by surprise. Teenagers had created an entire subculture based on attending dances on Friday and Saturday nights where sometimes as many as eight or nine local groups would play fifteen to twenty minute sets each. But when the music turned serious and profound, and when an extended blues solo took the place of a fifteen-second (Chuck) Berryesque guitar lead, dancing became passé. The Chicano performers that didn't go into retirement at that point were faced with a crucial career decision: To jam or not to jam? That was the question.

Bands that in 1964 and 1965 played rock and roll and rhythm and blues were inspired, or in some instances compelled to add Latin rhythms and melodies, timbales, conga, and other traditional Mexican instruments to their sound and repertoire. It was a gesture of political solidarity as much as it was a musical statement. A few years earlier, fledgling Mexican American rock and roll performers had wanted little to do with traditional Mexican music, which was pushed aside in favor of the Rolling Stones, Beatles, Motown, and James Brown. And besides, Mexican music was what their parents played in the house on Sunday afternoons. Rock and roll was for Saturday nights on the boulevard.

But by the end of the 1960s the streets contained demonstrators chanting "Viva La Raza," and newly formed organizations such as the Brown Berets marching under the Mexican flag. Chicano politics—also tied to

opposition to the war in Vietnam—was omnipresent in East L.A. beginning in 1968. The local bands couldn't have escaped it if they tried—the
activists and the musicians came from the same neighborhoods. A few
years earlier, members of the Brown Berets—the most visible young activists in East L.A. in the 1960s—had attended dances around Southern
California to see these same groups perform live. Local bands ignored
the movement at their peril. In this new climate, it could appear retro or
even self-loathing for a Chicano group to continue to perform its version
of classic American rock and roll and rhythm and blues.

Thee Midniters, formed in East L.A. in the early 1960s, had started
out with the goal of becoming the best rock and roll/R&B/hard
rock/slow ballad/Mexican American band with a horn section on the
planet. To note that they were the only one is not meant to diminish
their accomplishment. Thee Midniters left behind an excellent and
eclectic body of work, including a gutsy cover of Frank Sinatra's
"Strangers in the Night" from 1966, the year of *Revolver* and "Good
Vibrations." When the time came to shift to politics, Thee Midniters
were able to make a reasonably smooth transition, due to their musical
skills above all. In late 1968, a Latin-tinged instrumental that one of
the horn players had written a year or so earlier was recorded with the
title of "Chicano Power." To ensure that listeners got the point, the
band chanted "Chicano power" at the end of the song.

Sound was not the only indicator of having the proper politics.
Many Chicano groups that formed at the end of the 1960s took Spanish names, which had not happened before. These included Tierra, El
Chicano, and a few years later, Los Lobos who also like to call themselves "Just Another Band from East L.A." All of these groups were
influenced by Carlos Santana and the band Santana, which proved the
commercial possibilities of Latin rock with hits such as "Oye Como
Va" (number thirteen in 1971). White kids who couldn't pronounce the
Spanish lyrics and had no idea what they meant went out and bought
the song anyway. Executives began to see that maybe there was something to this Latin rock stuff. In 1972, the group Malo—which featured
Carlos Santana's brother Jorge on guitar—had a hit with "Suavecito."

The song's California sunshine groove has influenced white, brown, and black bands, most recently Sugar Ray.

Of course, the one single by a Mexican American that every Anglo rock fan knows, even if the lyrics are virtually incomprehensible, is "La Bamba." Weddings where neither the bride nor the groom invited a single guest with a Spanish surname will still feature a DJ playing "La Bamba" during the reception. College bands in regions of the country where sightings of Chicanos or Latinos are rare have performed the song during the obligatory halftime show.

Ritchie Valens, who recorded "La Bamba" in 1958, began his career in the late 1950s, when there were many Mexican American rock and roll fans, but very few Mexican American rock and roll performers. When Valens first started giving shows in the neighborhood around his San Fernando Valley home of Pacoima, he went by his real name of Richard Valenzuela. But then Bob Keane signed Valenzuela to a deal. Keane was an Anglo manager who vigorously pursued Southern California acts of any race, color, creed, or religion. Keane suggested to Ritchie that it might be better to drop the surname Valenzuela in favor of one not Spanish. According to Keane's later account, the problem was not so much that Anglo kids would refuse to buy rock and roll performed by a Mexican American (even racist kids purchased songs by black artists) but that they would assume someone named Valenzuela played that South of the Border junk. Whether or not Ritchie bought that argument, he agreed to make the switch. Teenage rock musicians just starting out don't have much say in these matters.

Valens went on to have a short-lived yet extraordinary career. He sang mostly in English, with the notable exception of "La Bamba." His 1958 single "Come On, Let's Go," later covered by the Ramones, was rock and roll in a punk mode years before punk was invented. The ballad "Donna" was an early example of the guitar-based slow dance numbers characteristic of the first wave of British Invasion groups. To white kids, Ritchie Valens was a seventeen-year old who played great rock and roll, but to Mexican American kids, he was that plus a symbol of hope to those trying to make it in the music business.

Valens died at the age of seventeen on February 3, 1959, in a plane crash that also killed Buddy Holly and the Big Bopper. Bob Dylan, Mick Jagger, and John Lennon had not even started writing songs at seventeen. After Valens died, Mexican American rock and roll took a leave of absence, more out of shock and mourning then reverence.

The arrival of the Beatles and the rise of Motown inspired hundreds of Chicano kids, some too young to remember much about Ritchie Valens, to get into rock and roll. Thee Midniters, Cannibal and the Headhunters, and the Blendells were among the Mexican American groups from Southern California, while Sam the Sham and the Pharaohs and Question Mark and the Mysterians hailed from other parts of the country. Together these groups released many quality singles in the mid-1960s, even though all but a few were and are unknown to the general public.

Chicano politics took some of the fun out of Chicano rock and roll, and yet the quality of music improved. For three decades, Los Lobos has represented the history of Chicano rock and roll in miniature. The group has sung in English, sung in Spanish, played rock, funk, and soul, as well as traditional Mexican folk from various regions of the country. They performed on the soundtrack to the movie *La Bamba*, and for their next act they recorded an album in Spanish, *La Pistola y El Corazón*, which won a Grammy. The members of Los Lobos continue to immerse themselves in American, Mexican American, and Latino popular music. Given current population trends, Los Lobos would seem to represent one vision of the future of pop music, and not just for Chicano performers.

AFRICAN AMERICANS AND ROCK

The Nixon administration (1968–1974) was not a good friend to black Americans, except perhaps those with lots of money. Thomas Byrne and Mary D. Edsall wrote that Richard Nixon in the 1972 campaign . . . "set out to establish positive grounds for the rejection of the kinds of social responsibilities that were raised by the civil

rights movement—presaging the conservative ideological framework articulated far more consistently by Ronald Reagan."[7] Nixon
was the first Republican presidential candidate to openly court those
white voters who believed that the civil rights movement, though
noble at the beginning, had gone too far. He also took the important
extra step of assuring them that they were not racists for feeling that
way. Simultaneously appealing to race and easing the conscience of
white voters has become a staple of Republican campaigns for over
three decades. Nixon gave the GOP a blueprint for running the
post–civil rights movement, race-based campaign strategy, which
eschews the "N word" and racist stereotypes but still conveys an us
against them message to working-class and suburban voters. For example, it's widely believed that Vice President George Bush won the
1988 presidential contest because his team skillfully used the story
of Willie Horton, a black criminal who raped a white woman while
out on furlough, against Democrat Michael Dukakis.

Soul and funk groups released a surfeit of political hit songs during
the reign of Nixon, few of which referred even obliquely to the president himself. Cause and effect is difficult to prove, but black performers seemed more willing to write about social and political conditions
during the Nixon administration then during the previous administration of Lyndon Johnson, who had an extraordinary record on civil
rights. As was the case with white groups and the Vietnam War, it
would seem that crisis conditions are required before pop artists will
record songs with social or political substance. The Nixon administration's "benign neglect" of the black community, and the leadership
void created by the murders of Malcolm X and Martin Luther King,
constituted one of these moments.

But before heading off into the 1970s, there were a couple of political songs recorded by tremendously popular black performers during
the 1960s that are worth discussing.

In February 1965, "A Change Is Gonna Come" by the soul singer
Sam Cooke rose to number thirty-one on the pop charts, and number
nine on the rhythm and blues charts, which gauged record sales in the

black community. Unfortunately, Cooke did not live to see the success
of this single, having been shot and killed in a bizarre incident at a Los
Angeles hotel in December 1964. Released a few months after President Johnson signed the Voting Rights Act into law, and a few weeks
after Martin Luther King received the Nobel Peace Prize, the title can't
help but convey a sense of optimism. The mood of the song, however,
is not celebratory but contemplative. Cooke's vocal style mixes gospel
and blues, and every word is sung with absolute clarity. In addition,
there are no specific references to events or political leaders of the day.

You could say this was politics on the cheap, except that Cooke
went beyond what other black performers were doing at the time. Motown was in the throes of young love singles—"Baby Love," "My
Guy," "My Girl," etc.—that featured instrumental backing from the
Funk Brothers and clever rhymes from Smokey Robinson. Memphis
soul sounded great—musical barriers were being broken—but steered
clear of anything that smacked of controversy. Under the circumstances, "A Change Is Gonna Come" was the R&B equivalent of a
manifesto.

Three and a half years later, with Malcolm X and Martin Luther
King dead, and Lyndon Johnson dead politically, James Brown entered
a studio in the lily-white San Fernando Valley community of Van Nuys
and recorded a single called "Say It Loud (I'm Black and I'm Proud)."
It went to number one on the R&B charts and number ten on the pop
charts. The song had all the necessary ingredients that make up the
James Brown oeuvre from the late 1960s, his greatest period: a thick
and ringing guitar sound, a beat that moves in fits and starts, and a desperate vocal that doesn't merely ask for but demands the listener's un-
divided attention.

In some quarters, the song had to have been perceived as a threat, especially since it was released in the summer of 1968, a few months after the riots that followed King's assassination and just one year after
Detroit and Newark burned. "Say It Loud (I'm Black and I'm Proud)"
could be interpreted as code for "we're coming to get ya." But for those
who looked past the title, or understood the title, the song is actually an

endorsement of self-respect and self-reliance—black power only in the sense of black empowerment. Here Nixon had not yet been elected president, and James Brown was taking a position that still resonated with conservatives and neo-conservatives—black and white. Indeed, the debate over whether big government or less government is the solution to the predicament of poor African Americans continues to this day. And yet "Say It Loud" represented a paradox; Brown was a hero in 1968 to the very inner-city teenagers and young adults most dependent on government largesse to make it through another day. They bought the record, but did they agree with the message? Like John Lennon's "Revolution," which came out a few months later, "Say It Loud" dared to question left-wing orthodoxy at a time when the Left seemed to hold all the cards in American politics. But then Nixon took office, which made James Brown appear to be some sort of political prophet. Ironically, sometime later Brown publicly supported Nixon, and that created problems for him with members of the black community.

One more note about "Say It Loud." Perhaps due to misunderstanding the message, or fear of being accused of inciting a second Watts riot so soon after the first one, the top soul station in Los Angeles, KGFJ, initially refused to play the song, which infuriated the James Brown camp. On August 29, 1968, his record label at the time, King, took out a full-page advertisement in the *Los Angeles Sentinel*, the newspaper that served LA's black community, blasting the station for its decision and calling for a listener boycott:

"If the Black People are going to stand up and let KGFJ do this then all the fighting that James Brown does for the Black People is wasted," read the ad. "It seems to be the policy of KGFJ to despise all Black men unless they are a 'Tom'." And this a few paragraphs later: "Black people we urge you to boycott this station. Get it off the air. Both Black and White (*sic*) can do without this type of prejudiced censorship."

You don't mess with a soul superstar at the peak of his powers. KGFJ had a lot of clout in those days, but not enough to take on James Brown. After the ad appeared, the station decided to include "Say It Loud" in its rotation.

Brown got better treatment thirty years later from a fellow Georgian, and a white one at that. In 1997, Congressman Charlie Norwood, a Republican, rose on the floor of the House of Representatives to offer his support for a pending resolution. A conservative, albeit with a populist streak on health care issues, Norwood was first elected in November 1994, when a "revolution" led by another Georgia Republican, Newt Gingrich, gave that party control of the House for the first time in forty years. Since his election, Norwood has voted to repeal the ban on assault weapons, in opposition to an increase in the minimum wage, and in favor of a constitutional amendment that would prohibit burning the American flag as a legitimate expression of political speech. As his voting record attests, Congressman Norwood is the embodiment of a Southern conservative politician at the end of the twentieth century.

Yet on one particular day, Norwood did not address his colleagues about the right to bear arms, or the pernicious power of unions, but the brilliance of James Brown. The congressman asked the House to approve a resolution "Recognizing the importance of African American music to global culture and calling on the people of the United States to study, reflect on, and celebrate African American music." Norwood also noted that he and James Brown both grew up in Augusta, though one presumes in different neighborhoods.

Yes, Norwood is a politician, and yes, he offered his resolution during Black History Month, but even allowing for expediency this was an extraordinary—if little noticed—moment in the history of race relations in the South. Thirty years earlier, Norwood would have been recalled, impeached, or simply run out of town if he had dared to publicly praise African American music, which after all had corrupted Elvis Presley and other white sons and daughters of the South. Indeed, Norwood probably could not have gotten away with this kind of public tribute through the 1970s and much of the 1980s as well. But by 1997, the South had evolved, James Brown was an American institution, and a conservative white congressman could take pride in the achievements of a black performer who for decades commanded a huge following throughout urban America.

⌒

Motown discovered politics two years into Nixon's first term.

In the spring of 1970, the label's prize act, the Temptations, re-leased "Ball of Confusion (That's What the World Is Today)," which rose to number three on the pop charts. "Ball of Confusion" is "Eve of Destruction" on speed. Not only is it faster-paced, but the Temptations reference seemingly every political and cultural issue of the day, while Barry McGuire got no further than nuclear war and race relations. The Temptations' song was like that scrawl that runs across the bottom of the screen on Fox News and CNN, jumping from topic to topic with no discernible frame of reference. "Ball of Confusion" touched on higher taxes, the Beatles, hippies, racism, organized religion, the empty promises of politicians, and more. In keeping with Motown's spirit of inclusion—the bigger the audience the better the sales, after all—the song added an issue or issues important to seemingly every social group, ideology, and race in America. Still, Motown played it safe. The only point of view was that planet earth resembled a "ball of confusion." We thank Berry Gordy and the folks at the label for clearing that up.

A few months later, Motown released "War" by Edwin Starr, which made it to number one. In terms of the music, "War" was the apotheosis of the hard rock and funk experimentation taking place in Motown's studios over the previous year. You couldn't get much heavier then "War" and still come out under the Motown name. This one was also for the white boys that dug Cream, Led Zeppelin, Black Sabbath, and Jimi Hendrix: heavy metal/soul/funk.

As for the lyrics, Vietnam is never mentioned, but no one in the targeted audience could have assumed that Edwin Starr was talking about World War II. The listener heard that "war" is a bad thing, but he was also thinking that this war, the one that featured every night on the 6:00 P.M. news, was a bad thing as well. Of course, Berry Gordy was not about to give radio programmers an excuse to remove the single from station playlists, even though by this time many Americans had turned against the war in Vietnam. With Nixon in the White House, you couldn't be too careful.

A couple of singles do not a trend make. But in 1971, Marvin Gaye released *What's Going On*, the first political *album* on Motown, and one of the few in the history of soul, funk, or rock and roll. After becoming a huge star in the 1960s, Gaye was not particularly productive for Motown for a couple of years, releasing only two top ten singles in 1969 and none in 1970. His clout diminished, Gaye didn't receive Gordy's unequivocal approval for the project: *What's Going On* was more politics then Motown was prepared to offer.

"It was one thing to release a single song with stream-of-consciousness lyrics about the state of the nation. But it seemed to Gordy far riskier to release an entire album of such stuff."[8]

But the boss eventually came around, and the story has a happy ending. *What's Going On*, which was released in June, sold millions, and has been revered by critics ever since, for both its music and lyrics. Since Marvin Gaye's death at the hands of his father in 1984, *What's Going On* has come to be regarded as a fitting tribute to its creator, and an account of personal and political anguish. The album is the product of an artist with the sense to recognize that he is not a politician. When you aren't worried about getting re-elected, you are not compelled to offer solutions. And Gaye doesn't. He suggests that we look around, which is the necessary first step in taking action. Like "Ball of Confusion," but with a sense of the tragic, *What's Going On* covers a range of issues, including ecology and the environment, the economy, and conditions in the inner city.

And then there was Stevie Wonder's "You Haven't Done Nothin'" (number one in 1974), which was merciless on the Nixon presidency, especially its policy of benign neglect toward the inner city. Again, Berry Gordy reads newspapers, if not polls. The song came out in the late summer of 1974, when Nixon was on his way to San Clemente, having turned the White House over to Gerald Ford. He was at that point a hugely unpopular president. Beating up on Mr. Nixon carried little risk at the time—even Republicans were sick of him. And yet this is another Motown political single in which the true subject could not be mentioned by name.

Motown made it safe for soul music as a whole to venture into the political realm. The O'Jays, a vocal group originally from Cleveland that recorded on the Philadelphia International label, had three Top 10 hits with a "message" in the early to mid-1970s. The first of these, "Backstabbers" (number three in 1972) was a fortuitous case of pop culture imitating life, having been released a few weeks after the June 17 Watergate break-in. Its theme of deception, lies, and dirty dealings seemed right in line with revelations out of Washington.

Having traded in cynicism, the O'Jays a few months later regained their faith in human nature, and released "Love Train," which went to number one in March 1973. This is the O'Jays version of "Imagine," the imagining of a utopian world where we all join hands and live in peace. The message harked back to white rock of the late 1960s ("Love Is All Around," "Love [Can Make You Happy]"), but the O'Jays' single speaks to a much broader constituency. The "Love Train" travels around the world, picking up like-minded passengers in England, Africa, China, and Israel. The song was released a few weeks after the last American troops departed Vietnam, another example where the O'Jays benefited from recent events. With Vietnam "behind" the nation, albeit not by much, there was more receptivity to a song that offered love as the antidote to war.

The O'Jays did almost as well by Watergate as did Woodward and Bernstein. "Backstabbers" came out around the time of the break-in, and "For the Love of Money" (number nine in 1974) was released a couple of months before Nixon waved good-bye to the American people and departed D.C. The idea that money corrupts is nothing new, and yet it doesn't always find a receptive audience. Some fifteen years earlier, Barrett Strong had a hit with "Money (That's What I Want)," a song that meant exactly what it said. But in the midst of Watergate, which among other things involved payment of hush money, illegal campaign contributions, and buying access to government, "the root of all evil" seemed to live up to its name. Ten years later, with Ronald

Reagan in the White House, money was once again something to honor, love, and cherish. And "For the Love of Money" became a staple at Old School dance nights.

⌒

By the end of 1974, disco was doing battle with funk, R&B, and soul for the mythical title of king of black music. In the beginning, before Donna Summer and the Village People, disco was an apolitical, easy-to-swallow alternative to the O'Jays, Ohio Players, and James Brown. "Rock the Boat" by the Hues Corporation, number one in July, and "Rock Your Baby" by George McRae, also number one in July, were danceable, smooth, and harmless. "Rock the Boat" is a terrific single, featuring a much-imitated style of rhythm piano, kind and gentle vocals, and a melody that's borderline lovely. If the genre had stayed like this, the anti-disco backlash of the late 1970s would have never materialized. "Rock Your Baby" is the quintessential well-made pop single: pleasant voice, risk-free production values, and double-entendre lyrics that nonetheless convey a feeling of sexual innocence.

Though recorded by black performers, both of these songs had much in common with middle-of-the-road pop, and were clearly intended to appeal to the musical tastes of the suburbs and the city. And given their final position on the pop charts, many white kids must have been pleased with what they heard. In the summer of 1975, Van McCoy, another black artist, had a number one hit with "The Hustle," one of the songs that disco haters regularly include in their chamber of horrors. "The Hustle" has its unfortunate moments, particularly a cloying riff that like the *Man Who Came to Dinner* refuses to leave, but on an obnoxious scale from one to ten, it ranks no worse then a six. "The Hustle" was another crossover hit, and among the first disco singles that celebrated a dance step.

One month later, KC and the Sunshine Band, an integrated group from Miami, reached number one with a great single, "Get Down Tonight," which presaged a split in disco. "Get Down Tonight" is much more funk-based then the singles mentioned above. It is, in short, an example of what might be called "black" disco, as opposed to the "white" disco of "Rock Your Baby." The contrast is predicated on styles of music, and not targeted audience. Black performers made white disco records, and on rarer occasions, white performers made black disco records. An example of the latter is Wild Cherry, which in 1976 got it together for one memorable song, the ever-popular "Play That Funky Music." And while it would not be entirely accurate to limit Donna Summer to the category of white disco, she did have a large white following, many of them gay men.

There was something terribly wrong with America in 1976. Our long national nightmare was not over. I'm not talking here about politics, but pop music. The number one song of the entire year was Rod Stewart's atrocious "Tonight's the Night," which was on top for a mind-boggling seven weeks. If it hadn't been for the Dick Clark hearings, I would have suspected payola. The number two hit for the year was another limp single by a much-celebrated English rock and roller, Paul McCartney's (Wings) "Silly Love Songs." Against this competition, disco actually sounded pretty good. At least you could dance to disco, which was precisely the point. In a purely musical sense, disco represented the revolt of happy feet against an anti-dance trend in rock music. Mid-1970s super groups such as Journey, Queen, Kansas, and Boston made records to be absorbed—some would say endured—but not to get you out of your seat. On the quieter side, the latest from Stewart and Wings, plus the continued popularity of Jackson Browne, James Taylor, and Carly Simon, further pointed out the decline of the beat. Since the mid-1950s, white kids that needed to boogie had turned to black performers for satisfaction. Disco singles by KC and the Sunshine Band, Chic, Tavares, the Trammps, and GQ, filled that need in the 1970s.

At the same time, disco was an unapologetic trumpeting of newfound affluence and newly obtained personal freedoms. Disco and the disco scene represented the triumph of 1960s liberalism. On the surface, that seems impossible, since disco is commonly regarded as the quintessential symbol of the 1970s. Furthermore, those people who swear by the "values" of the 1960s regarded and still regard disco as self-centered, materialistic, vulgar, and crass. Which might be true, but is also beside the point.

On the one hand, disco coveted the newly emergent black middle and upper middle class, professionals that in some cases benefited from affirmative action, a key component of Lyndon Johnson's Great Society. If group names such as Chic and GQ weren't enough, album covers with black men and women wearing beautiful clothes and, in some cases, driving beautiful cars erased any doubts. A song such as "Working Night and Day" from Michael Jackson's 1979 disco-drenched *Off the Wall* album, which featured the singer wearing a tuxedo on the cover, embraced the "work hard, play hard" ethos of the young and well-to-do, black, white, brown, or yellow. There was the strong suggestion in disco that the performers and their targeted audience inhabited roughly the same place on the socioeconomic scale, and that that distinction above all bound them together. The contrast could not be greater with a song such as James Brown's "Say It Loud (I'm Black and I'm Proud)," which used race to make a special connection between the performer and his fans. Disco did not target people living in Harlem or Watts, but those who had left Harlem and Watts for better parts of the city, perhaps never to return.

⌒

During the 1990s, as America debated the issue of same-sex marriage, many receptions following man/woman weddings included the 1979 song "YMCA" by the Village People. Probably 75 percent of the guests would know the Village People as a "gay group," with almost as many hip to the true meaning of "YMCA." The Village People's hits have aged well, compared with other disco artifacts such as the *Saturday Night Fever* soundtrack or Donna Summer. You won't hear "Night Fever" or "Enough Is Enough" at too many wedding receptions or baseball games these days. And while John Travolta in the famous white suit, striking that classic disco pose, is a figure of derision, younger audiences view the Village People affectionately. It's the advantage that comes from never having been taken seriously.

Long before the Village People, gays went to discos. "The New York disco scene from early 1971 to about the middle of 1974 was a true underground society and art form. The gays, long locked away in their bars, sought situations where they could party a little more frantically."[9] They continued to party frantically after "Rock the Boat" got the attention of the masses, and disco spread all over the country. Within a few years Studio 54 was the hottest club in America. Anybody could pick up a magazine, look at photos of 54, and correctly conclude that many men went there in pursuit of other men. The disco party scene was even featured in what the mainstream media liked to call family newspapers.

Disco was the first musical movement of the rock era in which so-called straight society emulated homosexual subculture. Films such as *Saturday Night Fever* and *Thank God, It's Friday* revolved in part around men going to discos to pick up hot, sexy women who knew how to dance. In 1979, Rod Stewart, who in the early part of the decade was considered the savior of rock and roll, had one of the top disco singles ever, the shameless "Do Ya Think I'm Sexy?" In an extraordinary feat of marketing, Rod transformed himself into a pretend homosexual for the occasion, releasing a promotional poster dressed in a "fem" outfit with the camera focused on his backside. David Bowie went from gay to straight, and Rod Stewart went from straight to gay. Indeed, Bowie got his disco song out of the way early—"Golden Years" in 1976—and spent the rest of the 1970s seeking new musical inspiration from the likes of Brian Eno. In the summer of 1978, the Stones had a number one hit with the disco-influenced "Miss You," although Mick Jagger didn't drastically alter *his* appearance. After all, he had passed through his effeminate stage several years before.

In retrospect it seems clear that disco changed forever the perception of homosexuality in America. The financial success of the Village People, and their acceptance by the mainstream, was the first in a long, inexorable process of making the country familiar with gay life, or the gay lifestyle. The impact has been cultural and political. Just about every reality show on television features at least one gay person speaking freely about his or her love life, or a contented gay couple. Gay characters are abundant on sitcoms, sometimes in lead roles. Rosie O'Donnell, whose lesbianism was one of the worst kept secrets in television, had a large following as a talk show host in the 1990s and early 2000s, even with little old ladies. The more recent memoirs of gay men invariably include statistics on the "thousands" of sexual encounters that they engaged in during their younger days. Gay sex has, since the late 1990s, been a hot topic on shock radio, which is getting less shocking and more predictable by the day.

At this rate, it wouldn't surprise me if some edgy network puts a gay version of *The Bachelor* on the air. If Hollywood made a World War II buddy picture today, it would most likely include a gay soldier in the standard mix of Jews, blacks, Italians, and Puerto Ricans.

Since the early 1980s, homosexuals have become much more visible and influential players in Democratic Party politics. Part of this stems from the need to confront the AIDS epidemic, but it was also a logical consequence of coming out, everywhere and all the time. By this point homosexuals have achieved parity with blacks, Latinos, and women on the identity politics scale. Issues such as same-sex marriage and gays in the military loom as large in the national debate as abortion or affirmative action. Both parties have openly gay members in the U.S. House of Representatives, and the time will come when a gay man or lesbian is elected to the U.S. Senate. As for president, if the current order of obtaining political power is adhered to, a woman or an African American will get there first. But to even speculate about an openly gay commander of chief is a sign of growing acceptance.

For gays as for blacks, disco represented a continuation of the politics of the 1960s by other means. Instead of riots and demonstrations—the conventional methods of a decade earlier—gains were achieved by private statements of "fuck you" to mainstream society. With gays, that translated into I will have as much a sex as I want, with whom I want, and where I want. Discos and bathhouses were Ground Zero for this next phase of what used to be termed gay liberation. Herein lies the advantage of a movement based on sexual orientation. One doesn't have to fight for the right to vote, or ride in the front of the bus, or smash through the glass ceiling. Claiming the right to be one's "true" self is sufficient. In the 1970s, gay politics never felt so good. But it was politics all the same.

Eleven years after the 1968 Democratic Convention, another widely reported and violent political protest occurred in Chicago, although with a very different purpose. In between games of a doubleheader at Comiskey Park—then the home of the White Sox—on July 12, 1979, fans participated in a pre-arranged "disco demolition rally." "Between ten and twenty thousand records were reportedly placed in the center of the field and blown up, to the delight of the crowd, which according to reports, went wild, tearing up the field and getting in fights, chanting 'Disco sucks.'"[10]

Through the years there have been various theories offered as to why a segment of society despised disco. The Chicago incident was the extreme manifestation of feelings held by others. Some have said hatred of disco was an outgrowth of homophobia. Others eschew the sociological explanation and argue that it was purely a response to mechanical, soulless, and dreadful music. There is truth in both of these views. What's missing, however, is any reference to class differences. With a subtext of expensive threads, overpriced nightclubs, and beautiful people, disco was an unusual merger of noblesse oblige and pop culture. The masses were free to buy disco records, but not to share in the nonstop sex and cocaine party that went along with the music, barred from participating because of limited means and access. As America moved ever closer to the Age of Reagan, disco anticipated the trend toward celebrity worship, superficiality, and crass materialism. The longhaired, middle-class kids that destroyed disco records on the playing fields of Comiskey could never have gotten into Studio 54 or the like, even had they wanted to. They were too vulgar, too unattractive, and too poor. On that night in Chicago the Angry White Male had his revenge, and not for the last time.

⌒

Whit Stillman's film *The Last Days of Disco* is set in 1981, which seems about right. Disco had five wildly successful years, from 1976 to 1981, more than could be expected given its preference for stock-in-trade overexperimentation. But disco had a knack for creating the illusion of having reinvented itself, whereas in reality pop culture was simply signing on to the winning team. When the Rolling Stones and Rod Stewart released disco records, it was done not out of musical appreciation but a mildly cynical attempt to keep current. Until the early 1980s, Mick Jagger was quite shrewd in adapting the Stones' sound to changed circumstances. The history of the Stones from 1963 to 1982 is the history of rock and R&B over the same period. The hippies of 1967 were the disco boys of 1978. The key to the group's success is that they managed to release many excellent records while chasing trends. The many bands that copied the Stones have never been able to match their versatility or feel for the market.

Since 1981 to 1982, there have been occasional attempts to launch massive disco revivals, but these have failed almost as quickly as they began. In that sense disco has been eclipsed by 1970s punk, which spawned a new generation of popular bands from the 1990s and into the twenty-first century. I have lost track of the number of teenagers or twenty somethings from 2000 to 2003 that I saw with spiked hair or Mohawk cuts and wearing Clash T-shirts. The public — including young men and women born after Chic's "Good Times" went to number one — will listen to disco songs on the radio, and pick up a disco anthology or two. And while these fans would go dancing at a club that specializes in hits from the disco era, they would not look favorably at a breakout of national disco fever any more then they would like to see hippies stage a comeback. There have been too many jokes at the expense of disco or hippies for younger people to take either seriously. Flower power and polyester suits are part of the dustbin of American pop history.

From 1955 to 1975, race is the predominant lens through which to
view the development of rock and roll. Class and other factors are either put to the side or disregarded altogether. The short definition of
the beginning of rock and roll, Elvis Presley et al., is that it represented a successful integration of black and white musical styles,
specifically country and blues. The British Invasion in 1964 and the
many subcategories that grew out of it—folk-rock, art rock, acid
rock—plus the rise of black nationalism served to divide the races
along musical lines. By 1966, if not sooner, various radio stations
were catering to the preferred tastes of black listeners, while others
courted white listeners. *Sgt. Pepper's*, the album that in mid-1967
"unified" Western civilization, made nary a dent in the black community, while the majority of whites were oblivious to the musical and
cultural significance of James Brown, who had god-like status with
his black urban fans in the late 1960s.

And yet race is not the best method of analysis for disco and punk
rock, the two major pop trends of the second half of the 1970s. Race
certainly played a part in disco—a big share of the audience and most
of the performers were black. But as I tried to show, class distinctions
and new money better explain disco's rise and importance, both in
terms of the support of its core fan base and the intense hostility of its
detractors. At the same time, race tells us little or nothing of the why,
what, and wherefore of the Sex Pistols, the Clash, and the Ramones,
other then to re-emphasize the point that rock is a hybrid of black and
white music. But even that notion is questionable when one listens to
the Pistols' performance of "Anarchy in the UK," where Johnny Rotten sings in a fashion that owes nothing to any black performer that I
can ever recall hearing. The same for the music of the Clash, at least
until the band's third album, *London Calling* (1979). Indeed, the Clash
grew tired of punk's anti-commercial stance and started recording
songs with the clear intent of cracking the Top 100. These singles dis-
played the obvious influence of rhythm and blues, soul, and funk. The

first release of this kind, the superb dance single "Train in Vain," reached number twenty-three in March 1980.

One of the reasons given for English punk rock was boredom. Working-class kids were bored with their lives, bored with the state of rock and roll, and so they invented punk to rescue themselves from a fate that was literally worse then death. Some American critics, seeking a political angle, blamed the economic situation on Margaret Thatcher, an ideal villain but, sorry to say, not yet prime minister when the Sex Pistols and the Clash were formed in 1975 to 1976. And since when did American rock critics become experts anyway on conditions affecting the English working class? Just because Johnny Rotten or Malcolm McLaren—the Pistols' manager—said something didn't make it true.

But skepticism toward the class-based explanation for punk does not rule out class as a major factor in its coming into existence. It's just that it's not class in the conventional sense of various strata of society that applies here, but class within the framework of rock and roll. Rotten and his cohorts hated what rock and roll had become by the mid-1970s, which in their not unreasonable view was fat music for fat, stupid, happy people. It was also priced well beyond their means. If a middle-class kid in England or the U.S. wanted to see a stadium concert by, say, Queen in 1977, he had to plunk down a good portion of his hard-earned income or else pay off a loan for weeks afterwards to his parents. A lower-middle-class kid would have to beat the crap out of the middle-class kid and steal the latter's tickets to get inside the gate. For rich kids, of course, money was no object, plus spare cash for designer drugs to enhance the concert experience. The more determined among them figured out how to get backstage later and party with the stars.

Punk was in open rebellion against the idea of rock and roll as it had evolved in the 1970s. The signs were there years earlier, but in the 1960s rock was too enamored of itself to notice. Back in 1967, when they recorded "Baby You're a Rich Man," the Beatles intimated in a wry fashion that rock and roll—the "peoples" music—had developed its own hierarchy, which resembled that of the class-conscious society that it was supposed to abhor. Still, "Baby You're a Rich Man" was a witty 45, and not the harbinger of a movement. By their next single, the Beatles had moved on to something else. But late-1970s punk rockers had nothing else. It was either save rock and roll or go get jobs in a factory.

10

FIGHT THE POWER

The Sex Pistols had an easy solution to the anxiety of influence: act as if it didn't exist. "The Sex Pistols claimed to have little interest in the music that preceded them, and (Johnny) Rotten, at least, hoped nobody would come after them."[1] Dismissing or ignoring the Founding Fathers of rock and roll was a radical break from the past. Until the late 1970s, punk and rock and roll performers had been unfailingly respectful in discussing the talents and accomplishments of their predecessors. The Beatles said nice things about Chuck Berry and Little Richard, Eric Clapton heaped praise on B. B. King and Muddy Waters, and the Rolling Stones complimented Slim Harpo, Jimmy Reed, and other blues or R&B performers who influenced their own sound.

Recognition was appreciated, not least because it brought some of these performers to the attention of white rock and roll fans, who might otherwise have never known about them. As Mick Jagger told *Rolling Stone* in 1968: "You could say that we did blues to turn people on, but why they should be turned on by us is unbelievably stupid. I mean what's the point in listening to us doing 'I'm a King Bee' when you can listen to Slim Harpo doing it?" In the late 1960s, the composition of B. B. King's audience changed from predominantly black to predominantly white, in no small part due to kind words from Eric Clapton and other English blues guitarists. B. B. would perform on the same bill as hard rock groups at the Fillmore (West or East) and other venues that catered to this audience. The hippies wanted to see him as much or more than they did Quicksilver Messenger Service or Moby Grape. The same went for Albert King, Freddy King, and other blues giants. Black musicologists and critics would occasionally grumble about white bands "stealing *our* music and getting rich," but you rarely if ever heard this view expressed by blues and R&B performers. In a perfect world, of course, B. B. King and the rest would have gotten rich on their own, without endorsements from their English admirers. But that's not how the system worked in the 1950s and 1960s.

Though not as deferential towards one another, competing rock and roll performers have generally gotten along through the years—the Battle of the Bands is merely a promotion thought up by radio stations. On those occasions when superstars did trade barbs, it was typically in response to a particular song, quote, or incident, and not as part of a wholesale condemnation of a body of work. For example, Mick Jagger and John Lennon said some unkind things in the 1960s and 1970s about their respective bands, but there was never the sense that Jagger didn't think well of the Beatles, or that Lennon was not a fan of the Rolling Stones. Lennon and Paul McCartney had a public spat in the years immediately following the breakup of the Beatles, but that was more in the nature of a family squabble. Rock and roll performers spend so much time talking about what they're against—the government, parents, high school, and corporate America—that they have to be for something. Otherwise, they leave their fans no reason to go on. That something is rock and roll. It changed their lives, and it can change yours too.

But Johnny Rotten wouldn't even concede that point. Everything was shit, including rock and roll. He didn't really mean it, of course, or he wouldn't be trying to save rock and roll. It was like Ronald Reagan running for president while blasting the culture of Washington. Indeed, this was punk's version of the postmodern political campaign. But Rotten's impertinence outraged the first wave of baby boomers, who demanded that the next generation pay the proper respect to the 1960s. How dare he refuse to acknowledge the genius of the Beatles, Stones, and Dylan? Just who the hell did the Sex Pistols think they were? If they wanted to mock Queen Elizabeth II, or rip the British government, that was fine, but stay away from the Beatles. What we have here is the rock and roll equivalent of political correctness.

The Sex Pistols and the Clash were in essence proclaiming 1976 to 1977 as Year One in the history of rock and roll. Whatever happened before was irrelevant. The Clash put out a one minute, forty second song—punk liked to get it done in less than two minutes—called "1977," which boldly proclaimed that there would be no "Elvis, Beatles, or Rolling Stones in 1977." How right they were in the case of Elvis, who died on August 16, 1977.

Baby boomers absolutely hated to be reminded that they weren't getting any younger. The advent of punk didn't just suggest they weren't getting any younger, it suggested they were getting old. For the first time in their glorious history, boomers found themselves on the wrong side of the generation gap. They had already been shocked to realize that life went on after 1969, and now they were confronted with the reality that not everyone believed the 1960s to be the greatest decade in the history of modern civilization. In fact, there were people born in the late 1950s and the early 1960s who were actually sick of hearing about hippies, Woodstock, peace, love, and this or that beautiful movement to make life better on Planet Earth. It just didn't seem possible.

Punk rock performers did disparage hippies, but for the most part they left alone other political and social remnants from the 1960s. But to boomers, an attack on the Beatles is an attack on the entire decade. The Beatles were the 1960s, and the 1960s were the Beatles. You can't have one without the other. Any written history of the 1960s includes the Beatles, as do television documentaries and timelines in museums that cover the same period. If the Beatles weren't included it would be grounds for condemnation. And so in a very real sense, punk rock was the first political, social, or musical entity to recognize the benefits of ripping into the 1960s. A line had been crossed.

More than ten years later, conservative Republicans adopted a similar strategy, although none of them to my knowledge claimed Johnny Rotten as an influence. Of course, Republicans in their official capacity didn't care one way or the other about the reputation of the Beatles or the Stones. It might even cost them votes to say nasty things about either group. Instead, they lambasted the political and cultural legacy of the 1960s without so much as mentioning *Magical Mystery Tour* or *Let It Bleed*. For this new generation of Republicans, mesmerized by the rhetoric of Ronald Reagan, the 1960s wrought bloated government, failed federal programs, moral relevance, promiscuous sex, widespread use of drugs, and an end to meritocracy. It all added up to the decline of America. The propaganda proved to be such a success that a conservative speaker merely had to say the name of the decade and a receptive audience would boo and hiss. It seemed there were a lot of Americans just waiting to go public with their disgust at both the 1960s and at hearing incessantly about how much better we were back then.

Republicans have not been as scathing in their criticisms of the 1970s. When they talk about that decade, they invoke one name: "Jimmy Carter." As far as they are concerned, nothing more need be said. But as was noted earlier, punk hated the 1970s rock scene, particularly its bombast and self-indulgence. Evidence of decline was everywhere. You could pick from Elton John's six-figure shopping sprees, massive stadium concerts, the excesses of the groupie/drug scene, interminable solos, the cult of musical perfection, "stardom," or soaring ticket prices. This stuff not only destroyed the soul of rock and roll, but, if you accepted the punk critique, it put the music in jeopardy. At the same time, it didn't take a Marxist to recognize that rock in the 1970s embodied the inherent inequities of capitalism. Middle-class kids helped make wealthy rock stars even wealthier by spending an ever-increasing proportion of their disposable income on records and concerts.

Like any populist movement, punk attracted supporters who despaired of ever seeing the status quo changed. The alliance of lawyers, promoters, and rock stars appeared to be unbeatable. But beyond the hype—and rock and roll at any level cannot exist without hype—the

Sex Pistols, Ramones, Clash, and Blondie insisted above all that "It's the music, stupid." Their approach was reminiscent of an expression from the 1960s, applied to the Best and the Brightest that steered the country into Vietnam: "Don't trust the experts." Instead of "brilliant" instrumentation aided by the creative genius of "brilliant" producers, punk would lay it out there with three chords and a breakneck pace. Yeah, they couldn't play their instruments especially well, but so what? Rock and roll isn't jazz, after all.

Bored kids took it upon themselves to restore excitement to rock and roll. Whether punk brought a new audience to rock and roll or converted Journey/Queen/Styx listeners that were waiting to be put out of their misery is hard to determine. It was probably some of both. I have observed a connection between fans of Ziggy Stardust period Bowie and fans of punk. In a typical American high school, it was risky to be openly pro-Bowie during his glitter days, and in the same environment it was risky to affect the safety pin and buzz cut look during the late 1970s.

A decade before video games, cell phones, and channel surfing, punk anticipated the short attention span of the American consumer. You could barely digest one Ramones' song before it was time for the next. The same was true for the Sex Pistols, the early Clash, and dozens of other bands. Playing the best of the Ramones is akin to watching two fast-breaking college basketball teams go and up and down the court for forty minutes.

The implicated groups from the 1970s barely acknowledged punk's existence. Maybe they were too busy planning their next gargantuan tours, which didn't disappear just because of Johnny Rotten's unflattering remarks. Punk did not, in fact, create a New World Order. But its spirit did have an impact on some remaining groups from the 1960s that had had prior experience shaking rock and roll out of its torpor. They saw in punk a version—but nothing more—of their earlier selves. But this was enough to cause a healthy re-examination of priorities. The Rolling Stones' 1978 album, *Some Girls*, the best from them in six years, was largely due to the World's Greatest Rock and

Roll Band hearing footsteps. Punk motivated the Stones to break away from their accountants, groupies, and assorted hangers-on and get down to serious work. The final song on *Some Girls*, "Shattered," is a litany of urban and personal horrors recounted by a man on the verge of a nervous breakdown. If Jagger does not sound as crazed here as Johnny Rotten, you've got to remember he was thirty-four at the time. But he passed the audition nonetheless.

⌒⌒

Punk saved rock and roll—just not right away. By 1982, punk started to fade, undone in part by its being ill-prepared for success or anything close. The Clash had two hits that year, "Should I Stay or Should I Go" and "Rock the Casbah," but the group would advance no further. The Sex Pistols had already disbanded a few years earlier. Blondie and the Ramones were past their best days. As soon as mainstream America showed interest, punk backed away, fearful of being compromised and also uncertain what to do next. In order to become a star, you have to want to become a star. Punk was at most ambivalent on this score, having been so adamant in its disgust at the selling out of rock and roll during the 1970s. In the end, integrity and apprehension won out over ambition.

Move ahead one decade. Bill Clinton has been elected president, ending twelve years in which Republicans occupied the White House. And a new crop of bands with members raised on the Sex Pistols, Ramones, and Clash are about to reinvigorate rock and roll, or if you prefer, rescue it from Grunge. Green Day, the Offspring, and others would release excellent albums in the 1990s, playing an admittedly market-friendly brand of punk that nonetheless reminded us what was so good about the original. And speaking of the original, in 1996 the Sex Pistols embarked on a twentieth anniversary international tour, which back in the day would have seemed about as plausible as Ronald Reagan showing compassion for the poor. The tour was not a critical success, but there was no denying that punk—even punk—had found a place at the rock and roll table. At the same time, boxed sets of punk cuts from the 1970s and 1980s are now available in a friendly music store near you, alongside the Beatles, the Stones, and all that stuff from the 1960s.

And in the late 1990s punk invaded the White House, or to be precise one former punk aficionado did by the name of Ted Widmer. In 1997, the Clinton administration hired Widmer to write speeches for the National Security Agency. Without having consulted the Congressional Research Service, I would be willing to bet he is the first and only openly punk rock fan to ever hold such a sensitive position in the federal government.

The combination of spectacle and music first attracted Widmer to rock and roll. There was no turning back once he saw and heard Sweet, David Bowie, and T. Rex, performers that blew away English audiences in the early 1970s but that only a certain kind of American could appreciate at that time. The notion of merging rock, camp, and theatrics might have literally been foreign to most teenagers on this side of the Atlantic in 1971 to 1972, but to Widmer it made perfect sense. In Widmer's case, glam could well have appealed to the politician within. As in successful modern campaigns, glam mixed a basic "message"—power chord rock and roll—with striking visuals. Marc Bolan all aglitter singing "Bang a Gong" gets your attention, and so does a candidate standing erect in front of a huge Stars and Stripes, or speaking to the heartland of America from the back of a train.

Widmer waited out the middle part of the decade—Queen, Aerosmith, and Boston—and then jumped back in with the emergence of punk rock. "I loved the energy and humor of punk rock," he explained. "The Ramones were the funniest band I ever listened to. And I thought that picture of Johnny Rotten flipping off Mick Jagger was hilarious."

A native of Providence, Widmer joined a few punk bands in the Northeast during the early 1980s, just as the rock audience was switching from punk to performers that looked good on a new channel called MTV. But Widmer wasn't in it for a career anyway. "We were pretty bad, but it was just so fun. Besides, the whole punk ethos was 'who cares'?" As a graduate student at Harvard, Widmer continued to play in a few bands, even though he had a lot of studying to do and A&R reps weren't exactly camping out in his driveway.

Still, Widmer kept at the rock thing long enough that eventually he and a friend put together a band that generated some regional interest. The original glam scene makers would have been pleased with the Upper Crust, which Widmer co-founded in 1994. A thinking man's Paul Revere and the Raiders, the members of the Upper Crust wore powdered wigs and knickers, just as French aristocrats did in the eighteenth century. The band recorded two albums and played numerous gigs on the East Coast. "We were getting enormous crowds in New York," recalled Widmer. "There is something about putting on costumes and makeup that excites people, especially when you're straight." David Bowie couldn't have said it any better.

They tried for a few more years, but the excitement of seeing straight boys in eighteenth-century French costumes did not, alas, translate into a coveted record deal. In 1996 the Upper Crust called it quits, and Widmer headed for Washington, where he subsequently got a job in the Clinton administration as director of speechwriting at the National Security Agency. The White House had no problems with Widmer's past, but the *Washington Post*, on what had to have been a slow news day, published one of its exclusive "scoops" about the new hire. "It said that Clinton's new speechwriter was in a cross-dressing band," said Widmer. "This did not make the transition to Washington any easier." But he survived—the Clinton administration had a lot of survivors by the end of the president's second term—and is today director of the C. V. Starr Center for the Study of the American Experience at Washington College. In this capacity Widmer has written on foreign policy issues for publications including the *New York Times*.

Ian MacKaye, one of the leaders of Minor Threat, a hardcore punk band from Washington, D.C., in the 1980s, had this to say about the

man that served as our president during most of that decade. "I fuckin'
hated (Ronald) Reagan. I've always hated the government. (But) I
guess what I felt like was it wasn't my domain. I didn't know enough
about politics to really sing about them. And I didn't know enough
about the world to really sing about it. But I knew enough about my
world to sing about it."[2] If a rock songwriter that "fuckin' hated Ronald
Reagan" couldn't or wouldn't put his feelings on paper, what hope was
there for rock lyricists that merely didn't like the president?

To hate a president, you need his cooperation. Bad policies help, but
aren't enough. He must also be smarmy, arrogant, or self-pitying to get
the public get really angry. In a nation where many men and women
are proud to say they don't pay close attention to politics, it's visual
images that often make the difference between triumph and tragedy for
a candidate at the polls. Consultants are supposed to be able to suppress those aspects of a candidate's personality that don't play well on
television. The rules are the same for both parties. Never appear per-
turbed on camera. The country could be going to hell, but if you're a
man, don't lose your temper over it—such macho displays might upset soccer moms. The results of these many instructions can be disastrous, as in the case of that plastic figure that goes by the name of Al
Gore. During and after the 2000 campaign Gore looked and acted as if
he was constantly trying to remember who he was supposed to be.
Every laugh, smile, and wave seemed to have been ordered up from a
place outside his physical being.

Reagan gave his enemies nothing to work with save a bad record.
He was a right-wing conservative with immense charm, and the combination baffled and frustrated his opponents. Who could blame them?
Liberals had never experienced anything like this before. Unlike
Richard Nixon, Reagan held up well under pressure, and unlike
George Wallace, he was not a bully. He also had none—or very little—
of Gerald Ford's physical clumsiness, Bob Dole's smoldering rage, or
the patrician immaturity of George H. W. Bush, who famously pouted
during a debate with Reagan in the 1980 New Hampshire Republican
primary. How do you goad the general public into opposing a guy with

a great personality? I recall attending a concert in 1987 by the Un-
touchables, a Los Angeles ska/new wave band, where the lead singer
repeatedly denounced Reagan as a "motherfucker." Outside of one
more example of left-wing political illiteracy, aimed at this president
that ugly word seemed uglier then usual. As far as I was concerned, the
lead singer's comment generated some sympathy for the very person
he intended to demonize. This happened with Reagan a lot.

Thrash metal, speed metal, and hardcore didn't stand a chance
against Reagan. Even rap, the most political of the popular music
styles borne in the 1980s, rarely attacked the president personally. If
the esteemed biographer Edmund Morris couldn't get a handle on
Ronald Reagan over hundreds of pages, how could a four or five-
minute song expect to bring it off?

The difficulty in capturing the essence of Reagan—a cynic would
say he has none to capture—is one explanation for the weak response
to this president from rock and roll, and other elements of pop culture
for that matter. But it's not the only one.

To employ an analogy that would please him to no end, Reagan
rewrote the political script that had been in use since the 1960s, specifically the belief that radical change necessarily comes from the Left.
This view was (and to some extent still is) propagated by rock fans in
the era of Jimi Hendrix, the Doors, and the San Francisco sound, which
explains how in their own minds they were able to link rock with the
"revolution." They opposed the war in Vietnam, and they lived for rock
and roll. Ergo, rock and roll opposed the war in Vietnam, as well as the
overhaul of society endorsed by the Left. They would permit no contradiction between their political beliefs and musical preferences. But
what happens when the "revolution"—another misapplication of the
word, but we'll leave that alone for now—is initiated by a conservative
in his seventies? Not a few pundits have called Reagan's rolling back of
the Great Society programs of the 1960s and his recasting the terms of
the political debate in this country a revolution. It's certainly been the
case that Democrats and Republicans—many of them thirty and forty
years his junior—have been profoundly influenced by his communica-

tion techniques and his critique of the role of the federal government. But can you have revolution in this day and age without rock and roll? Reagan was in his mid-forties when "Heartbreak Hotel" was released, and so were many of his supporters. Elvis and the Beatles meant little or nothing to him. And yet he and his followers symbolically marched through Washington with as much a sense of duty and purpose as the Armies of the Night that marched on the Pentagon in 1967.

In the 1980s, the best-selling rock acts were not aligned with the forces agitating for political change. A "Rockers for Ronnie" movement never materialized. But there were plenty of knowledgeable rock *fans* for Ronnie. This was a departure from the past for Republicans. In 1968, you couldn't imagine those clean-cut, well-groomed pro-Nixon youth listening to acid rock. They had the Johnny Mann Singers written all over their happy faces, and the Nixon campaign would not have had it any other way. They wanted only a certain kind of young person in their corner—no long hair allowed. Bill Clinton has said that campaigns are won by the candidate that best represents the future, but "retro" was a good thing for the GOP in 1968. If Nixon was the proper candidate for young people that rejected sex, drugs, and rock and roll, then it followed according to Republican strategy that he was the right candidate for their parents, and for America.

But in 1980, the year Reagan defeated Jimmy Carter, the counterculture was a fading memory, and rock fans could range in age anywhere from fifteen to fifty. Jimi Hendrix and Janis Joplin were long since dead, Sid Vicious had died the year before, the Rolling Stones were respectable, and Bob Dylan was apparently still a born-again Christian. John Lennon hadn't released an album for several years, and then he was murdered a month after Reagan's victory. Only paranoid Republicans would consider rock and roll a threat to the established order in 1980.

But what happened with Reagan and young people was enough to drive the 1960s crowd to the brink of suicide. Not only did many kids born after, say, 1960, like Reagan, they thought he was cool. They went to his speeches, cheered in the right places, laughed at his jokes about liberals, walked precincts on his behalf, and of course voted for him.

And not all of these youths for Reagan looked like the leadership of the Young Americans for Freedom. Some of them saw no contradiction between hitting punk clubs at night and going to work the next morning for a Republican politician. Punk was feisty, cutting-edge music, and under Reagan, the GOP had become the feisty, cutting-edge party. In the 1980s, the Democrats by contrast were retreating from liberalism, advancing few new ideas, and wallowing in the morass of identity politics. Given those alternatives, which do you think would look more attractive to a nineteen-year-old?

Older baby boomers were aghast. This notion of rock fans for Reagan upset their worldview, which had been formulated sometime between 1966 and 1969. But many of the 1960s-era boomers had stopped paying close attention to rock and roll since the Bee Gees went disco in the mid-1970s. (The boomers made an exception for Bruce Springsteen, who by a freak of nature didn't release his first album until 1973. And then—stranger still—he became the biggest rock star in the world during the 1980s.) They didn't know what was happening behind closed doors, nor did they want to, having petulantly determined that rock and roll ended sometime around 1977, if not a few years earlier. It's not easy for people enamored of their own times to recognize that times change.

By being this close-minded, they also failed to notice that the phenomenon of young Republican rock fans actually represented a triumph for the counterculture. By the 1980s rock had been burned so deep into the national consciousness that even enthusiastic supporters of a president who wanted to slash domestic programs for the poor, increase the defense budget, and maintain the rights of gun owners were checking out alternative bands. America had in fact, become a rock and roll nation, which as I recall was one of the dreams of the hippies.

⌐⌐

In 1984, the Reagan campaign overreached. Seeking to close off all avenues to Walter Mondale, their underdog Democratic opponent, Reagan's people started playing the Bruce Springsteen song "Born in the USA" at the president's public events. What better way to clinch the deal with America's youth, and draw in some older baby boomers as well, then blasting Bruce Springsteen's music at campaign rallies? The title suggested patriotism, pride in America, and although the lyrics were actually about a disgruntled Vietnam vet, who listens closely to lyrics anymore except critics? This was the 1980s after all.

The campaign had its way for a short period of time, until Springsteen vehemently protested, and they stopped playing "Born in the USA." There was nothing to be gained by getting into a prolonged dispute with Bruce Springsteen, one of the few men in America nearly as popular as Ronald Reagan in 1984.

In the 1980s, rock stars discussed politics even when they weren't asked. They *volunteered* their opinions, and urged us to join their causes. When you think back to the 1960s, there were not that many interviews where musicians commented on politics. Dylan, Lennon, and Jagger never endorsed candidates—not that they were being courted—and they seemed to avoid getting drawn into discussion on specific issues, which was fine with interviewers, who were there to talk about music. In the late 1960s, young rock writers were kept busy simply trying to keep up with new developments in the music field. Frankly, what John Lennon had to say about the *White Album* had to be of more import then what he might say about the White House. As Jon Landau wrote in his 1968 review of the Rolling Stones' album *Beggar's Banquet*: "On the surface, rock and roll moves at an amazing pace. The influence of a figure like the Maharishi can disappear in a matter of months. Talk about old fashioned rock and roll finds itself dead before it begins."[3] The publication for which Landau wrote that review, *Rolling Stone*, was launched in late 1967 to rescue rock journalism from daily newspapers and fan mags. It would be years before *Rolling Stone* covered political and economic issues on a regular or even semi-regular basis.

Twenty years later, rock and roll remained interesting, but was no longer essential. The rock press would certainly try to excite us with the information that some hot group was in the studio recording an album, or a big-name performer was set to launch a thirty-city tour. But it just couldn't provide the thrill of the Who recording a rock opera or Jimi Hendrix putting out a double album. Even today younger rock fans are in awe of the accomplishments of the leading rock artists from the late 1960s. They are astonished merely to hear the names of singles that were hits in 1968—one great song after another. The same will not hold true when future generations examine the rock scene of the late 1980s.

Still, the inclusion of politics made rock music and rock stars *seem* vital in the 1980s, which is not to say that the performers known for speaking out did so merely in an effort to get attention. There is no reason to think they were anything but sincere. "In the late 1980s, I was influenced and politicized to the point that I felt like I wanted to try to make some of these things (political and social issues) topical," explained REM's Michael Stipe in a 1998 interview. "I always said—and I don't think I'm being revisionary here . . . I don't think music and politics mix. However, I feel very strongly about this stuff. I mean after seven or eight years of the dark ages of our country, with Reagan and Bush. So there was that attempt."[4]

Bruce Springsteen, U2, especially the group's lead singer, Bono, REM, especially the group's lead singer, Michael Stipe, and Don Henley were not at all shy about expressing their opinions to rock writers. And the writers were only too willing to ask. Over the past twenty years it was not uncommon to read an interview with some rock musician where 25 to 50 percent of the text consisted of questions and answers relating to politics. The musicians usually sounded as if they had done their research—or at least commissioned someone to do their research—and carefully thought about when to take a stand. With the exception of Ted Nugent, who is rock's version of a political loose cannon, politically active rock stars tended to express positions more in line with those of liberals than conservatives.

Springsteen is the quintessential figure in what could be regarded as the golden era of rock and politics. On the basis of column inches, television and radio interviews, and his own output, Springsteen would win the award for the rock star that has expressed more political opinions than any other in history. His views are indicative of a staunch Democrat, including support for affirmative action, sympathy for the working class in urban and rural America, and skepticism about big business. He's certainly no radical in the mode of Johnny Rotten and the MC5. He believes in working through the system, and he believes in the system, which helps to explain why the Reagan people attempted to appropriate "Born in the USA." They felt safe aligned with Bruce.

He made his fans feel safe, too. They wanted change, but in the manner of Selma and not Watts, the Free Speech Movement and not the Days of Rage. In his politics and his music, Springsteen recalled pre–1966 America, when the civil rights movement was integrated and student protesters marched in an orderly fashion. Songs such as "Hungry Heart," "Tenth Avenue Freeze Out," "Born to Run" and "Badlands" revive the sound and spirit of rock and roll and soul music before *Revolver* and LSD, funk and black nationalism. You simply couldn't envision the audience leaving a Springsteen concert chanting "We Want the World and We Want It Now," but you could envision them singing "We Shall Overcome"—accompanied by an electric rather than an acoustic guitar of course. Springsteen offered rock and roll with a folk music sensibility. He never said he wanted a revolution, just improvements. And I can't see Springsteen calling Reagan a "motherfucker," even off the record. Indeed, he could become almost melancholic on the subject of Reagan and Reaganism. "But the difficult thing out there right now is that the social consciousness that was part of the '60s has become, like, old-fashioned or something," said Springsteen in 1984. "You go out, you get your job, and you try to make as much money as you can and have a good time on the weekend. And that's considered okay."[5]

In 1984, Reagan ran for re-election on the campaign slogan that "It's Morning Again in America." The implication was that after all the crap the Democrats had put the country through in the 1960s and 1970s, President Reagan had now returned us to happier and more prosperous times, just like it was back in the 1950s. With strong leadership and smart policies, his administration had wiped away twenty bad years—the essence of the Reagan revolution.

Springsteen could have toured in 1984 on the slogan "It's Morning Again in Rock and Roll." Not only did his music recall the 1950s and early 1960s, but his image did as well. Unlike the case with Gary Hart, reporters followed Springsteen around and found nothing. No drug use, no abuse of groupies, no temper tantrums, no millions won and lost or other typical tales from the files of rock stars since the 1970s. He kept himself in top physical condition. He divorced one woman because she didn't want to have children, and then married his backup singer, with whom he had three. He dressed in a simple black leather jacket and jeans combination, kept his hair at moderate length, and eschewed heavy make up, glitter, safety pins, and chains. He looked nothing like Kiss and nothing like the Clash. He was the epitome of an American rock and roll performer before the English came over here and messed everything up with their weird and bizarre styles. He was unmoved and seemingly untouched by the counterculture—in effect, he was the Ronald Reagan of rock and roll.

Political figures might want to think twice about being in the company of Bono. First he spent time with Jesse Helms, and then the North Carolina senator decided to retire. In 2002 he traveled to Africa with Secretary of the Treasury Paul O'Neill, but a few months later President Bush booted O'Neill out the door. Who is the next person to be felled by the "Bono curse"?

The singer is certainly not about to curb his activities. As a globetrotter on behalf of causes, he has no rival in rock and roll with the possible exception of Sting. Since the 1980s, Bono has protested against China's policies in Tibet, offered his views on the peace process in Northern Ireland (U2 is an Irish group), and has been a leader in the ongoing effort to either restructure or forgive debts that poorer nations owe the World Bank. I doubt that even 20 percent of U2's American fans were aware of the problems involving unpaid debts to the World Bank before Bono got involved. This is different from the late 1960s, when audience demand influenced the political activism of rock stars. Bono seeks to educate his fans, not the other way around.

Whether it's due to the Irish school system, stimulating discussions around the dinner table, good company, or having read widely and well, Bono invariably comes across as articulate and highly credible, rock's nearest thing to a public intellectual. In a special issue of *Rolling Stone* magazine devoted to the pending impeachment of President Clinton, Bono's contribution read as if he were writing the lead editorial for a respected political magazine of liberal bent:

> Stop it—America is better than this. Move on. Stop it by not voting for the politicians who have presided over it. The publishing of the Starr report on the Internet is a defining moment at the end of the twentieth century, like the paparazzi flies around the body of a princess, like a video-game war, like O.J.'s trial by television. Except this time, it's America itself that's in the docket.[6]

After Springsteen and Bono, Michael Stipe of REM is a close third on the list of rock stars that maintain dual lives as political activists. Like Bono, Stipe has become deeply involved in the plight of Tibet—he performed at the Tibetan Freedom Concert in Washington, D.C., in June 1998—as well as the issue of relieving Third World debt. In addition, REM, presumably at Stipe's urging, has at times acted like its own political action committee. In 1990, the band members gave money to a mayoral candidate in Athens, Georgia, the city where they had all met ten years earlier. REM also contributed to a candidate running for a commission seat in Athens, and at various times Stipe himself publicly opposed the expansion plans of a local hospital and the original architectural design for a civic center in the city.

Stipe also played the "is he or isn't he?" game in reference to his own sexual preference for much of the 1990s. When he finally went public and revealed the existence of a male lover, presumably on the advice of his manager, therapist, or both, he won points from gay rights groups, which now had a good reason to include his address and phone number in their data bases.

In the 1990s, younger bands followed the lead of Bono, Springsteen, and Stipe and took up political causes. One of these was Too Much Joy, which had a comical run-in with then-Speaker of the House Newt Gingrich that will be discussed in the next chapter. Another was the Los Angeles-based band Rage Against the Machine, whose motto could have been "Politics isn't everything, it's the only thing." Rage Against the Machine played benefit concerts on behalf of the Zapatista rebels of Chiapas, Mexico, and a black activist named Mumia Abu-Jamal, who was imprisoned for killing a police officer. The band also performed across the street from the Democratic National Convention in Los Angeles in 2000, until the police moved in to end the performance and disperse what officers considered an unruly crowd. Excitable reporters were hoping that this would turn out to be the much-anticipated L.A. Convention 2000 riot, but it never came close, although Rage Against the Machine received national media exposure for several days afterward.

⌒

In the spring of 1990, Steve Barr, a young man but veteran political organizer, flew from San Francisco specifically for a meeting in Beverly Hills with Jeff Ayeroff, then the president of Virgin Records. The ostensible purpose was to discuss financial support from the record label for Barr's latest effort to register new voters. When he arrived, Barr was quickly ushered into Ayeroff's office. The two chatted for a minute, and then Ayeroff asked Barr to join him for a meeting at the swank Four Seasons Hotel. A limousine transported the pair three blocks to the site.

When they reached the hotel, Ayeroff led Barr to a conference room. Barr later estimated that approximately 100 people, each in some way connected to the music business, were seated around a massive table. He recognized none of them except Frank Zappa, adorned like everyone else in the room in casual clothes. On the other hand, Barr was dressed like a law student going for an interview at a prestigious downtown firm. Since he is also 6-foot 4-inches, or thereabouts, Barr got noticed, even among this high-powered crowd. "I was wearing a Brook Brothers suit," he recalled. "I was the only guy in the whole place with a suit on. I looked like a Mormon missionary."

Near the end of the meeting, Ayeroff asked Barr to speak. Over the past hour or so, a general discussion had ensued about the best way to reach young voters, whatever that might mean. Barr was becoming restless, if not frustrated, by the lack of specifics. "When Hollywood gets involved with political causes, they have a knack for screwing them up," he recalls telling the group. "There's people starving in Ethiopia, so let's have a big concert. Madonna dances around, kids send in twenty bucks, and then it all goes away. Kids are left with the impression that they've fixed the problem." Barr went on to criticize Hands across America and others of the our-heart-is-in-the-right-place media events from the 1980s for being totally ineffectual. Instead, he stressed the comparatively mundane but much more practical step of getting young people to register to go to the polls.

When Barr finished, the crowd burst in applause, just the way it might have happened in the movies.

The meeting took place on a Friday. On the following Monday, Barr and two others were given cramped quarters in a corner of Ayeroff's office—the beginning of Rock the Vote. Barr's candor, charisma, and commitment had landed him a full-time position.

Rock the Vote was actually conceived a few weeks earlier, not in some swank hotel or record executive's suite, but in Ayeroff's shower. As he was getting ready for work, he started thinking about the recent arrest in Florida of the rap group 2 Live Crew on obscenity charges, which repulsed him. "I see on TV this guy get arrested, a black man in America handcuffed and taken away—put in jail—for rock and roll," he said.

Ayeroff's response was not to start a legal defense fund—which is often the way these things happen in the entertainment business—but to raise the possibility of using MTV to impress upon young people the importance of registering to vote and then urging them to actually do so. Suffice to say that Ayeroff was not hoping to swell the ranks of right-wing voters with his plan, but he carefully avoided any displays of partisanship in building support for the idea. "I felt that if kids start talking to politicians, then politicians are going to have to respond," said Ayeroff, "and they are also going to have to watch their mouths. They will be worried that in an election if you can get five percent more of the kids to vote, then they can swing the election."

Television reaches far more people than any ten concerts, and at a cheaper cost to the provider. Ayeroff had been one of the first music industry executives to recognize the potential of MTV; in the early 1980s, his marketing campaign for a new white soul/disco singer named Madonna included a healthy doses of music videos. By the middle of the decade, exposure on MTV had helped to turn Madonna into a superstar, and she in turn helped boost the network's popularity. MTV had reason to be grateful for Jeff Ayeroff.

After hearing Ayeroff's pitch, MTV executives agreed to air a few public service announcements urging young people to register to vote. Since television is the most effective and efficient means of communicating political information, far superior to concerts or records, MTV's agreeing to promote voter registration marked a new level of rock's involvement in the political process. Rock the Vote had a greater potential of reaching—and swaying—the eighteen to thirty segment of the population on political issues than any song or songs recorded by Springsteen, U2, Don Henley, or Bonnie Raitt, as Ayeroff knew well.

He assembled a team of graphic artists and video directors to both design a logo for the nascent organization and film some public service announcements. Ayeroff asked Madonna to participate; she recorded a spot wrapped in an American flag, surrounded by two shall we say flamboyant dancers from her entourage, in which she urged young people to get involved in the democratic process. It was pure Madonna, it was bizarre, and it worked. After all, one of reasons the youth turnout has often been anemic is because voting is something that one associates with parents and grandparents. The idea of being a good citizen, and doing one's civic duty, is not an easy sell to otherwise occupied college students, or adults in their twenties and early thirties. To counter this recurrent problem, Rock the Vote developed a very nontraditional spot to promote the most traditional activity in American society. Watching Madonna enveloped in Old Glory made voting seem downtown and hip, rather then suburban and square. "She (Madonna) did this one spot, and it ignited the whole thing," said Ayeroff.

Following the 1992 election, Hillary Clinton told Ayeroff that Rock the Vote's success in registering thousands of young voters, and encouraging those already registered to go the polls, made the difference between victory and defeat for her husband. Even allowing for the strong possibility that Hillary said the same thing to a number of people in the post-November glow, there is no question that Rock the Vote made a strong impact. In the 1992 presidential election, 20 percent more voters aged eighteen to twenty-four cast ballots than was the case four years earlier, when Democrat Michael Dukakis ran against Vice President George Bush. "Rock the Vote took credit for registering 350,000 new voters and sending two million young people to the polls (in 1992)."[7]

In 2001 Rock the Vote, which is headquartered in Santa Monica, California, had an annual budget of up to $5 million during election years and $2 million in off years. The organization is to some extent competing against itself; in 2000, 38 percent of eligible voters between the ages of eighteen and twenty-four went to the polls, down from 42 percent in 1992. One of the key goals of Rock the Vote is to return to that higher level of youth participation in the 2004 presidential election.

PUBLIC ENEMY?

Al Gore played the straight arrow many years before Bill Clinton's dalliance with Monica Lewinsky seemingly forced him into that role. In September 1985, he and his colleagues on the U.S. Senate Commerce Committee held hearings on the subject of "porn rock." Gore had a familial and political interest in the subject. His wife, Tipper, was co-chair of the Parents' Music Resource Center, an organization started earlier that year by a number of wives of powerful Democrats and Republicans in Washington. The PMRC "charged that rock music had become sexually explicit and pornographic."[1] The PMRC wanted labels on records warning parents about "offensive" lyrics contained therein.

One of the songs that upset Mrs. Gore, and indirectly led to the formation of the PMRC, was "Darling Nikki" by Prince, the one black artist from the 1980s who was popular with baby boomers—Tipper's crowd. During a time when much of the music by black performers was either over-emotive ballads or hardcore rap, Prince played primarily funk and rock and roll. But his musical style earned him no credits with Tipper, who was outraged by a line in "Darling Nikki" referring to female masturbation, or should I say to a female masturbating. Speaking with other wives in Washington, she discovered that the Prince song was one of many that were disgusting, sick, depraved, dangerous, and so forth. A proud fan of the Grateful Dead, a group not unfamiliar with the joys of LSD, Tipper felt she had to do something about "Darling Nikki," even though through the years acid has killed many more young people than has masturbation. One wonders how Tipper would have felt in the 1960s if a bunch of politicians' wives had mobilized to put warnings on Dead albums, or ban them outright. The PMRC was one of the early signs that baby boomer parents weren't becoming like their own parents—they were much worse.

The hearings on porn rock marked the first time since the days of "Louie, Louie" that Washington took such an active interest in sexually charged lyrics. These hearings also turned out to be a harbinger of the Senate confirmation of Supreme Court Justice Clarence Thomas six years later, when once again sex acts and "disgusting" language were tossed around within the august environment of the U.S. Congress. In the case of the PMRC, centrist Democrats and conservatives professed to be shocked by it all, while during the Thomas hearings, it was liberals that were deeply offended by remarks the nominee allegedly made to Anita Hill. More of the hypocrisy surrounding sex and politics in America continued.

An unlikely triad of Frank Zappa, John Denver, and Dee Snyder of the rock band Twisted Sister testified against warning labels on records. They were arrayed against a group of Washington wives and mothers, some who blushed and some who didn't, who outlined in graphic detail the new lows to which rock and roll and R&B had sunk over the previous few years. "Filth" and "tasteless" frequently came out of their mouths, words echoed by some senators on the committee. According to Martin and Seagrave, Tipper's contribution was a "slide show on demonic album cover art, bondage, and sadomasochism." In footage from the hearings, snippets of which are still broadcast now and then on VH-1, Tipper shows herself to be a skilled performer, adopting a look perfectly situated between piety, anger, and concern as she listens to the testimony of worried and angry women. It's the same look you see on Hollywood actresses when they are campaigning against smoking or major redevelopment projects.

In the end, the Recording Industry Association of America capitulated—some would argue caved—and agreed to put warning labels on particular releases. Since young people generally don't shop for CDs with their parents, and once purchased, CDs are easy to hide, one wonders whether the warning labels have proven to be a boon and not a deterrent to sales. Still, the question that lingers after all the years is why? Why did the Gores choose to go into the moral watchdog business? They must have asked themselves the same question fifteen years later, when Al was running for president. After all, Republicans are much better at this sort of thing. Within a few years, William Bennett had made his crusade the issue of pop culture's nefarious effects on young America, suggesting in his analysis the kinds of doomsday scenarios that are a staple of right-wing rhetoric. Republicans will invariably take the extra step and blame suicides, homicides, or murder/suicides on particular songs or groups. Democrats are unwilling to go that far. Instead, they talk about the potential for harmful effects without getting deeply into specific cases. Democrats regard offensive lyrics and blatantly sexual images as undermining parental authority, while Republicans describe them in terms of the breakdown of society. The latter is more easily communicated to voters.

Tipper Gore was not just another worried mother. When "Darling Nikki" bothered her, it became America's business. She and her husband, who by all accounts are political partners, had to have made a deliberate decision to embrace this cause. The fun-loving kids of the 1960s had grown up to be responsible parents, keeping tabs on their own brood in much the same way that parents have always done. The PMRC was a pre-emptive strike against the charges of permissiveness and immorality that conservatives often level against baby boomer Democrats. Whatever the Gores did during the 1960s—from what we've heard it wasn't much—that was a long time ago. In essence they were saying judge us by who we are today, and not by who we might have been back when "Light My Fire" was number one.

It's no mere coincidence that they exploited popular music in order to communicate this message. More than the movies, theater, or television, rock and roll defines youth culture of the 1960s. In taking on the music industry, the Gores were sending a signal that nothing was sacred in this effort. They would do what they could to bring about a "cleaner" world. Let others savor the irony of Grateful Dead fans leading a campaign against song lyrics.

~~

By the end of the 1980s and the beginning of the 1990s, Prince was no longer of value to the anti-rock forces. It's not so much that his songs had gotten tame, but he was less threatening than rap, which over the previous ten years had taken sex and violence way beyond anything contemplated by Prince. "Bitches" and "hoes" made frequent appearances in rap songs, as did the "F" word. "Since rap emerged in the late '80s, many have criticized hardcore rap for the genre's misogynistic treatment of women."[2] With the rise of gangsta rap around 1988 to 1989, urban warfare was added to the thematic mix. In 1992, the Ice-T song "Cop Killer" unleashed the full fury of right-wing America. According to Nuzum, President George Bush and Vice President Dan Quayle "both advocated censorship of Ice-T," while "Charlton Heston and the National Rifle Association attacked Time-Warner (Ice-T's record label) and Ice-T for glorifying the killing of law enforcement officials."[3] Of course, these are the same people and organizations that remain silent when paramilitary groups threaten to or inflict violence on officials of the United States government. But then again, Ice-T doesn't look like the guys who hide away in the backwoods of Idaho.

In the early 1990s, the chairwoman of the National Political Congress of Black Women, C. Delores Tucker, began a crusade against gangsta rap, which she detested for depicting negative stereotypes of black people. On February 11, 1994, the congressional subcommittee on Commerce, Competitiveness, and Consumer Protection held hearings on gangsta rap. Tucker was a key figure. "When I arrived at the hearing room the first thing I saw was a blowup of the inner sleeve of Snoop Doggy Dogg's *Doggystyle* CD, which had enraged many women with its salacious cartoon of a randy dog and his long tail. C. Delores Tucker was already sitting in the high-ceilinged, wood-paneled chamber looking queenly in her trademark turban—this one purple—surrounded by a coterie of black female retainers."[4]

Around this time, Tucker formed a partnership with the very same William Bennett, who during the Clinton years became a kind of Minister of Culture in exile. Together they assailed rap on familiar grounds. Ideological soul mates or not, this was certainly an alliance of convenience. Hooking up with a black woman insulated Bennett from charges of racism, while hooking up with Bennett enabled Tucker to establish credibility with powerful white conservatives. While Bennett/Tucker and like-minded advocates didn't succeed in eliminating rap, they did create a climate whereby some urban contemporary radio stations removed it from their playlists. In addition, particular record chains banned rap releases judged to be violent, anti-police, anti-Semitic, and anti-white.

Sounds change, but attempts to suppress rock and other genres transcend styles and generations. After all, during the late 1960s, various radio stations and record stores responded to public pressure and refused to play or stock singles with drug references. In this sense, the reaction to rap was not only a case of white politicians playing the race card, but another example in the history of rock where authority figures register their disapproval through various means. Unlikely as it seems, there is a direct line from "Lucy in the Sky with Diamonds" to "Cop Killer."

The politics and culture of rap and gangsta rap are typically filed under "Angry Black Male." "Hard-core or 'gangsta' rap as it became known, was an angry form of musical expression that openly discussed elements of the black inner city about which most Americans were not prepared to hear: guns, drugs, broken homes, injustice, gangs, murder, the breakdown of community, and police brutality."[5] But rap and hip-hop didn't start that way.

⌐⌐

"Rapper's Delight" by the Sugarhill Gang is the "Rock Around the Clock" of rap. Released in the fall of 1979, it reached number thirty-six on the *Billboard* pop charts—the first record in this fledging genre to make it into the top 100. The song features none of the menacing tone, vulgar lyrics, or angry politics that would come to be associated with rap in the 1980s. Good-natured and ribald, "Rapper's Delight" sounds like a Frank Zappa parody of African American braggadocio combined with the silly wordplay of such Dylan songs as "Leopard-Skin Pillbox Hat." "Rapper's Delight" begs not to be taken seriously, which is the source of its considerable charm.

The song came out during the nadir of the Carter presidency—high inflation, gas lines, and the Iranian hostage crisis—and yet there is no sense in either the words or music that the world is falling apart. It's as apolitical as most disco singles of the period, but without the attendant self-indulgence packaged as fantasy. Released on the Sugar Hill Label, the sound of "Rapper's Delight" does not quite attain musical independence. The vocals are unique, but the instrumentation is sampled from "Good Times," the hugely popular 1979 disco hit by Chic. The rhythmic intro sounds a lot like Taveres, which had a couple of successful disco/R&B hits, and every so often annoying disco production techniques can be heard in the background. Our litigious society compels one to think about litigation, and when I first heard "Rapper's Delight," I was sure Chic would sue the Sugarhill Gang and their label. How could these upstarts hope to get away with out and out musical thievery?

But "Rapper's Delight" and Sugar Hill Records did get away with it, which was our first clue that rap and hip-hop had an audacious, outrageous side. It was as if the powers behind "Rapper's Delight" were daring Chic to come after them. Chic represented the black music establishment, and Sugar Hill was the underdog, not unlike punk v. the rock and roll establishment.

In September 1980, Kurtis Blow had a modest pop hit with "The Breaks," a hip- hop song that maintains and in some places improves upon the humor of "Rapper's Delight." There are fewer nods to disco in this song than in "Rapper's Delight"—indication that musical styles were starting to change. "The Breaks" is not too far removed from Rick James or Prince, each of whom was on the verge of becoming a major figure in pop music. The title refers to both bad luck and the point in the song where dancers have the chance to let loose. The lyrics are funny and the mood is unsympathetic. If things go wrong, well, that's just the breaks. It's not the fault of the government, the Man, the PO-lice, or White America. Nobody is a victim and no one is allowed the luxury of self-pity. Accept your circumstances with equanimity.

Rap never completely lost its sense of humor. The Beastie Boys and other performers recorded some very funny songs in the late 1980s and 1990s. But the affectionate tone established by "Rapper's Delight" and "The Breaks" didn't last. The changeover officially occurred in 1982 with the release of "The Message" by Grandmaster Flash and the Furious Five, one of the earliest rap songs to offer a version of the urban nightmare. In time records of this type would hold great appeal for white kids, who were fascinated by the idea of the ghetto, even though they never wanted to visit one. In "The Message," the narrator warns us that he might go mad living day to day under harsh and brutal conditions. Who among us—whether white, brown or middle-class and black—wouldn't feel the same? One "message" to take from "The Message" is there but for the grace of God.

Released in the midst of the country's worst economic performance since the Great Depression, "The Message" is as much a symbol of the Reagan era as "Morning Again in America." According to Lou Cannon, author of *President Reagan: The Role of a Lifetime*, "By November 1982 more than nine million Americans were officially unemployed, a statistic that would rise to 11,534,000 by January."[6]

Cannon also noted that in January 1983, "20,000 people lined up in 20-degree weather to apply for 200 jobs at an auto-frame factory in Milwaukee."[7] As was the case with "Eve of Destruction," "War," and "For the Love of Money," successful politically oriented songs are those that can in some way be tied to current events. "The Message" had the double advantage of coming out in the midst of a brutal recession and during the reign of a president who had little or no inclination to provide help for poor black people, or support the overall agenda of African Americans. "But blacks, the most conspicuous dissenters in the 'Morning Again' landslide of 1984, never gave Reagan high marks."[8] Without ever mentioning Reagan by name, "The Message" capitalized on the sense of despair felt by the black community during those years. This was not unlike the early 1970s when the O'Jays released their grim "political" hits while another California Republican, Richard Nixon, was in the White House.

⌒

Disco postulated a guilt-free existence. The idea was to party all the time, and the world would either take care of itself or go to hell. Either way, it wasn't "our" concern, as we danced the night away. Gays were free to be themselves—and then some—once they were safely behind the doors of some hot club. They didn't have to apologize to anyone for their sexual preference, or how they chose to satisfy their desires. To this day, the legend perseveres about what it was to be a gay man in the 1970s. Disco and discos made that dream come true.

Middle-class blacks found their own refuge inside disco. The images on album covers and song lyrics made it OK to be black and materialistic, something that had not been a problem for whites. But middle-class or well-to-do black people could never entirely forget their brothers and sisters living in abject poverty. After all, this was the image of black American life that the media and African American elected officials emphasized. You couldn't escape it if you tried. Still, disco commanded that its fans leave their troubles behind, and march to the beat. Forget about whether your white colleagues suspect the firm hired you because of affirmative action, and don't feel guilty because you are scared to drive through the ghetto. Inside the disco, your personal traumas are of no concern to anyone. If you want to talk politics, go to a bookstore or coffeehouse.

But the release of the "The Message" and the subsequent proliferation of political rap made this position untenable for middle-class blacks. "The Message" put politics back into black music, from where it had been missing since the mid-1970s. Coincidence or not, the song signaled the end of a brief period of black political detachment. Two years later, the Reverend Jesse Jackson ran for president, and Louis Farrakhan became a national figure. By the end of the decade, Spike Lee, Public Enemy, and the cult of Malcolm X had injected a strong dose of black politics—historical and contemporary—into the popular arts. Most important, with Reagan inhabiting the White House it could seem downright cruel for the black middle and upper-middle class to ignore what was happening to their community. "When you look at the music of the 1970s—funk, R&B, and soul—that was escapism music, all about romance and party times," said Barry Benson, head of the rap music section for Rhino Records. Passive records that reflected the times. "What you found with a Republican administration coming in is that people had had enough." The comparative optimism of the Carter years permitted the luxury of adopting something of a laissez-faire attitude, confident of progress being made in economic justice and civil rights. That feeling diminished after the Gipper took over, followed by George Bush. Now the disco mentality seemed not ten, but a hundred years removed. The gap between Sister Sledge and Public Enemy was as wide as the one separating Journey from the Sex Pistols.

The relationship between punk and rap during the pivotal early 1980s has rarely been addressed: histories of punk and histories of rap and hip-hop tend to stay close to home. The approach is certainly understandable. Punk was an almost exclusively white scene, especially in the United States. You saw very few black faces at hardcore punk clubs, for both racial and aesthetic reasons. With the exception of late period Clash, punk rock had few obvious African American antecedents, and only a smattering of songs dealt with sex, which was of course a staple of the blues and rhythm and blues.

Still, the "roar" of punk anticipated the angry vocals and lyrics of rap and gangsta rap. Black music—disco—might have been self-satisfied and apolitical in the late 1970s, but not punk. "Anarchy in the U.K." cut through the bullshit of corporate rock and roll in 1977, and "The Message" did the same to disco a few years later. To the mainstream, Johnny Rotten was offensive and disturbing, and by the mid-1980s so were hardcore rappers. This pose accomplished its objective on two fronts. Many rock fans—but not rock critics—that came of age in the 1960s reviled punk, and the same happened with charter members of the "old school" generation and rap. Even sympathetic writers of black music such as Nelson George were deeply offended by the typical rap/hip-hop assessment of women. "As I assailed the 2 Live Crew, catcalls emanated from the back of the hall [at all-women Spelman College in Atlanta in 1989]," writes George. "Brothers from Miami were trying to shout me down, claiming 'Luke [Campbell, the leader of the group] knows these girls' and he's 'just rapping about freaks he knows in Liberty City.' Even more striking was that several Spelman students in the crowd spoke in Luke's defense. No matter how ill [his] views were on women, a number of Spelman's female students had no problem with 'Give Me Some Pussy' or 'Throw the Dick' as long as they were about hoes Luke knew."[9] At Spelman, George ran smack into the middle of the latest generation gap, which set 1960s' values against the "new reality." George was cast as the old guy—he was then in his mid-thirties—who just didn't get it. His political context was feminism, especially respect for black women, and his musical reference point was Motown, James Brown, and Stax, none of which would have ever released a track with the title of "Give Me Some Pussy." Yet to the young kids that was exactly the point.

Once it discovered politics, rap selected specific targets, in contrast to punk, which was enamored with anarchy and chaos for its own sake. "These songs were aimed toward the people in the streets first," said Benson. "They were going to wake up people, whether to the ills of the police as with NWA, or Chuck D on how the government deceived you, and that's why you should channel this rage and anger—gang members—you have toward other black people toward the government." Punk's politics were not usually issue-specific, especially in America. That's the kind of thing that was best left to Jackson Browne, Sting, Bruce Springsteen, and other stars that followers of punk either ignored or held in contempt. Punk hated the idea of save the whales or no nukes, not so much for political reasons, but because these causes were promoted with a kind of California gentleness that diluted the anger and spirit of true rock and roll. Sipping wine and listening to Jackson, Sting, or Bruce on a warm summer evening was not punk's idea of a good time.

But punk never had the responsibility—imposed from within or from without—of having to speak for all white people. At the most, punk was viewed as representative of a neglected, resentful, and perhaps oppressed working class—but only in Britain. In America, however, it was hard to feel solidarity with a teenager from the suburbs of New York or Los Angeles who gravitated toward punk because she was bored. And it was laughable when students at private colleges turned into punkers after dark in order to satisfy some sort of bohemian/radical yearning. By contrast, rap stepped into the void created by the rise of right-wing conservatism on the one hand and the concurrent decline and disarray of liberalism and a vibrant black political leadership on the other.

No one had come close in the 1980s to achieving the stature or respect of Martin Luther King and Malcolm X. Can you imagine *buying* the collected speeches of Al Sharpton—or Jesse Jackson, for that matter? In the 1960s, soul, and later funk, provided musical accompaniment to the movement. But in the 1980s, rap competed for space at the head table. A prime example is Public Enemy, which called its landmark album *It Takes a Nation of Millions to Hold Us Back* and a subsequent one *Fear of a Black Planet*. Both of these titles could be used as applause lines in a fiery political speech. If J. Edgar Hoover were still alive, he would have opened a file on Public Enemy faster than you could say FBI. Rap got off easy in just having to deal with William Bennett and C. Dolores Tucker, neither of who, as far as I know, had the power to authorize wiretaps.

It wasn't only black listeners that were attracted to rap and hip-hop as a result of its engagement with politics. Young white record-buyers, and in the case of Warren Beatty, a sixty-year-old white actor, found rap to be a desperately needed alternative to the politics of sound bites and photo ops. An unrepentant liberal and an unapologetic McGovernite,

Beatty was not pleased by the Democratic Party's rush to the center in the 1990s, particularly on the issues of economic justice and civil rights. His 1998 film, *Bulworth*, features an incumbent U.S. senator who can only speak hard truths after he is seduced by rap music and hip-hop culture. Under their spell he advocates positions far to the left of the post–Dukakis Democratic Party. The modern political industry, which includes lobbyists, consultants, and well-meaning but sycophantic staffers, is pushed to the side as the senator seeks a higher truth. Rap and black activists lead him there. The film is a progressive's dream to be sure, but is that so bad?

The sudden and total demise of punk in the early 1980s left politically inclined, three-chord-loving white rock fans without a viable option. The Sex Pistols and the Clash went quickly, the bodies buried before the coroner could render a definitive judgment as to cause of death. The most plausible theory is that punk suffered from its own ambivalence about fame and success. Bruce Springsteen apparently sees no contradiction between remaining pure and becoming rich, but punk performers couldn't or wouldn't reconcile the two. Once it seemed as if glory was within reach, then it was time to retire—until enough years had gone by to embark on a nostalgia tour.

Cast adrift, punk fans in the mid-1980s had few viable alternatives within rock and roll. You couldn't slam dance to REM, Bruce, Sting, and U2. And besides, each of them proudly embraced the spirit of the 1960s, which was not the favorite decade of true punks. An American indie underground scene thrived in the 1980s, and such groups as the Replacements, the Minutemen, and Fugazi had many fans. But only rap combined the hostility and antisocial tendencies of punk with an unmistakably aggressive political agenda. Rap had no ambivalence about attacking Reagan or his policies. White kids—especially college students or recent college graduates—welcomed the political element in rap, while suburban party animals and frat boys gravitated toward the Beastie Boys and 2 Live Crew. It must have seemed to confused parents in the 1980s that the different forms of rap and hip-hop resonated with the entire white population twenty-five and younger.

But rap was not bipartisan. In the 1990s, the Clinton years, political rap lost much of its edge. Black people once again had an ally in the White House, especially when compared with Reagan and Bush. Under Clinton, genuine progress was made against crime, crack, and teen pregnancy—the horrors of the inner city. Clinton offered hope to the black community, something that had all but disappeared with the election of Reagan in 1980. "Times are still tough for most black folk during Bill Clinton's second term," wrote Nelson George in 1998, "yet there is a yearning for a more humanistic, less nihilistic, but still acquisitive future reflected in the current music."[10] Rap could still find deserving targets, the police in particular, but the sense of crisis had dissipated, at least for the moment. Political rap needs an enemy or enemies in order to thrive. In that sense, the election of America's "first black president"—in Toni Morrison's words—was not good for business. Clinton was even forgiven for his gratuitous attack on Sister Souljah during the 1992 campaign, elevating this relatively obscure performer to celebrity status after she made remarks in the *Washington Post* suggesting a kind of logic behind black gang members attempting to kill white people during the Los Angeles riot.

In his review of *Can't Be Satisfied: The Life and Times of Muddy Waters*, Jon Pareles, pop critic for the *New York Times,* wrote: "The music, as Mr. (Robert) Gordon calmly documents, came from a milieu straight out of gangsta rap: guns, booze, knife fights, fast women, and sleazy deals."[11] Some rap stars made quite a nice transition from that milieu into films, television, and fashion, eventually achieving the inevitable respectability that in America comes with having accumulated millions—regardless of how one got there. A front-page story in the September 16, 2002, edition of the *Wall Street Journal* profiled the reinvention of Snoop Dogg, who in the 1990s seemed to spend an inordinate time in the vicinity of nearly naked women and gunfire, although not at the same time. The *Journal*'s upscale readership learned that Snoop Dogg had stopped smoking pot—a huge sacrifice on his part—was spending more time with his three children, and had expanded his business interests to include the production of soft-core porn videos and his own clothing line. He was being ably assisted in his financial endeavors by a team of advisers that included a recent graduate of the Wharton School of Business at the University of Pennsylvania. And so another "rebellious" performer found happiness down the line.

On the other hand, Muddy Waters was famous, just not *rich* and famous. Until his death in 1983 at age sixty-eight, Muddy Waters was performing in small clubs and at the occasional blues festival. Other blues performers have had similar experiences. They were revered for their artistry and their influence on post–World War II American popular music, but you never read about them on the front page of the *Wall Street Journal*. The one that comes closest is B. B. King, who nabbed a few commercials in part by outliving most of his generation of blues players and launching a chain of clubs. But it will take more than this for B. B. King to make it into Snoop Dogg's tax bracket.

Ice Cube transformed himself from angry young rap performer into an easygoing man of the screen. In 1990, he recorded an album called *AmeriKKKa's Most Wanted*, and he was at one time a member of NWA, the scariest of all gangsta rap groups. That was then. Today Ice Cube is a budding movie star, especially in the aftermath of *Barbershop*, a 2002 crossover hit in which he played the lead character. In interviews, Ice Cube is unfailingly polite and extremely friendly. And why not? Life has been very good to Ice Cube these last few years. He demonstrated that rapping about hopelessness is one path to a brighter future. That other Ice, Ice-T, went from "Cop Killer" to playing a cop in film and on television—take that William Bennett.

Of course, not all rap stars fared as well. Tupac Shakur and Notorious B.I.G. engaged in a feud that ended in the killings of both men. In the fall of 2002, Jam Master Jay of the seminal rap group Run-DMC was murdered in Queens. Indeed, rap must have set some kind of record for having the most performers die violently. The vast majority of rock stars that expire before their time overdose on drugs, with the notable exception of John Lennon, shot to death by a psychotic fan. But hip-hop can seem like a latter-day version of Aaron Burr v. Alexander Hamilton, albeit with someone else pulling the trigger.

Sociologists measure racial progress in terms of rising income and education levels. Politicians measure racial progress on the basis of legislation, legal rulings, and number of governmental appointments. Pop culture critics, without being facetious, could gauge the state of race relations in the early twenty-first century according to the value of Snoop Dogg's mansion or Ice Cube's contract. What Snoop pulled off is virtually unprecedented in American history, parlaying several negative stereotypes about black people—sex-crazed, prone to violence, appetite for drugs—into a wildly successful recording career and cozy "retirement" by the age of thirty. Like the dot-com nerds who are his peers, Snoop accumulated his millions in short order. In this sense, he has more in common with the entrepreneurial spirit of the 1990s than he does with the legacy of black music. No black performer in the past could have expected to get rich projecting these messages or images. Nor would they have wanted to. "Say It Loud (I'm Black and I'm Proud)" was not what Snoop Dogg and his fellow rap artists were peddling to America and the world.

The larger question is whether it's a joke on rap that white kids gobbled up songs about police brutality, mean streets, bitches and hoes, or a joke on the nation. After all, there is something quintessentially American about making money by trading on negative stereotypes. The comic Jackie Mason does a comparatively mild form of this in his routines about Jews. And he is just one among many examples, covering all ethnic and racial groups. Rap and hip-hop tell it "like it is" in a manner that many black people find insulting. But the formula has made a number of rap performers wealthy, which gets back to a sociologist's definition of progress. Snoop and the others made their money legally. It's not as if he was Superfly. Shouldn't those of us who want to see improvement in the lives of black people be happy at this development? Unless his financial advisers screw up, Snoop won't die broke and hungry, like far too many blues, jazz, and R&B musicians.

And yet it's still not clear whether rap represents the authentic voice of the angry and downtrodden or a wildly successful gimmick. How much of rap was legitimate, and how much of it was just another case of music industry manipulation, an *American Bandstand* for disaffected youths who wanted to piss off their parents? We may one day discover that the critics, academics, and occasional politicians who have testified to the artistic integrity of hip-hop culture are actually the ones who were naïve and misguided.

Eminem is the most popular white artist with black audiences since Elton John recorded "Bennie and the Jets" in 1974, which got him an historic gig on the television program *Soul Train*. Eminem is also a credit to his race, as opposed to Vanilla Ice, whose bubble gum raps were ridiculed by African Americans and a source of embarrassment to white hip-hop aficionados. An article in the October 28, 2002, edition of the *New York Times* quotes several younger black fans praising Eminem for being the real deal. Stephen Hill, vice president for music and talent at Black Entertainment Television, told the reporter, "Eminem is better than the best. In his own way, he is the best lyricist, alliterator, and enunciator out there in hip-hop music. In terms of rapping about the pain that other disenfranchised people feel, there is no one better than Eminem."[12]

With whites having purchased millions of rap music CDs since the early 1980s, it's only fair that blacks return the favor and stock up on Eminem product. His 2002 release, *The Eminem Show*, sold some 7 million copies during the year. The soundtrack from the film *8 Mile*, which starred Eminem and featured the story of a white rapper from Detroit and his personal and professional struggles, sold another several million. Presumably black consumers helped to boost the sales of both.

Eminem has become a kind of poster boy for integration, that word nobody uses any more. There is the racial composition of his fan base, as well as the natural and affectionate relationships between blacks and whites depicted in *8 Mile*. The rap performer's "creative team" in the film is biracial, and in the end, through sheer talent, he wins over an exclusively black audience that was prepared to hoot him off the stage. Although rap has gotten a reputation in some quarters for promoting Afrocentrism and polarizing the races, Eminem's message is just the opposite. Like Sly and the Family Stone, he is all about blacks and whites making music together. Given that his producer is Dr. Dre, a black man and a legendary figure in rap for twenty years, it can also be said that Eminem is true to the cause.

In this way, Eminem harks back to the spirit of the early 1960s, before pop music — with the exception of Motown — diverged along racial lines. At the same time, however, his material is a challenge to political correctness, which is above all a remnant of 1960s idealism. Criticized for homophobia and misogyny, another sign of his "legitimacy" as a rap performer, Eminem during his 2002 tour mocked and ridiculed his detractors. According to reviews, his young audiences loved him for this, which is another clear sign that political correctness is regarded by the current generation as another name for parental control. The preaching of tolerance can become insufferable, especially for young people who are trying to find their own way. Like Howard Stern, Eminem serves as a kind of safe house for those who are sick and tired of constantly watching what they say, or being told what to think.

Still, stuffy conservatives are not any better than uptight liberals in the Eminem playbook. "But the fun began before Eminem stepped on stage," wrote *Los Angeles Times* pop music critic Robert Hilburn of a concert Eminem gave in Los Angeles in August 2002, "as video screens featured images of politicians and others from Senator Joseph Lieberman (D-Conn.) to second lady Lynne Cheney denouncing the rapper's music with terms such as 'outrage' and 'shocking.'" Although Eminem has joked about being linked to Elvis — another white boy who did well reinterpreting black music — these denunciations sound a lot like what Elvis had to put up with in the 1950s. As the target of moral puritans and political puritans, one can only conclude that Eminem must be doing something right. The reaction to art is often worse than the source of the "problem." In his willingness to confront both sides on these issues, Eminem qualifies as something of a rebel in the context of contemporary America. He has given hope to those who believe that rap still has a bright future pissing off people in power.

The prevalence of female-headed households in poor, black neighborhoods and the macho environment of the streets have been given as reasons if not justification for the antiwomen and antigay lyrics in rap. In the court of public opinion this is the sociological defense, which is not permissible when used by others in the entertainment or political field. But the Angry Black Male reared in the inner city gets a pass because there's a fifty-fifty chance his life will be nasty, brutish, and short. We know this because we've heard it for decades from black politicians and white-owned media. Try to remember the last time you read or watched a story about something positive in Watts, the South Bronx, or the black neighborhoods of D.C. The vast majority feature instead crime, drugs, gangs, or chronic unemployment. Editors and publishers who live way up in the hills would tell you that their publications accurately represent ghetto life. Self-justification is second nature to people in the news business, even if they dance around the real reason for their decision, which in this case is that stories about black criminals, black crime, and black drug addicts fascinate suburban readers. Although not all or even most of these readers are racists, they have been conditioned to believe that the bad stuff constitutes most of what occurs in the "black" part of town. And very few of them are sufficiently curious or comfortable to get in the car to go have a look on their own.

A lot of rap—on CD and video—sticks to the one-dimensional view of black, urban America. Far from being a departure or a breakthrough, rap provides an image of the ghetto that's familiar even to white people living in regions of the country where African Americans are rarely seen. If this was a marketing ploy, it worked beautifully. "The perpetuation of stereotypical images of Black youth begs the question: Would white consumers be so interested in rap if more of the music and videos depicted Black Americans as multi-faceted human beings rather than as ghetto primitives?"[13] According to *Soundscam,* by 1997 approximately 71 percent of rap buyers in America were white, and, according to the *New York Times* on November 3, 2002, rap is a $1.6-billion a year industry, I would think the answer to the question is "no."

This is one area where rap and white America converged, to the delight of executive officers at rap-oriented record labels. Not as profitable, but just as intriguing, is the common ground between rap and right-wing politics in the 1980s and 1990s, even though they were frequently doing battle in public.

A good example is the seeming contempt for homosexuals evident both in certain rap and hip-hop songs and in remarks emanating from spokespeople associated with the Christian right. "(But) hip-hop is absolutely the most homophobic, macho culture that's influenced mainstream America in a lot of years."[14] At the same time, remarks by right-wing commentator Pat Buchanan and others that AIDS represented a kind of divine retribution rank pretty high on the homophobic scale. Antigay hate speech emanated from both the Left—in the form of rap, the sound of the inner city—and the Right. But this represented more than an attack on a particular group or lifestyle. After all, liberalism and the Democratic Party were and are on record as supportive of gay rights, and their legions are careful to employ just the right tone and politically correct language when discussing various "oppressed" groups, including homosexuals. You can lay odds that the person over there sporting an AIDS ribbon is a registered Democrat, and a head count isn't necessary to make the assumption that liberals have outnumbered conservatives in the various AIDS walks that have been held since the 1980s. A successful effort in Congress to legislate against gay marriage, originated with the ultraconservative wing of the Republican Party. Dick Armey, the former leader of the Republicans in the House, once made a self-described slip of the tongue and called Barney Frank, a Democrat congressman from Massachusetts who happens to be gay,

Barney "Fag" on the floor of the House of Representatives. I don't recall Armey's excuse for mangling Frank's surname, but I do recall that
his colleague wasn't buying it. Republicans are indignant when their
party is called racist, but they more or less take in stride the GOP being labeled "homophobic," which suggests that they believe the majority of American voters feel the same way. I can't imagine that powerful Republicans would have forced Trent Lott out of his position as
Senate majority leader had he made remarks insulting to gays, instead
of African Americans.

Unlike right-wing conservatives, rap did not pursue an antigay political agenda. But throwing around derogatory terms in various rap
songs could not have made it any easier for gay rights groups to convince teenage males—black, brown, and white—of the importance of
tolerance. This was not a problem for the Christian Right, which itself
had no patience for the tolerance of homosexuals, opting instead to label homosexuality sick or abnormal. Indeed, on this issue—but little
else—black rap performers and fundamentalist churchgoers had something in common. Rap moved back and forth across the great American cultural divide. Leftist on economic issues and police brutality, rap
performers could sound almost reactionary when the subject was gays
or women.

Having spent much of the 1970s and 1980s training men to call females "women" instead of "girls," "chicks," or "broads," feminists
now have to deal with something far worse: references to "bitches" and
"hoes" blasting from stereo systems in the middle of busy intersec-
tions. The predictable and unfortunate reaction of some concerned
leaders is to advocate censorship, voluntary or otherwise. There is no
better technique of splitting apart the already fragile liberal coalition
then to pit free-speech absolutists against proponents of a prevent defense. Still, there is no denying that some rap songs projected ugly and
vile images of women, which must have been a rude awakening for
those who believed that American society had, in fact, "come a long
way, baby." Not even during the dark days of the 1950s were women
subjected to this level of verbal abuse. And it doesn't stop in the
recording studios or concert halls. Wherever American teenage boys

gathered—parks, locker rooms, or gyms—you can hear the words "bitches" and "hoes," sometimes in reference to one's own (conveniently absent) girlfriend.

Rap posed a particular dilemma for professional black women, who wanted to be supportive of the "authentic" voice of the inner city but were repelled by the use of derogatory terms to characterize their gender. As a result, rap took itself out of the running as the soundtrack for conventional campaigns. It would have been an act of political stupidity in the 1980s and 1990s for a serious Democratic candidate of any color to play a rap song at a rally, even if the lyrics or themes were comparatively benign. (Republican candidates would never think of going there.) The association of rap with antigay and antiwoman slurs was enough to eliminate that possibility. Democrats couldn't risk undermining their coalition simply to appear contemporary to young people, most of whom probably weren't intending to vote anyway.

12

THEY DIG ROCK AND ROLL MUSIC

Democrats suffered in the 1980s, especially young Democrats with no memory of the time when their party controlled the White House. The 1980, 1984, and 1988 presidential elections ended in easy victories for Republicans Ronald Reagan (twice) and George Bush. Throughout the decade, the Democratic Party at the national level lacked strong candidates, smart ideas, and, most damaging of all, a coherent campaign strategy. The Michael Dukakis/George Bush race in 1988 is still regarded by Democrats as one of the low points in their post–World War II history, worse then George McGovern's landslide loss to Richard Nixon in 1972, or Ronald Reagan's crushing defeat of President Jimmy Carter eight years later. At least Reagan and Nixon were masters of the electoral game . . . but George Bush? How could the Democrats lose to George Bush, an insecure politician and weak candidate?

You could start with having Michael Dukakis strap on a helmet and take a ride in a tank, the campaign's answer to the charge that the Democratic nominee was vulnerable on defense issues. The tank ride didn't make Dukakis look tough, or decisive, but utterly ridiculous, and even worse, quite desperate. He probably regretted it immediately, but by then it was too late. No matter how hard he tried to move on, Dukakis couldn't escape the absurdity of having played tank commander for a day. A desperate campaign is a doomed campaign.

Among the angry and frustrated young Democrats at that time was Sean Landes, who turned eighteen in 1991. Since the second grade, Landes had lived only under Republican rule. In spite of that fact, or more likely because of it, he registered as a Democrat when he reached the legal voting age. Even before he cast his first ballot, Landes had openly expressed his impatience with the recent election defeats of his new party, and his desire to do his part to reverse the trend as quickly as possible.

Landes knew who he didn't want to be president in 1992, but not who he did. During the summer of 1991, when he returned to California after completing his freshman year at Columbia University, Landes spent part of each day watching C-SPAN, the fledgling channel that actually believed Americans would enjoy nonstop coverage of politics, policy hearings, and the deliberations of Congress. It certainly worked for Sean Landes. C-SPAN that summer served as his personal Home Shopping Network for candidates, allowing him to compare the strengths and weaknesses of the various Democrats then considered serious contenders for 1992.

Landes was looking for a centrist with star power, an exciting candidate with safe ideas. Though he admired many leading Democratic politicians from the 1960s, he rejected 1960s liberalism, especially the rise and expansion of the welfare state. He was attracted to the notion of "personal responsibility," and more to the point, he recognized that backing the welfare state was a losing stand in the 1980s and 1990s. Landes and many other Democrats believed their party had to adjust to the reality of post-Reagan politics, or it would continue to collapse in presidential elections.

One day Landes turned on C-SPAN to watch a conference being sponsored by a group called the Democratic Leadership Council. Landes had heard of the DLC, which was formed in 1985, but he knew next to nothing about the keynote speaker, Arkansas governor Bill Clinton, who had already indicated his interest in running for president in 1992.

Though started by Democrats decades older than Landes, the DLC espoused a philosophy of government and policies with which he was entirely comfortable. The DLC believed that "the private sector, not government, should be the primary engine for economic growth and opportunity"; and that "America needs a renewed ethic of civic responsibility in which people who receive government assistance have an obligation to give something back to the country." The DLC master plan for victory in 1992 stated that it was time for Democrats to clamp down on the welfare state, jettison the idea of unlimited government, and adopt a more conservative and more politically popular approach to taxes and spending.

Bill Clinton delivered that message, or one much like it, to the DLC convention. Landes admired the speech and the speaker; when Clinton came to Southern California to speak a few weeks later the nineteen-year-old made a point of going to hear him. This time Clinton was scheduled to appear before the Coalition for Democratic Values, a group that Landes later described as well to the left of the DLC, and openly skeptical if not contemptuous of moderate Democrats. A tough crowd, as Landes acknowledged when he approached Clinton a few minutes before the opening to offer his support: "Excuse me governor, I'd just like you to know that you have at least one sympathetic listener." Clinton stopped walking, shook his hand, and asked him his name.

Landes recalls that loud boos greeted Clinton when he took the podium, but by the end of his speech, most of the audience applauded. Although several new fans now trailed behind the governor, Landes got close enough to congratulate him on his successful performance. When he stuck out his hand, Clinton grasped it, and added, "Thank you, Sean." "I was pretty floored that he remembered my name," said Landes.

Landes was not the first, and certainly not the last, voter seduced by Clinton's ready-made warmth and gift for putting names to faces. A day or so later, Landes phoned DLC headquarters and offered to volunteer for Clinton's nascent presidential campaign. He had no trouble getting in. The Clinton team was not inundated with potential volunteers in California in 1991. A few days later, the DLC called Landes and asked if he wouldn't mind driving Clinton around Southern California during an upcoming fund-raising trip. Landes said it would be no trouble at all.

Anyone who has traveled the crowded freeways of Southern California would know that Clinton and Landes spent a lot of time together in the car. Landes liked to talk as much as Clinton did—the trips were not spent in awkward silence. The pair discussed politics, of course, and they also discussed music, specifically rock and roll music. It was a conversation between two fans; Clinton grew up with rock and roll, and so did Landes. Where rock and roll once separated the generations, it could now unite them, which was a detail not lost on the Clinton campaign team as it prepared for 1992.

Like an eager producer hawking a hot new record, at one point during a long, slow automobile ride Landes urged Clinton to listen to a song by Fleetwood Mac called "Don't Stop," which had made it to number three on the *Billboard* pop charts in September 1977. (The official name of the song is "Don't Stop," but many people refer to it as "Don't Stop Thinking about Tomorrow"). Clinton had probably heard "Don't Stop," but in any event, he told Landes to put it in the cassette deck. What Landes didn't tell Clinton, at least not right away, is that he believed "Don't Stop" would make a great theme song for the 1992 campaign. He thought it hit all the right political notes—seize the future, and forget about the past. Clinton was not only a New Democrat, but he was a young Democrat, especially compared to recent party nominees, such as Walter Mondale and Michael Dukakis. Landes considered Clinton "one of us," although the two of them were some twenty-four years apart. "It was important to me that the words of the song were clear, that you could hear them, you could understand them, you could sing along with them," said Landes.

After the song had finished, Landes shared his plan for the song. Clinton didn't say yes, but he didn't say no, either.

In October, Landes, now back at Columbia for his sophomore year, received a message on his answering machine from a man named Bruce Lindsey, Clinton's lawyer and closest political confidant. Lind-

sey suggested that Landes watch Clinton officially announce his candidacy on television the next day because "we are using your song."

In July 1992, Landes was sitting near the top of Madison Square
Garden when Bill Clinton received the Democratic Party nomination for president. As soon as Clinton finished his speech, balloons
and confetti reigned from above, and the song boomed over the
sound system, "prompting" Hillary and Bill Clinton and Tipper and
Al Gore to dance around the stage. As a scene in *The Big Chill*, a
bunch of forty-plus people with questionable rhythm dancing to a
hit from fifteen years earlier looked embarrassing, but not at a political convention, where long-winded speeches are typical. Why not
Fleetwood Mac? "It was an incredible feeling," said Landes, who
this time had no advance notice the song would be used. Eight years
later, Clinton concluded his speech at the Democratic Convention in
Los Angeles by reminding the delegates and the nation "Don't stop
thinking about tomorrow." The five-word song title is his trademark,
conveying a message with which he and his presidency will always
be identified. To provide memorable lines or campaign themes, John
Kennedy had Theodore Sorensen, Richard Nixon had William
Safire, and Ronald Reagan and George Bush had Peggy Noonan.
Bill Clinton had Fleetwood Mac.

On a Sunday morning in March 1998, the three Democratic candidates
for governor of California addressed delegates attending the state party
convention. One of them, Lieutenant Governor Gray Davis, would not
have been out of place among the statues in a wax museum. Davis is ra-
zor-thin, straight-laced with seemingly no sex appeal—an obvious contrast to Bill Clinton, who only a few weeks before publicly declared that
he "did not have sex with that woman." The vanilla image had not hurt
Davis, who kept winning elections, even in Republican years. But this
time, he was going for the big prize, one of the most visible and prestigious elected offices in America. After all, Ronald Reagan and Jerry

Brown had both served as governor of California—and neither of them was boring.

Rock and roll is an easy and cheap way to inject some pizzazz into a campaign, and by extension, the candidate. When Gray Davis took the stage that Sunday morning, the sound of Wild Cherry's "Play That Funky Music (White Boy)" (1976) filled the auditorium. Now Davis is a white boy, rather pale as a matter of fact, but otherwise this hard rocking/funk song featuring a blistering guitar solo did not bear any resemblance to the person advancing to the podium. When the music began, more than one delegate wore a look of bemusement, as if nothing could be more preposterous than the idea of combining that song with this candidate. And yet many of the delegates also tapped their feet or clapped their hands. "Play that Funky Music" does that to people, regardless of the context. Mercifully, Davis didn't attempt to dance or clap; upon reaching the podium, he smiled to the crowd, and waited patiently for the music to stop. As it faded, the audience was in a good mood, and prepared to give the candidate their full attention, which he might not otherwise have received. Even hung-over delegates sat up in their seats. The speech went surprisingly well, filled with well-delivered applause lines and pumped-up asides. In June of that year, Davis easily won the Democratic primary. Still, I don't recall that his victory speech included a special thanks to the members of Wild Cherry.

But rock and politics don't always mix so well. Four years earlier, the Democrats nominated Kathleen Brown for governor of California, who was the daughter of one former governor and the sister of another. Her opponent in 1994 was Pete Wilson, the feisty Republican incumbent known primarily for his staunch support of the death penalty and his intense hostility toward illegal immigrants and their children. Kathleen Brown that year faced a not atypical problem for female candidates, especially on the Democratic side. She had to prove that she was as tough and decisive as her male opponent. Brown's opposition to the death penalty made her challenge in this regard that much more difficult.

Luckily for her and her campaign advisors, Aretha Franklin recorded a number one hit in 1967 called "Respect." Though first re-

leased by the male soul singer Otis Redding, "Respect" has become
something of an anthem for female candidates. "Respect" suggests
women power without the political baggage of feminism, unlike "I Am
Woman," which is just too close for comfort to the *Ms. Magazine*
crowd. Kathleen Brown's campaign team pulled out "Respect" for her
massive 1993 fund-raiser at the Beverly Hilton Hotel in Beverly Hills.
The huge throng, three-fourths of whom were women in their thirties
and forties, came to support Kathleen Brown, but also to hear the guest
speaker, Ann Richards, then-governor of Texas. The event was a celebration of female political power—actual and potential—as much as it
was a fund-raiser for a particular candidate. It occurred just one year
after the much hyped "Year of the Woman," when female candidates
around the country lashed out against the men in Washington who "just
don't get it," and when the concerns of mothers, daughters, and working women dominated the national agenda as never before. Few in the
room that day doubted that 1994 would be even better, with Kathleen
Brown becoming governor of California and Ann Richards defeating
her opponent, George W. Bush. A woman president, anyone?

When Ms. Brown was introduced, and the famous opening riff of
"Respect" came over the ample sound system, two thousand people
rose from their seats and began a kind of rhythmic clapping, trying to
stick to the beat. Since this was a weekday afternoon, and the wine
supply was limited, nobody went crazy, but they clearly were having a
good time. Female attorneys wearing power suits, studio publicity reps
wearing short skirts, and a sprinkling of Democrat Grande Dames were
all doing the R-E-S-P-E-C-T thing. A few men gamely tried to play
along, but this was not their moment. Like white politicians swaying
to gospel music, males in the audience were merely hoping not to
make fools of themselves.

A minute into the song, and Kathleen Brown appeared, making her
way through the middle aisle to the podium, a spotlight following her
every step. Hollywood analogies are common and cheap, but it sure
seemed like Kathleen was about to receive a Golden Globe Award. She
wasn't walking exactly, but she was bopping and groovin', shaking

some outstretched hands and high-fiving others as she made her way to the podium. Aretha played at a loud volume, however, couldn't disguise the fact that this was no soul sister. Ms. Brown appeared to have never heard the song, or worse, to have never danced to this kind of music. Just what kind of baby boomer did we have here? How about one trying much too hard to show she could "get down" with the best of them. It was a relief when Kathleen finally reached the podium.

Over the next several months, Ms. Brown's candidacy suffered a series of missteps, as Governor Wilson built an insurmountable lead. That embarrassing entrance to the strains of "Respect" could be interpreted as an early warning sign, an indication that this campaign would never find its footing.

And then there is the issue of guilt by association, which is not confined to rock and roll and politics. "With a news cycle that never ends, one of the big things is playing error-free ball," said Eli Attey, chief speechwriter for the 2000 Gore campaign, "which includes vetting everything you can possibly vet. You need to make sure that nobody has any nanny problems, and that no one associated with you has written or said anything offensive." Every consultant knows to be extra careful, and yet there have been times when ex-racists, ex-potheads, current drug dealers, or white-collar crooks have slipped through a campaign's security system. Even a rock band that does not subscribe to middle-class morality on matters sexual might get through.

One of the 1980s teenagers that went gaga over Ronald Reagan was a Michigan high school student named Jeff Holland. He had a lot of company on campus. Holland recalls in the fall of 1984, 1,963 students at Holland's high school supported Reagan in a mock election, and thirty-seven backed Walter Mondale, a margin of victory that invoked the memory of those periodic elections that the Kremlin would hold to validate the rule of a particular Soviet premier. "He (Reagan) was a cowboy and cowboys are cool," said Holland, explaining Reagan's appeal to young voters.

In January 1985, Holland traveled to Washington to witness the swearing-in of Ronald Reagan for a second term as president. Although nothing could ruin this special day for Holland, he was pretty damn embarrassed when Kool and the Gang and Jerry Lee Lewis performed at the youth gala. If Reagan represented the future in American politics, the dismantling of 1960s liberalism, then what were these tired acts doing on the stage? Why not instead hire some contemporary performers? As the acts did their show, Holland cringed, but he also made a personal vow to make sure this never happened again to young Republicans. "I thought: come on, this isn't right. We must do something different." Ten years later, Holland got his chance.

In the early 1990s Holland, still a staunch supporter of the GOP, gravitated toward an alternative band called Too Much Joy. The members of this group were like fledgling dot.com entrepreneurs, minus the venture capital. They recorded their first album on their own, promoted it on their own, and booked their own concert tour, a shining example of the economic self-reliance touted by 1990s politicians from both parties.

Too Much Joy devised clever ways of getting noticed. In 1990, for example, the band traveled to Hollywood, Florida, to perform in a concert they had arranged in support of 2 Live Crew, a rap group that several weeks earlier had been busted on obscenity charges in that same city. MTV, CNN, and representatives from Warner Brothers, the label that had signed a contract with Too Much Joy, were all in attendance. The crowd also included a couple of undercover agents, distinguished by their loud Hawaiian shirts. The band, however, had been expecting—indeed hoping—they would make it to the show.

Too Much Joy had rehearsed a 2 Live Crew set, and planned to perform the same songs the rap group had performed the night they were busted. This was a publicity stunt, an expression of solidarity between musicians, and a statement about race in America all rolled into one. A

perfect event for rock journalists—who did, in fact, swarm to the concert—as well as those familiar talk shows that trade in controversy.
You can imagine the host's opening lines: Can a group of white guys
from a rich suburb in New York get away with doing the same thing
that got black rappers in trouble with the law? If not, what does it say
about America? If so, what does it say about America?

The outcome of the appearance was never in doubt. The moment
that Too Much Joy performed the song that had upset the authorities
before, the guys in the Hawaiian shirts rose from their seats, climbed
on stage, and busted the band—equal opportunity justice. As the members were being led away, they made sure to turn toward the cameras
and yell "Freedom of Speech" and "Fuck the Police." The subsequent
trial, in which they were found innocent of obscenity charges, generated wide coverage in the media.

None of this mattered that much to Jeff Holland. He was initially
drawn to Too Much Joy because they had the audacity and sense of humor to record a cover version of "Seasons in the Sun." This lightweight
and rather grating pop song from 1974 was about a guy bidding his
family and friends farewell as he prepares to die, presumably from natural causes. Holland went on to purchase the band's CDs, play them
assiduously, and attend several of their concerts.

Holland's discovery of Too Much Joy coincided with an upswing
in his political career. In the summer of 1994, he landed a plum job
with the National Republican Congressional Committee (NRCC),
writing direct mail pieces sent to targeted groups of voters around the
country. Two years earlier, the Clinton campaign had dubbed its central headquarters the War Room. Holland was working in the GOP
version of the War Room, along with other ambitious Republican
twenty-somethings who firmly believed that this was the year their
party would, after forty long years, finally win back control of both
houses of Congress. A frequent visitor to the office was Newt Gingrich, Holland's latest Republican hero now that Reagan had retired
from public life. Gingrich did a masterful job of keeping the troops at
the NRCC motivated by convincing them that total victory was not

just possible, but probable. Holland gladly put in long hours at not much pay to craft the messages that would help achieve the glorious triumph Newt predicted for November.

After Vietnam, Watergate, the Arab oil embargo, the Iran Hostage Crisis, rising crime, rising deficits, and what was viewed as the "moral breakdown" of American society, toughness, or the appearance of toughness, became a necessary part of the campaign pose of candidates from both parties. Republicans did this the best, for reasons that are not entirely clear. Ronald Reagan and Newt Gingrich set the standard for acting tough, and in so doing helped to attract young white males like Jeff Holland to the GOP. Among this crowd, the Republican Party acquired the reputation as being more "kick-ass" then the Democrats, who didn't even have the backbone to say no to feminists or gays, for God's sake.

But there was one category in which Holland readily conceded victory to the Democrats, and it irked him no end. "I was sitting in the offices of the NRCC with some people who were around my age," he said. "We were talking about how the Democrats always had cooler songs. They just did. We talked about how we might combat that, and how we could get past the 'coolness factor.' The Republicans never seemed to get it." Fleetwood Mac, which had not had a hit in years, seemed cutting-edge compared with Kool and the Gang and Jerry Lee Lewis. Even that brilliant strategist Gingrich seemed to have no idea how to graft an image of cool onto the Republican campaign machine. When it came to the link between pop culture and politics, the GOP was still stuck in the Eisenhower era, or maybe all the way back in the time of Calvin Coolidge.

Jeff Holland decided that he alone could fix the problem. After spending long days at the NRCC, he would go home and listen to his CDs in an effort to find the perfect song to match the Republican effort in the 1994 campaign. One night he put on a Too Much Joy CD, although he later recalled that this was more out of personal preference than any political motive. But when he listened to the Too Much Joy theme, which included a line about having to destroy in order to create, he had his answer. Wasn't this the whole idea behind the GOP crusade? Eliminate the vestiges of 1960s and 1970s liberalism, and replace them with a new philosophy of government based on politically and socially conservative themes and values?

Holland posted that particular line on a wall at the NRCC, partly to reassure his peers that the GOP could also be cool, and partly as an incentive to keep working hard. He also eventually got the chance to play the song for Gingrich, just as Sean Landes had played "Don't Stop" for Clinton. As Holland wrote in the fall 1996 edition in the Too Much Joy newsletter: "Newt didn't stay long, but we knew the song sank in, because the 'to create you must destroy' theme became apparent in his campaign stump speeches for GOP candidates."

The Too Much Joy theme never came close to achieving the political fame of "Don't Stop," but Holland was satisfied that he had made his point. On election night 1994, when the Republicans achieved their goal of winning back both houses of Congress, a tipsy Holland and his tipsy co-workers sang the Too Much Joy song at the top of their lungs in the bar of a swank Washington hotel.

After the election, Holland took some much-needed time away from politics to follow Too Much Joy from city to city on their latest concert tour. One night he mentioned to the lead singer that the Too Much Joy theme had meant a lot to young Republican strategists during the 1994 campaign. The lead singer, by no means a Republican, found this hard to believe. But just in case, he challenged Holland to produce some hard evidence of the song's impact. He specifically asked Holland to obtain a letter on stationary with official Republican letterhead attesting to this fact. He didn't expect to get such a letter, but if he did, he knew exactly what he was going to do with it.

Holland dutifully approached Gingrich's office and made the request. A few weeks later, he got what he wanted, courtesy of an eager-to-please and newly installed staff. The opening read: "Thanks in part to Too Much Joy, our party accomplished a feat few thought possible." And it concluded this way: "Your song—through the spirit it created—had a tremendous impact on the 1994 mid-term elections, and as a result, will have a tremendous impact on the future of our great nation."

Once they received the letter, it probably took less than a minute for the press-savvy members of Too Much Joy to plot their next move. Copies were sent to the editorial offices of *Time* and *Newsweek*. The band had a pretty good idea how this would play out in the media. Of course, if Gingrich had bothered to look closely at Too Much Joy, he would surely have had to reject any association with the band. In addition to that famous theme song, Too Much Joy wrote and recorded several others that took what might be called a laissez faire approach to sex and drugs. Even worse, one of their CDs featured a drawing of a young, naked (heterosexual) couple relaxing after having just had sex. To reporters even remotely cognizant of the tensions in the Republican Party between fundamentalist Christians and libertarians or moderates, the letter was a gem, an entry in a political column or maybe even a separate story—everybody loved exposing puritans as hypocrites. How could the GOP reconcile praise for Too Much Joy with the band's embrace of hedonism and decadence? Reporters called Gingrich, the newly crowned Speaker of the House, and demanded an explanation. Gingrich denied knowledge of the letter, which Holland considers plausible given the amount of constituent mail that is sent from the typical political office. But he pointedly didn't deny having heard the song, and the damage was done. The perception of Gingrich as a flawless operative, which was honed in the aftermath of the landslide, had suffered a blow. As it turned out, Gingrich would make many more mistakes over the next few years.

And there are the politicians who just can't help themselves. In the November 23, 1998, issue of *The New Republic*, a publication that usually favored Al Gore, there appeared a story about a "rap" the then-vice president had recited in public. The article may well have been intended as a warning to Gore to never try such a thing again. Apparently he didn't make anyone forget the Beastie Boys, Vanilla Ice, Eminem, or other popular white rappers, let alone Ice-T or Ice Cube. Instead of denigrating gays, women, or the police, as is common in rap, Gore skewered Republicans, specifically Republicans in Congress. His particular gripe was that GOP politicians cared more about the impeachment of President Clinton, and Clinton scandals in general, than they did about the good of the country.

It didn't get airplay, never appeared on a CD, and to my knowledge no film of it exists. But thanks to *The New Republic* we have what I presume to be the full text of the Gore rap, for lack of a better title:

> We say "legislate;" the Republicans say "investigate."
> We say, "educate"; they say, "instigate."
> We say, "illuminate"; they say, "interrogate."
> We say, "protect our children"; they launch more inquisitions.
> We say, "make the decisions"; they take depositions.
> We know our future is nearing; they hold more hearings.[1]

Even the shameless one, Bill Clinton, never transformed into a rapper. It's too bad for Gore that he didn't know how to play the saxophone.

Perhaps due to *The New Republic* article, Gore curtailed his rapping, and he and his campaign went about the business of picking the ideal song for the 2000 contest, eventually settling on "You Ain't Seen Nothin' Yet" by Bachman Turner Overdrive (1974). Within this context, the meaning of the title was obscure; was it a reference to the economy, the exercise of presidential power, environmental regulations, or all of the above and more? From the perspective of 2002, "You Ain't Seen Nothin' Yet" was a brilliant choice, especially given the history-making set of circumstances surrounding the disputed vote in Florida.

⌒

If George W. Bush rapped during the 2000 campaign, he did it outside the earshot of a journalist from *The New Republic*. No record exists of his launching into hip-hop verse to excoriate liberals, atheists, congressional Democrats, or other groups that would arouse the ire of a right-wing Republican. Indeed, there is precious little evidence that President Bush has any interest in the music of his generation—rock and roll—let alone rap. He has never repeated the behavior of his father, who under the tutelage of blues guitarist/ political guru Lee Atwater played about five seconds of air guitar at the 1989 inaugural party. If you've never seen it, it's worth trying to find the tape, filed perhaps under the heading "Poppy plays the blues."

In reference to his mysterious past, George W. Bush has said that he was "young and foolish," which is presumed to mean that he drank and partied too much. Some of his critics have also suggested that he snorted too much, but Bush has never acknowledged cocaine use. And with that, he closes the book. His comments on rock and roll are brief and bereft of emotion, which is in stark contrast to Bill Clinton, who could talk about the subject passionately for hours. During the 2000 campaign, Bush told Maureen Dowd, columnist for the *New York Times*, that he liked the Beatles until they entered their psychedelic period. He offered nothing more about particular Lennon/McCartney songs that moved him or what the Beatles meant to his generation. And I can't recall that he said anything one way or the other about the Rolling Stones, Bob Dylan, the Grateful Dead, or Motown. Too bad Dowd or some other enterprising reporter didn't find a source that could reveal the contents of George W.'s record or CD collection. It would be interesting to know if he feels he has something to hide. Does he listen to Pink Floyd when no one is around? Was he once young and foolish for Zeppelin? Or was there maybe a time back in 1977 and 1978 when Bush, thoroughly disgusted with his privileged position in life, turned to the Sex Pistols and Clash for solace and satisfaction? Did he ask himself more than once the question: What would Johnny Rotten do? We may never know.

The public President George W. Bush has even less of a connection to rock and roll than Bob Dole or Ronald Reagan had. Whereas those older Republicans, or their consultants, turned to rock to pump up the campaign, Bush's people seemed intent on stifling any suggestion that he was a live human being during the 1960s and 1970s, as if he jumped from the 1950s to the 1980s with no stops in between. Then again, if you want to limit reporter curiosity about sex and drugs, it makes some sense to keep rock and roll locked in the closet, even at the cost of not appearing as cool as your Democratic opponent. Along with middle-age abstinence and frequent expressions of his love of Jesus, maintaining distance from rock and roll might be part of the remaking of George W. Bush into a man of impeccable character—according to the standards of contemporary America.

There's no reason to expect that the Bush campaign will change its tune in 2004. After all, they didn't need rock and roll in 2000, and this time their candidate will be running as a popular incumbent. Since September 11, 2001, the success of the Bush presidency has been predicated on national paranoia and national security, a combination that also worked for Republicans during the mid-1950s, the height of the Cold War period. There was no rock and roll until 1955. If the Bush people want to rekindle the national mindset that prevailed in the immediate aftermath of the Soviet Union testing a hydrogen bomb, then rock and roll on the campaign trail could actually be a liability. I'm not predicting that the campaign will play Perry Como or Patti Page at rallies, but they might be able find some songs suggestive of that "simpler time" fifty years ago. If you're going to bring back the Cold War, you might as well take a stab at bringing back Cold War culture as well.

As for the Democratic candidates, we should expect a veritable rockfest in 2004. Democrats run away from some aspects of the political and cultural legacy of the 1960s, but not from rock and roll. The positive repercussions that continue to flow from playing "Don't Stop" at the 1992 convention virtually ensure that Democratic strategists will continue to look for rock hits that define the campaign and the candidate. With the possible exception of North Carolina senator John Edwards, the candidates lining up to run against Bush in 2004 are all from the generation for whom rock and roll was everything. But what will happen in 2008, 2012, 2016, and 2020? Will rock continue to rule the political charts?

Recall that earlier in this book I noted that at the beginning of the twenty-first century rock and its various derivatives could he heard everywhere. Television advertisements, supermarkets, sporting events, before, during, and after films, talk radio promos, campaign rallies for candidates of both major parties and the minor ones as well. Rock follows you wherever you go. I suspect that long ago employers gave up trying to ban rock in the workplace; the internet and portable CD players have made it very easy to sneak a listen at your desk. Besides, who in 2003 wants to be the old fogy that tells the members of his or her staff to turn that damn thing off?

Still, if rock is omnipresent, why do many veteran fans, and some younger ones as well, seem so glum? Hasn't it been the case since Elvis was tamed for mass consumption that rock and roll sought the widest possible audience? Yes, but . . . Today it seems as if the rock we hear on the radio and in public spaces has been reduced to about 100 songs, many of which are repeated so often that you might well find yourself wishing for the return of Beautiful Music. Between tight playlists on oldies stations and the steady elimination of diverse and adventuresome contemporary rock radio, you could conclude that this genre is heading toward oblivion. I don't mean literally; there will continue to be new rock bands, some of them no doubt very good. Indeed, *Rolling Stone* in 2002 awoke from its hibernation just long enough to feature a cover story on the return of rock. But thus far in the twenty-first century, rock is just one more form of entertainment. Its latest re-emergence had no discernible impact on politics, society, or pop culture.

The comparatively cavalier approach of today's fan even extends to the music itself. Teenagers don't argue as heatedly about the relative talent of various groups, lead guitarists, or bass players as they did in the 1960s and 1970s. In some circles, Clapton v. Hendrix was just as significant as Nixon v. Humphrey, and justifiably so. There was once a time when discussions about rock music would go on for hours, in dorms, living rooms, cars, planes, or over the phone. But these days rock is one more easily disposable commodity in a world full of the same.

Which brings us back to the future of rock and politics, or to be more precise, the future of rock in politics. In a word: shaky. Beginning with 2008, it can no longer be assumed that a huge portion of the audience will glom on to a particular theme song as they did with "Don't Stop." The problem, not uncommon in politics, comes down to demographics. In a decade, maybe sooner, classic rock will no longer garner the votes. By 2008, the people for whom *Sgt. Pepper's* truly mattered at the time of its release in 1967 will be fifty-five and above. How many times can they tell their children and perhaps even their grandchildren where they were when they first heard "Day in the Life"? And how many times can their children and grandchildren hear these stories before they run screaming out of the living room?

Eventually politicians looking for songs to impress young voters will need to select from the 1980s and beyond. It won't be easy. Do you go for grunge, and drudge up unpleasant memories of Nirvana? Do you opt for Guns and Roses, and risk charges of sexism and misogyny? As for the 1990s, good luck picking a song that doesn't include at least one obscenity or trade in alienation and anger. If the idea of a rock campaign song is to lift the spirits of the audience, the 1980s and 1990s weren't especially helpful to the cause.

Yes, of course, a young intern will be dispatched to the local CD outlet, and he or she will return with an appropriate and modern song. It's not impossible to come up with *something*. But whatever that is will not resonate with the children of the 1980s and 1990s like the Beatles, Dylan, and Fleetwood Mac resonated with baby boomers and near-miss baby boomers. There's no sense in arguing that rock meant more in the 1960s than it has ever since, or in lording it over people who had the misfortune of being born later then 1975. And if you're a political aide deciding which song to choose, that whole discussion is beside the point anyway. You care about nothing except getting your candidate elected.

Rock and roll will never die, and rock and roll as an opening act for a campaign speech will never die either. Journalists will continue to search for the meaning in a campaign's choice of theme music, and ask a politician what he thinks of rock and specific performers. But once you get beyond the 1970s, rock is no longer a common pursuit, unifying people of a certain age regardless of their politics. That music is also not a matter of life and death—or anywhere near—to Generation X and whatever comes after. Before contemporary politicians would consider rock a major asset to their campaigns, there would have to be a resurgence of it strong enough to force *Rolling Stone* to stop writing about fashion and teen sex. With rock and roll now taken for granted and talented bands excluded from the radio, the chances of this happening grow ever more remote.

Still, don't lose hope, young frustrated rock and rollers. After all, nobody in America in 1962 could have predicted where or when the next big thing would emerge.

EPILOGUE: FREEDOM

Following the events of September 11, 2001, rock and roll mobilized quicker than did the United States military. It took almost a month before the bombing commenced in Afghanistan, but the telethon *America: A Tribute to Heroes*, aired on September 21. I was in Washington during the week of September 11, and within a couple of days after the terrorist attacks the local classical music station was running promos urging people to tune in because it would help them relax. (I'm assuming that Wagner was shelved for a while.) Music filled the gap between "attack on America" and "America strikes back"—the period in September and early October when we waited for the United States to make its move. While the music featured on the telethon was not as soothing as the music of Vivaldi, it was as solemn a series of performances as has ever been given in the history of rock and roll.

The roster was top-heavy with the icons of classic rock, such as Tom Petty, Paul Simon, Bruce Springsteen, and Neil Young. Each of these musicians was at least in his teen years at the onset of the counterculture, and has vivid memories of the war in Vietnam. Young and Simon were actually making records at a time when many people considered rock un-American and even subversive. If the number of rock songs indirectly or directly opposed to war in Vietnam was small, the number of those backing the U.S. effort was much smaller. It wasn't cool in the 1960s to mix rock and patriotism. Think of what would have happened at Woodstock had Country Joe come out with his guitar and sung about sticking it to the Vietcong. The crowd would have put down their joints, pulled up their pants, and rushed the stage in anger.

But outside of Noam Chomsky and a few others, America was the recipient of considerable sympathy and compassion after September 11. The telethon, put together to raise money for the United Way's September 11 Fund, enabled rock to become a part of what seemingly every talking head in the United States was referring to as "the healing process." The timing of the event could not have been better. The peace movement was virtually nonexistent since America had not yet gone to war. Rock musicians didn't have to feel they were abandoning their traditional base in order to support the policies of the government. Most people were in no mood to party, which made staying at home and watching television an attractive option, even on a Friday night. And endless media coverage loaded with dire predictions and frightening scenarios had for the moment turned an essentially apathetic populace into news junkies. No one doubted the importance of this event, or the need to come together. The telethon was a Woodstock for all Americans, the Right and the Left, young and old, and even black and white. *That* was unusual.

A few weeks later, with bombs falling on Taliban positions, "The Concert for New York City" took place at Madison Square Garden. No longer a strictly American affair, this event featured several British rock stars: Paul McCartney, the Who, Mick Jagger, Eric Clapton, David Bowie, and Elton John. The performance included one of the first post–9/11 songs about 9/11, McCartney's "Freedom." Like President Bush, McCartney reduced the significance of the terrorist attacks to a single word. For the president, that word was "evil"; Paul's choice was rather more uplifting. Then again, he wasn't trying to rally the American public in support of war. "Freedom" was not a song of much depth, and suffered by comparison with "Revolution," which had a sense of irony and did not simply follow the crowd. McCartney took no chances with "Freedom"—an accurate reflection of the national mood at that time. The type of freedom was not defined; was it political, religious, or artistic? But none of this really mattered. Suffice to say that, according to the song, freedom was this thing that separated us from them: We had it, and we were not going to give it up without a fight. You got the feeling that "Freedom" will not age well.

"Freedom" was not the last word. Within a year, the number of songs "about" 9/11 had expanded, including several that either advocated peace—a little late for that—or took a position that questioned American actions. In the latter group was "Shoot the Dog" by George Michael, who if nothing else has to be regarded as one of the more unpredictable musicians in pop music history. Still, music in 2002 had been relegated to a position in the entertainment hierarchy somewhere below film, video games, and reality television shows. Not many people cared that the Michael song or "John Walker's Blues" by Steve Earle didn't echo the administration line. Bill Maher got into a hell of a lot more trouble for remarks he made in the fall of 2001 about the relative courage of the suicidal hijackers and American bomber pilots on his late-night television program *Politically Incorrect*. Maher's remarks signaled the beginning of the end for his show on ABC.

The first officially certified 9/11 album came from Bruce Springsteen, as if anyone was surprised. Like politicians and priests, Bruce is expected—no required—to interpret the events of our lives. Anything less would be a disappointment to the many older critics who have invested so much in his career. For his part, Springsteen is too much the consummate professional to give any hint whether he considers this role a burden. Neither the Stones nor the Beatles ever fell into the "political trap"—"Street Fighting Man" and "Revolution" are proof. But The Boss keeps churning out songs that hit us where we hurt. It appears there are no term limits for political songwriters. Of course, in the case of the attacks on the World Trade Center, Bruce also had to respond because he is the favorite son of New Jersey.

The Rising was released in July 2002 to overwhelmingly positive reviews. In August, Springsteen went on a nationwide tour to promote the record. Articles and/or reviews in both the *Los Angeles Times* and the *New York Times* included "9/11" in the headlines. So did a piece about the album in the *Wall Street Journal*. The *Washington Post* review of Springsteen's concert at the MCI Center included this sentence: "We needed Bruce Springsteen even more than we thought, and we thought we needed him a lot."[1] In 1975, Bruce represented the future of rock and roll; with *The Rising* he has been crowned the savior of baby boomer civilization. How much higher can he go?

The best song by far on *The Rising*, "Let's Be Friends (Skin to Skin)" has nothing to do with 9/11, and as such garnered nary a line in the many reviews I read of the album. "Let's Be Friends" demonstrates, along with "Tenth Avenue Freeze Out" and "Hungry Heart," that Springsteen understands the mechanics of mid-1960s soul better than any other white man on the planet. He listened and he learned. Most white rockers through history have emulated the great black blues and R&B guitarists, but Bruce focused on the vocalists, rhythm, keyboard, and horns of the Chicago and Detroit stable circa 1963 to 1967. Had Springsteen made the entire album in this vein, it could have been one of his best ever.

In little more than a year following the terrorist attacks, rock did more for the country than it did in any one year on behalf of the peace movement in the 1960s and early 1970s. None of the anti-war rallies featured an array of talent comparable to "The Concert for New York City." Whether this was due to personal beliefs, professional responsibilities, commercial pressure, or a combination we may never know for sure. After all, there wasn't much of a risk in performing songs to raise money for the families of firefighters killed on September 11, 2001.

Still, if it wasn't obvious before, it should be obvious now: the politics of rock and roll are elusive. For every "I-Feel-Like-I'm-Fixin'-to-Die-Rag" there is "Freedom." We all want to change the world, but not in the same way.

NOTES

CHAPTER 1

1. James Miller, *Flowers in the Dustbin: The Rise of Rock 'n' Roll, 1947–1977* (New York: Simon & Schuster, 1999), 349.

2. Roger Kimball, *The Long March* (San Francisco: Encounter, 2000).

3. Max Lerner, *America as a Civilization* (New York: Simon & Schuster, 1957), 358.

CHAPTER 2

1. Cathleen Decker, "Lungren, Davis Still Marching to Different Drums," *Los Angeles Times*, September 7, 1998, p. 1.

CHAPTER 3

1. Linda Martin and Kerry Segrave, *Anti-Rock: The Opposition to Rock 'n' Roll* (New York: DaCapo Press, 1993), 163.

CHAPTER 4

1. Newt Gingrich, *To Renew America* (New York: HarperCollins, 1995), 7.

2. Anatol Lieven, "The Push for War," *London Review of Books*, October 3, 2002, 10.

3. Nick Bromell, *Tomorrow Never Knows: Rock and Psychedelics in the 1960s* (Chicago: University of Chicago Press, 2000), 7.

4. Gingrich, *To Renew America*, 24.

5. David Halberstam, *The Fifties* (New York: Villard, 1993), 514.

6. Morris Dickstein, *Leopards in the Temple: The Transformation of American Fiction 1945–1970* (Cambridge, Mass.: Harvard University Press, 2000), 87.

7. J. A. S. Grenville, *A History of the World in the Twentieth Century* (Cambridge, Mass.: Belknap, 1994), 428.

8. Halberstam, *The Fifties*, 98.

9. Joshua Micah Marshall, *The American Prospect*, March-April 1999, p. 56.

10. Donald Clarke, *The Rise and Fall of Popular Music* (New York: St. Martin's Press, 1995), 311.

11. Allan Nevins and Henry Steele Commager, *A Pocket History of the United States* (New York: Washington Square Press, 1968), 528.

12. Eric Hobsbawm, *The Age of Empire: 1875–1914* (New York: Pantheon, 1987), 6.

13. Bruce J. Schulman, *The Seventies: The Great Shift in American Culture, Society, and Politics* (New York: Free Press, 2001), 5.

14. David McGee and Carl Perkins, *Go Cat Go* (New York: Hyperion, 1996), 204.

15. McGee and Perkins, *Go Cat Go*, 204.

16. Wes Smith, *Pied Pipers of Rock and Roll* (Longstreet, 1989).

17. Martin and Segrave, *Anti-Rock,* 77.

18. Martin and Segrave, *Anti-Rock*, 29.

19. Ann Powers, "No Last Hurrah Yet for Political Rock," *The New York Times*, Arts and Leisure, December 31, 2000.

20. Wilfred Howard Mellers, *Twilight of the Gods: The Music of the Beatles* (New York: Viking, 1973), 27.

CHAPTER 5

1. John Jackson, preface to *American Bandstand: Dick Clark and the Making of a Rock'n'Roll Empire* (Oxford: Oxford University Press, 1997).

2. Jackson, *American Bandstand*, 57.

3. Jim Miller, ed., *The Rolling Stone Illustrated History of Rock and Roll* (New York: Random House, 1976), 96.

4. Darrell Satzman, "Singing the Praised: Christian Rock Growing as Economic, Social Force," *Los Angeles Business Journal*, March 19-25, 2001, 1.

5. Religion News Service, "Rock: Shaking Pews but also a Spirit unto Itself," *Los Angeles Times*, July 27, 2002, B15.

6. Miller, *Rolling Stone Illustrated History*, 102.

7. Miller, *Rolling Stone Illustrated History,* 103.

8. Smith, *Pied Pipers of Rock and Roll*, 6–7.

9. Miller, *Rolling Stone Illustrated History,* 103.

CHAPTER 6

1. Philip Norman, *Shout! The Beatles in their Generation* (New York: Simon & Schuster, 1981), 201.

2. Greil Marcus, "The Beatles," *The Rolling Stone Illustrated History*, 1976, 174.

3. Dwight MacDonald, *On Movies* (New York: Da Capo Press, 1981), 400.

4. "Flying, East and West," Stanley Kauffman, *The New Republic*, December 25, 2000, 22.

5. Meg Greenfield, *Washington* (New York: Public Affairs, 2001), 83.

6. Nelson George, *The Death of Rhythm and Blues* (New York: E. P. Dutton, 1989), 139.

7. Mary C. Brennan, *Turning Right in the Sixties: The Conservative Capture of the GOP* (Chapel Hill: University of North Carolina Press, 1995), 118.

8. Morris Dickstein, *Gates of Eden: American Culture in the Sixties* (New York: Basic Books, 1977).

9. Miller, *Flowers in the Dustbin*, 224.

10. Kathleen Tynan, ed., *Kenneth Tynan Letters* (New York: Random House, 1994), 328–29.

11. Dave Marsh, "The Who" *The Rolling Stone Illustrated History*, 268.

12. Stanley Karnow, *Vietnam: A History*, 2d ed. (New York: Penguin, 1997), 454.

CHAPTER 7

1. *USA Weekend*, 4.

2. Peter Biskind, *Easy Riders, Raging Bulls: How the Sex-Drugs-and-Rock-'n'-Roll Generation Saved Hollywood* (New York: Simon & Schuster, 1998), 20.

3. Norman, *Shout!*, 293.

4. Rickey Vincent, *Funk: The Music, the People, and the Rhythm of the One* (New York: St. Martin's, 1996), 108.

CHAPTER 8

1. Nik Cohn, *Rock from the Beginning* (New York: Pocket Books, 1970), 188.

2. Donald Clarke, ed., *Penguin Encyclopedia of Popular Music* (New York: Penguin, 1990), 221.

CHAPTER 9

1. Karnow, *Vietnam: A History*, 609.

2. Melinda Herneberger, "Tough and Self-Controlled, Dole Gets Ready to Be '00 Contender," *New York Times*, March 11, 1999, 1.

3. Gillian G. Garr, *She's a Rebel: The History of Women in Rock & Roll* (Seattle: Seal Press, 1992), 116.

4. Schulman, *The Seventies: The Great Shift*, 180.

5. David Handleman, "Is the Return of Glam Real or Just a Glittery Fantasy?" *New York Times*, October 19, 1998.

6. John Storm Roberts, *The Latin Tinge* (Oxford: Oxford University Press, 1979), vii.

7. Thomas Byrne Edsall and Mary D. Edsall, *Chain Reaction: The Impact of Race, Rights, and Taxes on American Politics* (New York: W.W. Norton & Co., 1997).

8. Miller, *Flowers in the Dustbin*, 284.

9. Peter Knobler and Greg Mitchell, eds. *Very Seventies: A Cultural History of the 1970s, From the Pages of* Crawdaddy (New York: Simon & Schuster, 1995), 115.

10. Vincent, *Funk: The Music, the People,* 215.

CHAPTER 10

1. Robert Palmer, *Dancing in the Street: A Rock and Roll History* (London: BBC Books, 1996), 274.

2. Michael Azerrard, *Our Band Could Be Your Life: Scenes from the American Indie Underground, 1981–1999* (New York: Back Bay Books, 2001), 134.

3. The editors of *Rolling Stone*, *The Rolling Stone Record Review* (New York: Pocket Books, 1971), 97.

4. Bill Forman, "Diminished But Unafraid: REM Talks about the Passion," *Pulse!* November 1998, 34.

5. The editors of *Rolling Stone*, *Bruce Springsteen: The Rolling Stone Files* (New York: Hyperion, 1996).

6. "Voices from the Culture: The Clinton Conversation," *Rolling Stone*, November 12, 1998, 70.

7. Geoff Boucher, "A Rocky Political Period for the Rock the Vote Campaign," *Los Angeles Times*, February 20, 1999, F2.

CHAPTER 11

1. Martin and Segrave, *Anti-Rock*, 292.

2. Eric Nuzum, *Parental Advisory: Music Censorship in America* (New York: Perennial, 2001), 158.

3. Nuzum, *Parental Advisory*, 100.

4. Nelson George, *Hip Hop America* (New York: Penguin, 1999), 188.

5. Nuzum, *Parental Advisory*, 109.

6. Lou Cannon, *President Reagan: The Role of a Lifetime* (New York: Touchstone, 1991), 232.

7. Cannon, *President Reagan*, 233.

8. Cannon, *President Reagan*, 524.

9. George, *Hip Hop America*, 176–77.

10. George, *Hip Hop America*, 211.

11. John Pareles, "Untangling Mudddy Waters and His Blues," *New York Times*, July 30, 2002, B7.

12. Lynette Holloway, "The Angry Appeal of Eminem Is Cutting Across Racial Lines," *New York Times*, October 28, 2002, C2.

13. Norman Kelley, ed., *R&B: Rhythm and Business: The Political Economy of Black Music* (New York: Akashic Books, 2002), 231.

14. Russell Simmons and Nelson George, *Life and Def: Sex, Drugs, Money, and God* (New York: Crown, 2001), 171.

CHAPTER 12

1. Dana Milbank, "It's a Rap," *The New Republic*, November 23, 1998, p. 11.

EPILOGUE

1. David Segal, "Thanks, Boss. Bruce Springsteen Rises to the Occasion at the MCI Center," *Washington Post*, August 12, 2002, C01.

INDEX

Roe, Tommy, 72, 121
Roe v. Wade, xvi, 198
Roll Call, 29, 30
Rolling Stone (magazine), 11, 85, 115, 159, 243, 292–93; founding of, 119; readers of, 121
Rolling Stone Illustrated History of Rock and Roll, The, 54, 105–6, 114, 144
Rolling Stones, xii, xvii, 1, 2, 4, 6, 7, 11–12, 18, 29–33, 37–38, 40–41, 43, 45, 52, 57, 83–84, 86, 91, 94–95, 99, 110, 123–24, 127, 134–35, 139–44, 151, 153, 155, 160, 166, 176, 195, 204, 206, 209, 223, 226, 231–36, 241, 297
romance novels, 74
Ronstadt, Linda, 18, 74, 200
Rorem, Ned, 119
Rotten, Johnny, 130, 142, 227–28, 231–33, 236–37, 245, 261, 289
Rubber Soul (Beatles), 2, 132–33, 159
Rubin, Jerry, 178
Run-DMC, 266
Russia, vi
Rydell, Bobby, 96–98, 120

Sadler, Barry, 155
Safire, William, 279
Saigon, xvi, 126, 149, 150, 152
Sam and Dave, xi–xii, 124
Sam the Sham and the Pharoahs, xii, 212
Sandinistas, 102
San Francisco, 165, 181–82, 187, 240
Santana, 210
Sartre, Jean-Paul, vi
Saturday Night Fever (film), 222–23
Saturday Night Massacre, 40
Savoy Brown, 37, 184
Schlesinger, Arthur Jr., 135
Schulman, Bruce, 67
Schwarzenegger, Arnold, 158
Seeger, Pete, v, vii–viii, 129–31, 134, 171–72
Segrave, Kerry, 76, 254
segregation, 68, 71, 104
September 11, 2001, 53, 82–83, 89, 116, 295–98
September 11 Fund, 296
17 Magazine, 115
Sex in the City (TV show), 75
Sex Pistols, 2, 28, 54, 82, 142, 227, 228, 231, 233, 235, 261, 264, 289; anniversary tour, 236
Sexual McCarthyism: Clinton, Starr, and the Emerging Constitutional Crisis (Dershowitz), 61
sexual revolution, 73

Sgt. Pepper's Lonely Hearts Club Band (Beatles), xv, 2, 4, 6, 13, 37, 94, 119, 134–35, 161, 163–65, 227, 292
Shakespeare, William, 6
Shakira, 74
Shakur, Tupac, 266
Shangri-Las, 199
Shannon, Del, 108
Sharpton, Al, 263
Shepard, Sam, 47, 52
Sheridan Square Entertainment, 80, 169
Sherman, Bobby, 96
She's a Rebel: The History of Women in Rock and Roll (Garr), 201
Shout!: The Beatles in Their Generation (Norman), 114
Simmons, Gene, 203
Simon, Carly, 221
Simon and Garfunkel, 138, 203
Simon, John, 118
Simon, Paul, 295
Sinatra, Frank, 13, 18, 62, 107, 210
Sinclair, John, 178, 189
singer-songwriters, vii, 206
Singing Nun, 108, 110
Sister Sledge, xvi, 205, 261
Sister Souljah, 265
Six Crises (Nixon), 189
sixties, 5, 7, 8, 42, 47, 49, 52, 54, 124, 135, 145, 234
Slick, Grace, 200
Sloan, P. F., 43, 137
Sly and the Family Stone, 269
Small Faces, 18
Smith, Wes, 70, 104
Smokey Robinson and the Miracles, 156
Snoop Doggy Dogg, 256, 265–67
Snyder, Dee, 254
socialism, vi–vii
Some Girls (Rolling Stones), 235–36
Songs of Protest, 152
Sorensen, Theodore, 279
soul, xiv, xix, 127, 263
Soul Survivors, 123
Soul Train (TV show), 268
South, the, 67, 137, 154
Southeast Asia, xv, 38, 126, 178
Southern Baptists, 154
Southern California, 78, 146, 209
Southern Christian Leadership Conference, 129
South Korea, 60
South Vietnam, 137